D1125653

HAYES

OF THE

TWENTY-THIRD

HAYES

OF THE

TWENTY-THIRD

The Civil War Volunteer Officer

by T. Harry Williams

University of Nebraska Press • Lincoln

Copyright © 1965 by T. Harry Williams
All rights reserved
Manufactured in the United States of America

First Bison Book printing:
Most recent printing indicated by the last digit below:
10   9   8   7   6   5   4   3   2   1

Library of Congress Cataloging-in-Publication Data
Williams, T. Harry (Thomas Harry), 1909–
Hayes of the Twenty-Third: the Civil War volunteer officer / by T. Harry
Williams.
p. cm.
ISBN 0-8032-9761-0
Previously published: New York: Knopf, 1965.
Includes bibliographical references and index.
1. Hayes, Rutherford Birchard, 1822–1893. 2. United States. Army.
Ohio Infantry Regiment, 23rd (1861–1865) 3. United States—His-
tory—Civil War, 1861–1865—Regimental histories. 4. United
States—History—Civil War, 1861–1865—Campaigns. I. Title.
E682.W73   1994
973.7′4771—dc20
93-47268 CIP

Reprinted by arrangement with Alfred A. Knopf, Inc.

∞

to **J**ohn **D**oles, *Jr.*

ALSO A UNIT OFFICER

Preface

Rutherford B. Hayes, colonel and brigadier general in the volunteer army of the Civil War and regimental, brigade, and division commander, had a favorite remark he liked to make at the reunion meetings of veterans, where the reminiscent talk of battles seemed to wax louder and longer with the passing of the years. "As we grow older, and the army stories grow larger," he would say to his comrades with gentle irony, "we thank God that we are enabled to believe them." A man of sensitive perception and probing curiosity, Hayes, as he reflected on what participants in the war were saying about it, sometimes wondered if the true record of the war could ever be told from the sources available to historians. He was human enough to think occasionally about his own record and to compose a few short accounts of it. Yet he was honest enough to concede that even he did not know everything about scenes in which he had been a central actor. He discussed the problem with a friend who was trying to write a book about the war, and this man answered, in words that were an echo of Hayes's own thoughts: "I often wonder what the historians of the future are going to do if we who 'were there' cannot tell what was done."

That a historian of the future would ever want to write about his war career was a thought that would never have occurred to Hayes, who was a singularly modest individual. He left behind him, however, abundant materials for a book. Every day of the war, as he did every day throughout most of his life, he penned an entry in a diary, and practically every day he wrote at least one letter, to his wife or to some other member of his family. Since his death, the Rutherford

B. Hayes Library at Fremont, Ohio, has collected a mass of sources bearing on the war period. If ever the stuff of history was available to a writer, it was ready to hand for one who chose to write of Hayes the soldier.

But for the historian of today a question will arise that has to be answered. Does Hayes the soldier merit a special study? Or, to put the doubt another way, does any man who commanded only a regiment for the greater part of the war and a brigade and a division for short interludes deserve a book-length treatment? Are not important generals the figures who should dominate history? It would not be enough to answer that although Hayes was a relatively minor personage during the war he was a big one after it, a President of the United States, even though a good case could be made that unless he had compiled a war record to support his political aspirations Hayes would never have reached the highest office. A book about Hayes's war service must stand on its own merits, must tell us through the man something we need to know about that great conflict and the Americans who fought it.

A good unit commander who kept good records can tell us a good deal, can, indeed, tell us the things we now most need to learn about the war. Practically all of the previous writings about the military events have concentrated on the top generals and the strategy. This was quite proper, because top generals are a vital part of the military structure, and unless they are understood the battles cannot be understood. But in the process of looking only at the leaders of armies we have ignored the leaders of units, who in the crisis of a battle may be quite as important as any general. In the battle of the Opequon, for instance, General Philip Sheridan devised an excellent plan, but at the crucial moment the execution of that plan came to rest on brigade officer Hayes; and if Hayes had not done the right thing Sheridan's grand scheme would have collapsed and that general might have gone down in the historical ratings as a failure.

But it is not just because unit commanders may determine the course of a battle, and indirectly of a war, that they deserve attention. Of equal, perhaps greater significance, they can impart to us something we have to know about the Civil War and about the whole history of war as well. It is by studying them, and only by studying them, that we can ever find out how Civil War armies were operated and marched and fought and how Civil War battles were actually conducted. The story of any army of the war is the story of its units, from the regiment to the brigade to the division and finally on up to the corps. Unless all of these units functioned, the army would not function, no matter how high the genius of its commander. We need very much to know more about these units, and almost the only way we can secure the knowledge is to come upon a unit officer like Hayes who wrote freely about how he ran his unit. Hayes is especially rewarding because he was for the most part a regimental commander, and the regiment, although the smallest of the units, was the basic element in a Civil War army. The writing of unit histories, units like Hayes's Twenty-third Ohio regiment, is a new field in the literature of the war and one that should be exploited.

There is a final reason to justify the study of a unit officer and especially of one like Hayes who came out of civilian life. A vast amount of nonsense has been written about the controlling role in the war of the professional soldiers. It is true that the West Pointers dominated the army and the corps commands and that at the highest level the Civil War was a West Pointers' war. But this is only a part of the story. At the division, the brigade, and especially the regimental level, the volunteer civilian soldiers dominated. It could not have been otherwise. There were simply not enough trained soldiers available to command the units in the armies. These positions, at the beginning of the war and throughout its course, were held by volunteer officers, and if it had not been for such men, civilians like Hayes, who had the intelligence to master the rudiments of military knowledge and the natural ability to lead, the Civil War armies could not have operated. It was a mark of the raw robust vigor of American democratic society that it could produce the needed men in the required numbers, and it is through a man like Hayes that we can best see how the United States lumbered into war in 1861—awkward, inefficient, wasteful, and yet somehow grand and irresistible.

Volunteer officer Hayes was a good deal like the society he represented. Innocent of military knowledge at the start of the war, he had to learn a lot of things fast. He learned them, as did hundreds of others like him, the hard way, by his own efforts, from the lessons of history, and sometimes at the expense of his men. But the point is that he learned, and before long he became a competent officer within the limits of his unit responsibility and his own capacity. He made some mistakes, but they were few and not too serious. In most situations he came to the right decisions.

This evaluation is not meant to imply that Hayes could have been anything more than he was. Although he briefly commanded as large a unit as a division, he acted for most of the war as a regimental leader. His most important battle experience was as commander of a brigade. He did well with all three units. Whether he could have commanded the next largest aggregation, a corps, is doubtful. He had enough mental capacity to enable him to master the techniques of corps direction. But he did not possess the other qualities that would have been required—imagination, inner toughness, a willingness to bear the lonely responsibility of high command. He was a competent and courageous unit officer but nothing more. He lacked a certain spaciousness of spirit, lacked, perhaps, the ambition or drive to reach too far. Even when he became President, he did not enjoy the office too much and eagerly retired to private life. History ranks him slightly above the average among the Presidents, and by coincidence this should be his rating as a soldier—above the ordinary but not among the great. He would have been the first to accept both judgments.

I have to express my thanks to a number of people who helped in the preparation of this book. First on the list by any standards is Watt P. Marchman, director of the Rutherford B. Hayes Library. Mr. Marchman, devoted student of Hayes's whole career, has long believed that of that career the war phase was the vital period, because it made Hayes a figure of importance, launched him into politics with the reputation of a military hero, propelled him, really, into the presidency. For as long as he has had this concept, Mr. Marchman hoped that someday some writer would want to do a book on Hayes as a soldier, and his desire and my rising interest in unit history coincided. The Hayes Library provided generous and intelligent support—financial assistance, research materials, and constant and courteous service. With all this, at no time did Mr. Marchman or anybody connected with the Hayes Library attempt in the slightest to influence in any way any conclusion I reached as to Hayes's virtues or faults. It is a library for scholars, and it respects the scholarly method.

Also desirous to see a book about Hayes of the Civil War was the late Admiral Webb C. Hayes, a grandson of Rutherford B. Hayes and a student of military history. Because of his paternal and professional background, Admiral Hayes took a special interest in my study from the beginning. I regret that he did not live to see it completed. I think he would have liked the volume, although he would not have hesitated to disagree with parts of it.

The late Dr. Roy Bird Cook of Charleston, West Virginia, compiler and champion of the history of his state, made available to me, with his customary generosity, large chunks of valuable source materials. Mr. Boyd B. Stutler, also of Charleston and also an authority on West Virginia history, read virtually the whole manuscript and caught several errors and made many expert suggestions for improvement. Mr. Charles Shetler, curator of the West Virginia Collection at the West Virginia University Library, was constantly alert to supply items that he thought might escape my attention. Mr. Sam Neal of Chatham, Virginia, genial friend and student of the mountain campaigns, shared his knowledge with me and acted as a personal guide over many of the fields where Hayes fought. Robert M. Reilly, Civil War buff and scholar, made the maps.

Others who responded to my requests and who provided help of varying degree—large or small, it always was graciously given—are Miss Ethel L. Crandall, the Reverend Clarence Shirley Donnelly, collector and writer, C. E. Dornbusch, Cecil D. Eby, Jr., William K. Kay, who knows as much about Civil War tactics and formations as anyone should know, David C. Mearns, Richard Miller, and Harlow Warren, the chronicler of Beckley, West Virginia. Some of these individuals are cited more specifically in the notes. I must also record my gratitude to the anonymous staffs of the following libraries: the University of California at Los Angeles, the Ohio State University, the Indiana State Library, the Indiana Historical Society, the Library of Congress, and the Illinois State Historical Library. All these people, and others, have lightened my burden of research and made easier my writing of this book.   T. Harry Williams

August 1964

Contents

Illustrations

[*Except where noted, illustrations are by courtesy
of the Rutherford B. Hayes Library, Fremont, Ohio.*]

Maps

HAYES

OF THE

TWENTY-THIRD

Chapter 1

The Golden Years

ON MARCH 1, 1877, Rutherford B. Hayes stood on the rear platform of the special railroad car that was to bear him from Columbus, the capital of Ohio, to the national capital at Washington. He had been twice elected to the national House of Representatives and three times to the governorship of his state. He was governor now and he was also President-elect of the United States. But he did not know with certainty that he would be inaugurated to the highest office in the land. The election of 1876 was in dispute, and as yet no final disposition of the doubtful votes between him and his Democratic opponent had been made. Still his friends thought that the issue would be resolved in his favor and that he should be in Washington when the decision arrived, and he was willing to go. As he looked over the faces of the large crowd that had come to the station to see him depart, he was moved by the evidence of their support and friendship, and he began to speak.

"*My Fellow Citizens,*—I appear to say a few words in bidding goodbye to you. I understand very well the uncertainty of public affairs at Washington; I understand very well that possibly next week I may be with you again to resume my place in the Governor's office and as your fellow citizen. But I also understand that it is my duty to be at Washington, prepared to assume another position higher and more responsible and with more difficult duties." Then the serious, bearded face took on a firmer expression, and the strong and rather stocky figure straightened, assuming a martial appearance only partially visible before, and the voice rang out more vibrantly. "I have thought, as I looked upon this great audience and as to-day I gazed on the people who thronged our route to this depot, of a similar occurrence six-teen years ago. A little less than sixteen years ago I marched down High Street with one thousand men to pass to the East and to the South to do what we could to restore the Union of the States, and to reestablish the authority of the Constitu-tion. In that work we were eminently successful, so far as it was possible to be successful by force of arms. . . . Of my comrades, one third and over never returned to their homes."[1]

Hayes was not threatening to employ in 1877 the same kind of physical force that had been resorted to in 1861. On the contrary, he went on to plead for a peaceful acceptance of the results of the election, for a union of hearts and not of bayonets in the federal Union. But in this crisis of his career it was inevitable that he should recall his Civil War experience and seek to draw some feeling of security from his onetime association with the "one thousand men" of the Twenty-third Regiment of Ohio Volunteers. Throughout his life he would remember the regiment and the larger units in which he ultimately served. Somehow the vision of those surging ranks gave him, as they gave him now, an inner strength and courage to face up to any trial. He would be-come President in 1877, and it is as President that history gives him a place. But for Hayes the four years he spent in the White House were decidedly secondary to the four he knew in the war. In truth, for Hayes everything that ever hap-pened to him was secondary to the war. It was, as it was for

[1] Charles Richard Williams, *The Life of Rutherford Birchard Hayes* (Colum-bus, 1928), II, 4.

countless other men, young and not so young when they entered it, the great central event. The war years, he told a gathering of veterans in 1885, were "the best years of our lives. Those years are indeed golden."[2]

It would be easy to dismiss Hayes's frequent apotheoses of his army experience as merely the self-seeking of a politician. All veterans, and especially those running for office, regularly reminded the populace of how they had held the field at Chancellorsville or won the day at Chattanooga. And Hayes's political career prospered because he had been a soldier, because he could say that he had volunteered and had been wounded and had risen on merit to be a general. Indeed, it is quite probable that without his military record he would never have been President of the United States. But any suspicion that Hayes was trading on his record fades when subjected to analysis. He was a politician but not a particularly avid one and in some ways not a very good one. He voluntarily renounced more than a single term in the presidency, thus lessening his influence in the office, and after leaving the White House he deliberately assumed a largely passive political role. Most of his many and almost mystical tributes to the golden army years were delivered when he was out of politics and had no motives of self to serve. It was not the pursuit of votes that impelled Hayes to exalt the martial past but a search for something deeper, something that he himself probably could not have defined. There was a kind of aura emanating from a military group, its comradeship and its sense of entity, that warmed and elevated Hayes. It was as though he had encountered in the war a largeness of the human spirit, courage, generosity, sacrifice, that disappeared in the peace, and he could not endure to lose it. He sought to recover the quality or the mood by attaching himself to men

[2] *Fifth Quadrennial Congress, Military Order of the Loyal Legion of the United States* (n.p., n.d.), no pagination.

who had shared it with him and who must perforce still
practice its virtues. He belonged to all the veterans' organi-
zations he could join and he spoke at all their campfires year
after year—the Military Order of the Loyal Legion, Ohio
Commandery, of which he was commander in chief, the Society of the Army of West Virginia, and, largest and best
loved, the Grand Army of the Republic.

He spoke and always the audiences listened deferentially,
because he spoke well and because they respected his record
as a soldier and because he had been President. But the
veterans, now grown stout and successful and sometimes
cynical, must have been puzzled at times by Hayes's eulogies
of the unselfish spirit generated by military comradeship.
And only the more sensitive among them could have understood what was in his mind when he talked about their
lustrous heritage from the great past. (Oliver Wendell
Holmes, Jr., who said it better, would have known instantly:
"Through our great good fortune, in our youth our hearts
were touched with fire.") Hayes never tired of reminding his
hearers that they had been a part of a unique experience
whose memory would never leave them. Recalling the scenes
of the war for the Society of the Army of West Virginia, he
exclaimed: "I have had my share of the good things of this
life. . . . We have been fortunate men. It is something to
make us happy as long as we live and approach the grave
with a calm feeling of trust and gratitude."[3] Some observers
might have seen a certain pathos in Hayes's constant journeys
to the encampments, in his ceaseless invocations of a mood
long since gone. But if the past was lost, Hayes could not
realize it, or if the disturbing thought sometimes came to

---

[3] *Eleventh Reunion of the Society of the Army of West Virginia, 1887* (Wheeling, 1888), 104–5; *Proceedings of the Twenty-fifth Annual Encampment of
the Grand Army of the Republic, Department of Ohio, 1891* (Steubenville,
1891), 142.

him, he put it away. To the last he was a veteran. In 1892, just short months before his death, the Grand Army of the Republic marched in Washington, the survivors of many armies of the war trying with their own brand of pathos to recapture the glory of the Grand Review of 1865. Former President Hayes trudged in the ranks, not as onetime commander in chief of the armed forces, but proudly as colonel of the Twenty-third Ohio. William McKinley, who had also been a member of the regiment and who would also attain the presidency, saw him then and seemed to catch some sense of the identification his comrade had always sought for. The search had been rewarding, McKinley decided. He told a veterans' gathering after Hayes's death: "And he was always with you. He kept near to you in peace as he was close to you in war. He was never above his comrades. . . . I heard him once say that the Grand Army button he wore on his coat was the grandest decoration he had ever had."[4]

Nobody who saw Rutherford B. Hayes as a boy or youth would ever have predicted that someday he would lead men in battle, ride a horse across a slough in the face of enemy fire, or become a general. "Ruddy" Hayes was delicate and serious and seemed destined for a sedentary and perhaps a scholarly life. His parents had moved from Vermont to Delaware, Ohio, and here on October 4, 1822, Hayes was born, three months after his father had died. His mother, made fearful by the accidental death of another son, raised him in a smotheringly protective feminine atmosphere. The only masculine influence he encountered was that of his mother's brother, Sardis Birchard, a man of some substance, who tried to fill the place of the boy's father and who on occasion augmented the family income with generous contributions.

---

[4] *Proceedings . . . Twenty-seventh Annual Encampment, Grand Army of the Republic* (Sandusky, 1893), 142.

Young Hayes was educated at private schools and at Kenyon College in Ohio. Already in his student days he displayed many of the characteristics he would exhibit as a mature man. He was solemn and industrious and intense. He kept a diary and to it he confided his ambitions—he would seek constantly to improve himself in every way, and he would regulate his life by imposed rules of discipline. Attracted to the legal profession, he was able, with help from his uncle, to attend the Harvard Law School. On completing the course, he did not begin practice in Columbus, where his mother had removed, but in the small town where Sardis Birchard lived, Lower Sandusky, now Fremont.

For a period Hayes endured the life of a rural lawyer, trying petty cases and receiving small fees. When the Mexican War broke out in 1846, he thought of volunteering, but doctors told him he could not stand the rigors of a campaign. Then in 1850 he made what he must have considered a decisive move, a break of some kind with the past. He transferred his office to the bustling metropolis of Cincinnati. Almost immediately new and broader vistas opened before him. He won some important cases, gained a name as an adept lawyer, and increased his income. And now that economic security was promised he at last married, his long-time sweetheart, Lucy Webb. She was intelligent, socially assured, and had a will fully as strong as his. Along with professional reputation and social status there came an opportunity for political preferment. Inevitably people talked about running the rising young lawyer for office. Hayes mixed in politics, but his interest was more dutiful than ardent. He was first a Whig, and when that party broke up he became a Republican. At no time did he throw himself completely into the political game or play at it with passion. Nor did he seem intrigued with any possible official rewards. He was a firm but not an extreme antislavery man. He stumped for his party in campaigns, but he did it with no great show of feeling or urgency. Even in the fateful election of 1860, although he supported Lincoln, he manifested little apparent concern over the outcome.

Thus stood Hayes on the eve of the Civil War—moderately successful, widely respected, and reasonably certain of a stable future. Everything about him seemed solid and assured. He was five feet eight and a half inches in height and weighed around a hundred and fifty pounds. Auburn brown hair crowned a rather large head. The face was strong rather than handsome and of a ruddy complexion and was set off with a reddish full beard. He looked satisfied but not arrogant, serious but not stuffy. He also looked like a man who had never given himself completely to anything, who had dreams that he had never realized.[5]

For Hayes, as for thousands of other men in the North, the fall of Fort Sumter had the impact of an emotional explosion. It changed drastically his outlook on the events that had followed Lincoln's election just as it would soon alter violently the whole tenor of his life. Even beginning of the secession movement had failed to jar Hayes very much out of his customary calm. He expressed only an irritated conviction that if some states were foolish enough to secede, they should be permitted to go out. But as the situation developed—as the parade of states continued and as the seceding units formed their own government and assumed the stance of a nation—his attitude hardened. He spoke with growing bitterness of the Southern effort to break up the concern. Then came Sumter and the firing on the flag, and Hayes suddenly saw the issue in a clear new light. The Union had to be preserved, no matter what the cost and if

---

[5] Hayes's career is best treated in Harry Barnard, *Rutherford B. Hayes and His America* (Indianapolis, 1954).

necessary by war. If war came, he decided, he would have to play his part in it. Characteristically, he arrived at this conclusion after a good deal of communion with himself and consultation with others. He discussed his course with Lucy, with Sardis Birchard, and with his friend Stanley Matthews, another lawyer. So that he would know something about military procedure, at least, as he said, how to do "eyes right and left," he joined a volunteer home company made up of members of a literary club to which he belonged. Finally he and Matthews agreed they would volunteer their services to the state and try to go in as officers in the same regiment. In his diary Hayes recorded the depth of his feelings, which he said were also Matthews's: *"I would prefer to go into it if I knew I was to die, or be killed in the course of it, than to live through and after it without taking any part in it."*[6]

Hayes and Matthews had high motives, and being men of pride and some position, and having important political connections, they naturally felt that their proffered service would be valuable and should be suitably rewarded. Unlike many ambitious civilians, they did not believe they were immediately competent to command regiments as colonels. But they did think that they were capable of performing passably in an intermediate rank from which, if they showed merit, they could work their way up, and they so informed Governor William Dennison. The governor was more than willing to oblige the aspirants, but like other harried executives in those first hectic days of the war, he was having organization problems. The state was bending every argument to induce

---

[6] Rutherford B. Hayes, MS. Diary, May 15, 1861, Rutherford B. Hayes Library, Fremont, Ohio; Hayes to Sardis Birchard, April 20, 23, 25, May 12, 16, in Rutherford B. Hayes MS. Letters, Hayes Library. These basic sources will be hereinafter cited as Hayes, MS. Diary and Hayes MS. Letters. Hayes was an inveterate diary keeper and letter writer from his youth until his last days. The Hayes Library kindly furnished me with typed copies of the diary and letters for the war years. I have also examined large portions of the original manuscripts.

the host of three-months men, who had answered the first call, to volunteer for three years in state units in the national service. Paradoxically, for Hayes and Matthews the danger was that too many regiments might enlist, thus exceeding the state's quota and cutting them out of a chance for present service. But the result was exactly as they wished. On June 7 Hayes received a telegram from Dennison asking if he would accept a majority in a regiment of which William S. Rosecrans, formerly of the regular army, would be colonel and Matthews lieutenant colonel. Instantly Hayes wired his acceptance, and two days later he and Matthews, pursuant to directions from the governor, entrained for Columbus.[7]

At the capital they learned that Dennison had put together a regiment made up of companies from the northern and northeastern counties and to be known as the Twenty-third Ohio Volunteer Infantry. It was the first Ohio regiment in which the field officers were appointed by the governor instead of being elected by the troops. The company captains did not take readily to the prospect of being placed under strange officers from another area and made their feelings known in a somewhat tense interview in Dennison's office. But the refusal of the governor to change the arrangement and some tactful words from Matthews and Hayes stilled at least for the moment any overt resentment. The fledgling officers realized, however, that they had their work laid out— they would have to convince the men that they knew their business. They took a hack out to Camp Chase, four miles west of Columbus, where their own and other regiments were being assembled. Because Rosecrans had not yet arrived, Matthews, as the ranking officer, had to muster the companies into service. With Hayes assisting, the work was completed by June 11, and the Twenty-third Ohio was a reality.

---

[7] Hayes to Sardis Birchard, May 26, June 5, 10, 1861, Hayes MS. Letters.

The next night Hayes for the first time slept under a tent and found the experience refreshing. In fact, he was exhilarated by everything in this strange, new life. He was much happier, he wrote Lucy, than he could be "fretting away in the old office near the Court House. It is living."[8] In a few days Colonel Rosecrans, all energy and regular army, appeared and made his presence felt. Drills and parades were inaugurated, even though the troops were still without uniforms or weapons. Hayes loved every part of it—the long lines, the noises of the camp, and, above all, the sense of being associated with men united in a common endeavor. The hitherto reserved man confided to his diary: "I am more affected as I look at the men on parade than I expected to be; not more embarrassed, but an agreeable emotion, a swelling of heart possesses me." He learned things quickly, almost intuitively. What he and Matthews did not know, he confessed in a letter, they guessed at and they were kept busy guessing. One day, when all the ranking officers went to Cincinnati, he was left in command of the whole camp. A captain with a West Point education, who had been named officer of the day, came to Hayes's tent and asked for his orders of the day. Hayes was completely confused but met the situation perfectly: "I merely remarked that I thought of nothing requiring special attention; that if anything was wanted out of the usual routine I would let him know."[9]

---

[8] Hayes, MS. Diary, June 7, 10, 12, 1861; Hayes to Mrs. Hayes, June 10, Hayes MS. Letters. Dennison's order appointing Hayes a major was dated June 7, and Hayes was sworn in on June 12; printed documentary forms in Hayes Library. The scene when Matthews and Hayes confronted the protesting officers in Dennison's office is also described in Russell Hastings, MS. Genealogy and Autobiography, typed copy from Hayes Library. This source from a man who became Hayes's adjutant will be hereinafter cited as Hastings, MS. Autobiography. According to Hastings, Mrs. Hayes accompanied her husband to Camp Chase, and both of them made a point of visiting all the officer quarters.
[9] Hayes to Sardis Birchard, June 14, 1861, Hayes MS. Letters; Hayes, MS. Diary, June 13, 16.

Already he had grasped one of the first rules for getting along in the army—if you don't know what to say, say nothing.

Hayes was now a member of one of the most remarkable military assemblages in history. The volunteer citizen army which in 1861 gathered all across the country represented in every facet the democratic society from which it came, the raw, brute strength of that society and its youthful self-confidence and its transparent idealism and its gawkish materialism. And because it was a volunteer body, composed of men who had rushed forward in the first fine blush of patriotism, its rolls exhibited an astonishing range of personal abilities and professional skills. A typical Northern regiment contained more men who could do more things than did an average Southern regiment, for the simple reason that the Northern units were made up of men from a more complex social and economic system.[1] Lincoln caught this quality of the army he had summoned forth and recorded it in a message to Congress. There were many regiments, Lincoln said, whose members possessed full comprehension of all the known arts, and there was scarcely a one from which could not be selected "a president, a cabinet, a congress, and perhaps a court."

Lincoln's analysis was more prophetic of the Twenty-third Ohio than he could have possibly known. Assuredly this regiment contained among its commanding and ranking officers more names that would become famous than any other regiment in the Northern armies. Its first commander,

---

[1] In one Ohio regiment a survey based on the official papers of each member disclosed approximately one hundred trades and occupations. The historians of the regiment remarked with little exaggeration: "Whatever duty might have fallen to our lot—from selling a paper of pins to building a steamboat or railroad—plenty of men could have been found fully competent for the work." Joshua H. Horton and Soloman Teverbaugh, *A History of the Eleventh Regiment* (Dayton, 1866), 211-12.

William S. Rosecrans, "Old Rosy," was a West Pointer and
regular army man who had resigned his commission and was
in the oil-refining business in Cincinnati when the war
began. Rosecrans had but a short tenure with the regiment.
In June, 1861, before it took the field, he departed to assume
a larger command post, but shortly as an army commander
in West Virginia he would see it marching again under his
orders.[2] Rosecrans eventually rose to command one of the
largest Northern field armies and seemed about to emerge as
one of the great captains of the war—before his star sank in
controversy and in the red afterglow of Chickamauga. His
postwar career was almost as distinctive as his war record.
Engaging in political and business ventures in several states,
he held the offices of minister to Mexico, congressman from
California, and Register of the Treasury. Rosecrans was succeeded as regimental commander by Eliakim P. Scammon,
also a West Pointer and also something of a controversial
personality. A mathematics professor before the war, he was
a competent enough soldier but too fussily insistent on military protocol to be popular with a volunteer regiment. An
irritable person himself, he irritated Hayes and other officers
no end. Coming out of the war a brigadier general, for years
he represented the United States as consul at Prince Edward
Island. Hayes was the third commander of the Twenty-third
and after him came James M. Comly, a steady soldier who
had been a Columbus lawyer and journalist. He played an

---

[2] Rosecrans was made a brigadier general in the regular army and ordered to
General George B. McClellan's army in West Virginia. When McClellan
was summoned east in July, Rosecrans succeeded him. At this point it is
necessary to clarify a matter of geographical terminology. The Twenty-
third began its career and spent most of its service in the extreme western
part of Virginia, the part that in 1863 would become the new state of West
Virginia. It would be awkward and confusing to write about operations in
western Virginia and then midway in the story to suddenly shift gears, so
to speak, and begin to discuss operations in West Virginia. Therefore, regardless of the time period involved, whenever this region is referred to as a
military theater it will be called West Virginia.

active role in politics after the war and became the American minister to Hawaii. Stanley Matthews transferred to another regiment and then in 1863, deciding he was not cut out for military life, resigned his commission. His capabilities were for the law, and in the postwar era he fashioned a notable reputation in that field. After a term in the United States Senate, he was named in 1881 as a justice of the Supreme Court, and on the highest tribunal he wrote some significant decisions that enlarged the power of the national government over the states. Even in the lowest ranks the regiment had a name destined for fame. A frail youth of eighteen enlisted in 1861 as a private and rose to the grade of major. His name was William McKinley. He would enable the regiment to go Lincoln's prognostication one better. The Twenty-third contained not one future President but two.

It was a remarkable regiment and not just because of the great names on its rolls. When first mustered in, it numbered around 950 men, which was an average strength for a regiment, and when mustered out in 1865 it numbered 732, which was an unusually high figure for a unit after the depletion of war and which reflected a recruiting method that kept replacements flowing in.[3] Its casualty quota was respectable, not high enough to rank it among the twenty or so Northern regiments suffering the highest rate of battlefield deaths but sufficient to place it on a select list of 300 fighting regiments. Out of an aggregate enrollment of 2,230, it lost in killed or died of wounds 159 men and from disease and other causes 131, for a total of 290.[4] It performed some of the hardest

---

[3] Hayes to General W. C. Hill, adjutant general of Ohio, April 3, 1863, MS. in Hayes Library, fixed the original size of the regiment at 955. Whitelaw Reid, *Ohio in the War* (Cincinnati, 1868), I, 7, stated the number as 927. The minimum size of a regiment was 845 and the maximum was 1,025.

[4] William F. Fox, *Regimental Losses in the Civil War* (Albany, 1889), 317. Its total of killed and wounded was 567.

marching of the war in what was without a doubt one of the most rugged theaters, West Virginia, and in this same region it did some of the meanest if not the most spectacular fighting of the war. It was the lot of the Twenty-third to spend the bulk of its service in what was essentially a pocket of the war or a sideshow to the main event. West Virginia, as a Union-sympathizing area in the Confederacy, had a real political and propaganda value in the Northern scheme of grand strategy, and, lying on the flank of Virginia proper, it posed a potential if not always an actual military threat to vital rail-road lines of communication uniting the eastern and western parts of the Confederacy. By any measure it was important for the North to occupy and hold West Virginia, and the Twenty-third was one of the units that did the job. The work was necessary to the ultimate triumph of the Union cause, but it was small and nasty work—fighting in pygmy battles, chasing guerrillas, patrolling lonely mountain roads, repressing civil-ian sympathizers of the South. It was dull routine, unexciting war, and it offered few opportunities for anyone to make a reputation. Only twice did the occupying troops in West Virginia emerge from behind their misty mountain barrier into the bright light of the "big war," in 1862 when they fought in the Antietam operation and in 1864 when they fol-lowed Phil Sheridan in the Shenandoah Valley. Units such as the Twenty-third experienced the worst side of war, the very hardest to endure, the kind that required duty, dirt, and devo-tion and that offered little glory in return. In the end, the most remarkable thing about the Twenty-third was not that two future Presidents and a collection of lesser figures served with it but that it came through the oppressing obscurity of its war years still a proud regiment.[5]

---

[5] For chronological histories of the record of the regiment, see Frederick H. Dyer, *Compendium of the War of the Rebellion* (New York, 1959), I, 206, III, 1507; "Military History of the 23rd Regt. O. V. Inf.," MS. prepared under the direction of James M. Comly, Hayes Library.

From the beginning and to the end Hayes and the Twenty-third were inextricably united in a physical and spiritual association. Going in as a major, Hayes was promoted to lieutenant colonel on October 24, 1861, when Matthews left the regiment, and thus became second in command to Scammon. Then in November Scammon was elevated to brigade command, and Hayes took over the regiment. He led it for almost a year before receiving the grade of full colonel, which came to him on October 24, 1862, a year to the day after his first promotion. After that, responsibility, although not rank recognition, came faster. In January, 1863, he was given command of a small brigade of two regiments instead of the usual four, and later in that year a full brigade. When at the opening battle of the Shenandoah Valley campaign of 1864 the commanding officer of his division fell wounded, Hayes assumed command on the field and led the division through that battle and two more. For his services he was commissioned a brigadier general of volunteers as of October 19. On the return of his superior, he reverted to brigade command, although because of the poor health of that individual he often exercised temporary control of the division. Right at the close of the war he was assigned to the command of a new division, comprising 5,000 men, but hostilities ended before he could take over the direction of this unit. He was named brevet major general of volunteers as of March 13, 1865, but the promotion was made a year after he had resigned his commission.[6] Curiously, although he directed brigades and divisions, Hayes never fought in battle as a general. His brigadier's commission was not announced until December, 1864, when active operations in his theater had ceased. Actually, as a battle leader, he acted as a colonel and regimental

---

[6] Francis B. Heitman, *Historical Register and Dictionary of the United States Army* (Washington, 1903), I, 515; printed forms and official manuscript letters in Hayes Library.

commander. When he controlled larger units, of which the Twenty-third was a part, he was still a colonel. He was quite satisfied with his status. Although he might well have complained of his tardy advancement, he made no particular effort to push himself, and he never employed the political and personal influences at his disposal. He held back partly because he had qualms about exercising a command beyond his background and capacity. And, although he did not fully realize it, he would rather be a colonel of a regiment than hold any other post. He liked to say: "I prefer to be one of the good colonels to being one of the poor generals."[7] Good colonels were vital to the mass armies that swarmed to the field in the Civil War. Without these colonels, men like Hayes just out of civilian life but who were able to master the art of war, the armies could not have operated.

---

[7] Williams, *Hayes*, I, 273–4. Like many other regimental commanders, Hayes was wounded in battle, a total of four times. MS. note by Hayes in Hayes Library. Except for James Monroe in the Revolution, he is the only President who had been wounded.

Chapter 2

The Good Colonels

GOVERN AT WILL nearly a thousand men, each one of whom leaps to perform my bidding, and some, perhaps many of whom would count it small cost to spill his blood for me," wrote one regimental commander to his wife. "A soldier is always guarding the door of my tent, a line of soldiers always surrounds it, all my individual wants are supplied, the most of my wishes anticipated." Around him in the tent, this officer continued, were weapons, uniforms, a bottle of whiskey, pipes, and manuals on tactics and regulations. It was all "a paradise of delight," he imprudently declared. "No woman to bother me. . . . Nary baby to keep awake o' nights. The fact is, camp life to a field officer is a bachelor's paradise." His reactions, although playfully put for the benefit of his correspondent, were typical of those of other volunteer officers suddenly transported from civilian life to the ways of war. It was a new and strange world they found themselves in, a man's world, and at the start most of them were utterly captivated with it. The change was "almost magical," another officer observed, and he, like many others, was not quite sure how he had got there.[1]

The colonels of regiments came into the army with various motives. Some entered because of a sense of duty or patriotism;

---

[1] Walter George Smith, *Life and Letters of Thomas Kilby Smith* (New York, 1898), 179–80; Milo M. Quaife (ed.), *From the Cannon's Mouth: the Civil War Letters of General Alpheus S. Williams* (Detroit, 1959), 18.

some, because they were carried away by emotion in the surcharged atmosphere following Sumter; and some, because they were ambitious and saw in a military career publicity for some other kind of career; many, it may be suspected, acted because of a combination of reasons. And they were a various lot. Some soon found that they were not competent to command but never admitted it; and if not detected from above and discharged, they blundered their way to the very end. In the first year of the war it was possible for unqualified men to attain responsible command posts. Colonels and other field officers and company officers were usually elected to their position by the vote of the troops or, more rarely, as in the case of the Twenty-third, appointed by the governor. But the election method was the only available way to obtain quickly the large number of troop leaders required. The North raised during the war a total of over 2,000 volunteer regiments of all arms, and colonels and lesser officers had to be inducted immediately. Election sometimes produced good choices—the men knew the candidates and selected shrewdly. Sometimes it descended to a personal or political contest—the men picked the aspirants who promised the most or talked the best. Regardless of the type of man elevated, the election system invested regiments and even larger units with a uniquely democratic cast. Officers who had been elected often seemed to feel that they could hold their place only if they continued to please their constituents. One Ohio colonel orated to his regiment at the beginning of a campaign: "I am, by your choice, to lead you. I am but a machine in your hands. . . . If you see fit to place confidence in me, obey my commands, and follow me where I lead, I shall feel proud of the command of the Seventh Regiment."[2] A governor could, of

---

[2] Lawrence Wilson, *Itinerary of the Seventh Ohio Volunteer Infantry* (New York, 1907), 41. In the second year of the war a system of examinations was instituted that made it possible to weed out incompetent officers.

course, make the same wrong kind of decision as a regiment, could, for example, throw a colonelcy to an individual who had no other recommendation than political influence. But he was more likely to exercise some discretion and name at least some men of ability or standing.

Both modes of selection violated every known principle of military procedure. But, surprisingly, they worked. They brought in at the start, along with some misfits, a large number of capable men who became regimental commanders immediately or who, like Hayes, began in secondary roles and worked their way up. Only a society of immense innocence could have sanctioned such methods of providing military leadership and only one of infinite vigor and diversity could have produced such abundant and able officer material with these methods. These men were the good colonels, and without them the nation could not have officered its armies. An overwhelming majority of them were civilians. In 1861 there were in the regular army, after the departure of Southern sympathizers, about 440 graduates of West Point. These men would have made admirable training directors for the volunteer hosts, and an act of Congress authorized their employment in such a capacity. But precious few of them got out of the regular service. For one thing, the War Department resisted the transfer of its best personnel, and even if this attitude had not existed a regular officer could not have secured a state commission unless offered one by some governor. Of the 508 West Point graduates in civil life, 115 re-entered the regular service and 393 accepted commissions from their states in the volunteers. Many of the latter, like Rosecrans, began as colonels but were soon jumped up to the grade of general. By any computation, then, most of the 2,000 volunteer regiments, probably 1,600, had to be commanded by men with no professional military background. The Civil War is always considered a West Pointers' affair, and this is true in the largest sense. In the sixty biggest battles graduates of the academy commanded both armies in fifty-five, and in the remaining five a graduate commanded one of the opposing armies. No civilian general demonstrated the capacity to direct an army of combined arms, nor did a civilian often command the largest unit in an army, the corps. But many civilians led brigades and even divisions, and they dominated the regimental commands. On the regimental level the Civil War was a civilians' war, and this was of moment for commanders of larger units, for generals commanding armies, and for directors of the highest strategy. The regiment was the basic unit of an army. If the regiments operated efficiently, the army could operate; it could even sustain its identity against bad leadership at the top. In the end, much of the effectiveness of a Civil War army came down to the personal qualities of its colonels.

A regiment consisted of ten companies and averaged in size from 900 to 1,000 troops and officers. This was its number when it marched off to war, but it was never as large again. Battle losses, disease, and desertion took their toll, and since practically all states put their recruits into new regiments instead of filling up veteran units the strength of most regiments steadily declined. By the end of 1862 the average strengths were down to 500 or 600, and later some regiments shrank to an even lower total. The command organization for a regiment was simple but adequate for the purpose. Regimental headquarters comprised a colonel, a lieutenant colonel, a major, and a staff of twelve commissioned and noncommissioned officers. The guiding spirit of the system, the man who had to oversee everything all the time, was the colonel. He had to educate his subordinates and the men under him, and in the process he was likely to get something of an education himself.

One of the first facts a regimental commander had to learn

was that his men were citizens first and soldiers second. Because they were civilians who happened to be wearing uniforms, they could behave in ways undreamed of at West Point and create situations never treated in the textbooks. One colonel out of the academy found that in his unit were two companies known as the Montgomery Guards and the Sarsfield Guards. On the day before a parade a Sarsfield lieutenant came to ask the colonel how the men should turn out, as Montgomery or Sarsfield Guards. Patiently the lieutenant explained the problem: "I am a lieutenant of the Sarsfield Guards and orderly sergeant of the Montgomery Guards, and the captain of the Montgomery Guards is orderly sergeant of the Sarsfield Guards." Even when this colonel recorded the incident after the war, his bafflement was obvious: "And so the two companies, in the most friendly manner, were made up of each other, and when paraded at different times were beautiful to behold, one clad in hibernian green and the other in our national blue; but when paraded together one of them was not there."[3] The citizen soldiers had a sharp eye for the stuffed-shirt officer or the pretentiously solemn order. They were likely to laugh at such instructions as those contained in an official pamphlet issued to the Ohio volunteers: "Be regular in the calls of nature"; "Swearing profanes the name of the God of battles. . . . The habit is unmanly, useless and degrading"; "Drinking—unless under medical advice, is your greatest curse"; and "Lewdness makes beasts of men," followed by the ambiguous exhortation: "Be as pure as when at home."[4] On the other hand, they were in some things as

---

[3] Joshua H. Bates, "Ohio's Preparations for the War," in *Sketches of War History, 1861–1865. Papers Read Before the Ohio Commandery of the Military Order of the Loyal Legion of the United States* (Cincinnati, 1888), I, 129–30. Six volumes of this valuable series were published between 1888 and 1908; hereinafter they will be cited as *Sketches of War History, Ohio Commandery.*

[4] Henry B. Carrington, *Ohio Militia and the West Virginia Campaign of 1861* (Boston, 1904), 23.

careless or helpless as children and had to be watched over like children. The good regimental commander knew this and acted accordingly. The records of any regiment will show that the colonel had to attend to even the most elementary detail —order the preparation of sanitary sinks, prohibit the discharge of firearms in camp, and force the men to wear only their prescribed uniform. Hayes openly told his men he regarded them as children, his children, and they liked the idea of this relationship because they liked him.[5]

Before he could do anything else, a colonel had to make his men like him. This was difficult, because he had to seem democratic and human, a man like themselves, and yet remain distant enough to preserve an aura of authority. He must view every man in the regiment as an individual with individual problems. A Jewish soldier once came to Hayes to ask transfer to another company. The men in his unit were ridiculing his religion, and he wanted to be in a certain company that contained a number of Jews. Hayes accomplished the change, and this man never forgot it. Even after suffering eight bullets through his body, he insisted on coming back to serve under the colonel.[6] A regimental commander had to persuade his men that he cared for them when they were ill or wounded by visiting the hospitals and passing out delicacies and words of cheer. If his wife accompanied him on these tours, the men were doubly impressed. Mrs. Hayes, who spent much time in camp, became a beloved figure to the men of the Twenty-third.[7] A colonel had to be able to mingle with

---

[5] Regimental Order Book of the Twenty-third Ohio, MS. in the National Archives, orders by Hayes of April 26, May 2, December 15, 1862; Joseph A. Joel, in New York *Daily Graphic*, June 23, 1876.

[6] Joel to Hayes, May 21, 1873, Joel Papers, Hayes Library; Joel, "Passover in Camp," in *The Jewish Messenger*, March 30, 1866.

[7] Journal of the 23rd Regiment, Ohio Volunteer Infantry, p. 14, typed copy in Russell Hastings Papers, Hayes Library; *Tributes to the Memory of Rutherford Birchard Hayes* (n.p., n.d.), 18, pamphlet published by the Ohio Commandery of the Loyal Legion.

the men on a familiar basis without inviting liberties. In effect, he had to act like a superior civilian. One soldier recorded an incident that revealed Hayes's technique and also something about the quality of the enlisted men: "Colonel Hayes came along looking in the company quarters; walked in cordially and laid down on our patent sofa—Indian bedstead; . . . I was trying to ask him to read a passage in Caesar, as the latin was a tough sentence, and he was a graduate of Kenyon. After resting awhile he went out. . . . Colonel Hayes seems to be pleased at our skill in fixing up things to make things homelike; but Colonel Scammon always wants things like West Point—*military*."[8] Many West Pointers were like Scammon. They wanted things military and they acted military, and these men simply could not command volunteers. The citizen soldiers could be persuaded and pleased and then led, but they could not be driven. If the colonel was liked and trusted, he could lead. If he was not, he might as well get out. In the last analysis, the discipline of a regiment depended largely on the personality of the colonel. The intelligent civilian leader was better fitted in almost every way to arouse the devotion of his men than the average West Pointer.

But winning devotion was only the first step in a colonel's progress to leadership. The colonel who was liked just because he was folksy and kind would not last. Sooner or later he would find himself in the situation for which he and his unit existed, battle, and it was here that he would make or break himself. The first quality that a regimental commander had to exhibit in battle was fearlessness, sheer physical courage displayed in the most spectacular fashion. The men would follow an officer who led them and try to execute his orders, not because of his rank, but because they accepted his leadership. But even a general who showed signs of fright would

[8] E. E. Henry, Diary, August 10, 1862, typed and printed copy in Hayes Library.

lose control of his troops. Hayes seemed to recognize instinctively this requirement of command and he always acted
on it. One of his officers wrote: "This implicit trust in the
man extended down through the brigade, the different regiments constituting it, and thence on down to the shortest
man in the rear rank. We all knew no foolish movement
would be ordered . . . but wherever we were our leader was
a leader in the full acceptance of the term, and we always
found him well to the front, with the orders, 'Come on boys,'
not 'Go on boys.' " In one engagement Hayes with the regimental colors and a portion of the regiment somehow got
beyond the formed line of battle and to the extreme front.
An officer who ranked him called: "Bring the colors back
to the line of the brigade." Hayes turned and shouted:
"Bring the brigade up to the colors." Without any orders the
brigade sprang forward with cheers to the advanced position.[9]
By modern standards such exhortations as Hayes's may seem
romantic and even incredible, but they were of the stuff
that inspired Civil War soldiers to perform impossible feats
of valor. When uttered by an officer exposing himself in the
very front of battle, they did not sound like empty rhetoric
to the men hearing them. It was an attribute of the good
infantry commander that he could spontaneously employ
language as an element of leadership.

But a colonel had to do much more in battle than strike
brave poses or shout inspiriting commands. Not even the most
headlong exhibition of courage would in itself carry the
field. A colonel was the director of an organized unit of
several hundred men, and he had to so dispose those men
as to attain the maximum effect of their numbers. In short,
he had to think as well as to act. The problem was perfectly
described by one officer: "Now the regiment becomes a

---

[9] Hastings, MS. Autobiography; *Proceedings . . . Twenty-seventh Annual
Encampment, Grand Army of the Republic*, 239.

machine, and now comes the hour of trial for its commander
—he must ascertain where the enemy is the best way he can—
he must see and think for that whole regiment, must direct
every movement, and watch every movement of the enemy.
. . . He must be cool when all others are excited, must stand
when all others are disposed to run." What this officer was
saying was that the regimental commander must have the
apparent ability to see through the terrain ahead of him and
to know what was coming. It has been called the gift of great
infantry officers.[1] In part, it meant only studying the ground
and envisioning what might happen and preparing contingent
plans. But a colonel could not do these and other things unless
he knew something about the art of war. The final quality
of a good colonel, and perhaps the most important one, was
that he had to be a technician in a highly specialized subject.
If he knew nothing about the subject, as was the case with
every civilian officer, he had first to educate himself, and he
had to do this not in an atmosphere of academic leisure but
in the heat and haste of war itself.

The colonel just out of civilian life had to learn about many
new and strange things—military rules and regulations,
military administration, and, most puzzling of all, tactics.
The only way he could learn them was by studying the
books. "Study the Army Regulations," a regular officer advised a civilian, "as if it were your Bible!" The serious
and ambitious colonels needed no prodding. "I *study*, I tell
you," one told his wife, "every military work I can find."[2]
Fortunately there were plenty of books available, most of
them pocket-sized manuals that could be carried in a sad-
dlebag or tucked away on a tent table. A colonel's basic

---

[1] Paul M. Angle (ed.), *Three Years in the Army of the Cumberland: The
Letters and Diaries of Major James A. Connolly* (Bloomington, 1959), 78;
John J. Pullen, *The Twentieth Maine* (Philadelphia, 1957), 111.

[2] Jacob Dolson Cox, *Military Reminiscences of the Civil War* (New York, 1900),
I, 20; Willard M. Wallace, *Soul of the Lion* (New York, 1960), 44.

library would probably consist of *Regulations for the Army of the United States, 1861,* H. L. Scott's *Military Dictionary* or a similar compilation, perhaps a translated edition of Napoleon's *Maxims* or Jomini's *Art of War* to provide a sampler of strategy, and one or more books on tactics. The tactical manuals were many but essentially the same in content. In 1855 the War Department had adopted William J. Hardee's *Rifle and Light Infantry Tactics.* The book, really three compact volumes, was reprinted freely and pirated variations appeared abundantly in 1861. The War Department sponsored a uniform revision of Hardee, and this work, compiled by Silas Casey, was published in 1862 in three small volumes. Entitled *Infantry Tactics,* it was universally called *Casey's Tactics,* and it became the most widely used manual of the war. Hayes, like other volunteer officers, found it invaluable. Interestingly enough, its detailed instructions did not refer to the regiment as a tactical unit. Casey, like Hardee and other writers before him, called the basic unit a battalion. But as his battalion comprised ten companies and was identical in size with a regiment, it was easily adaptable to the requirements of the volunteer forces.[3]

First a colonel had to master his manuals; he was a pupil educating himself. But even as he studied he had to become a teacher and impart his knowledge to others. The effect of the volunteer system was to ensure that practically all the officers of a regiment would know nothing about war or their

---

[3] A good discussion of the war manuals is in Francis A. Lord, *They Fought for the Union* (Harrisburg, 1960), 39–52. The full citation for Casey is Silas Casey, *Infantry Tactics* (New York, 1862). In preparing this summary of military literature, I have benefited from material supplied by William K. Kay. Mr. Kay has also rendered valuable assistance to my discussion of the whole matter of troop training. Hayes apparently did not own a copy of Hardee but seems to have had a similar manual published in 1861. Later he acquired a copy of Casey. List of Hayes's military books supplied by the Hayes Library.

jobs. The civilian colonel who was learning his business had to instruct other civilians—civilian lieutenant colonels, majors, and staff officers; civilian company commanders, perhaps the most important of all, because they had the closest disciplinary contact with the men; and civilian noncommissioned officers. Finally, under the supervision of the colonel, all of these had to instruct 1,000 civilian soldiers. And so the regiment became a huge school, with faculty members teaching each other and each trying to stay a lesson ahead of his students. The mechanics of instruction were effectively simple. An order of Colonel Scammon's read: "On *Monday,* next, and until further orders, the company officers of the 23rd Reg't, not otherwise on duty will assemble at 3 p.m. for recitation in Infantry Tactics and instructions in matters relating to military *discipline.* It is to be understood that this is not a matter of choice, but that the attendance is required by *order.* . . ." Another Ohio colonel, who had to whip a regiment into shape quickly, organized what in a later era would be called an accelerated program: "Officers recite in three classes on alternate evenings at my quarters—non-commissioned officers recite at company Headquarters divided into convenient sized classes."[4] The classes were concerned with regulations, tactics, and training; but at the same time a colonel had to oversee a vast amount of administrative detail that would continue to demand attention after the educational process had ended. To provide an orderly and permanent control of this area, a colonel would set up a "council of administration" consisting of the next three senior officers. The council dealt with all kinds of matters and lifted a heavy routine load from the

---

[4] Regimental Order Book, Twenty-third Ohio, October 18, 1861; J. Warren Kiefer to Mrs. Kiefer, November 12, 1862, in Kiefer Papers, in Division of Manuscripts, Library of Congress.

colonel, leaving him in the formative period of a regiment's life time to prepare it for the fundamental mission of combat.[5]

In the writings of Civil War colonels, whether these be official orders, private letters, or diaries, there is one word that occurs and recurs. It is "drill," and no infantry officer could give his men too much of it. Colonels drilled their outfits when they were breaking them in and continued to drill them throughout the rest of the war. "You will remember," one officer recalled to his men after the war, "whenever I had the opportunity, I drilled the regiment thoroughly. I took it out, exercising it in firing, in movements, and even taking it through the brush and timber so as to give them practice in conditions they might meet." The men had not liked it, he recalled, but it had paid off when they got into battle.[6] The routine for this drilling was rigorous. Reveille was at five or five-thirty in the morning. The Twenty-third while under Scammon in 1861 engaged in squad drill for an hour before breakfast, in company drill in the morning, and in drill with arms and regimental drill in the afternoon. This schedule was typical of many regiments in the first year of the war; later it would be cut to a morning and afternoon period.[7] An Ohio colonel detailed in his diary the duties of an average day. In the morning he supervised company drill. At two in the afternoon the officers recited tactics to him and then went out to take over squad drill. "Daily drills—daily

---

[5] Regimental Order Book, Twenty-third Ohio, June 21, 1861, March 13, 1862.

[6] Grenville M. Dodge, in *Fiftieth Anniversary, Fourth Iowa Veteran Infantry* (Council Bluffs, 1911), 10. One regimental commander even as late as December, 1864, drilled his regiment two hours every afternoon. Otto Eisenschiml (ed.), *Vermont General: The Unusual War Experiences of Edward Hastings Ripley, 1862–1865* (New York, 1960), 279. See also Quaife (ed.), *From the Cannon's Mouth*, 31.

[7] Regimental Order Book, Twenty-third Ohio, July 8, 1861; Hastings, MS. Autobiography; Horton and Teverbaugh, *Eleventh Regiment*, 210–11; Augustus Van Dyke, "Early Days; or the School of the Soldier," in *Sketches of War History, Ohio Commandery*, V, 20.

recitations in tactics—take the starch out of some, and others are learning fast. And now I superintend,—select an officer to drill the others in the morning, one squad drill, company drill, and Battalion [regimental] drill in the afternoon. . . . I drill the sergeants daily, in length of step, time and preserving distance."[8]

The first form of drill to which the recruit was introduced was squad drill or the "school of the soldier." Here he learned such fundamentals as how to stand at attention and salute and face right and left. He learned how to load and fire a musket. As prescribed in the manuals and as actually practiced, a soldier had to go through nine motions before he could discharge his weapon. The process was complicated and had to be thoroughly drilled into the recruits. Once mastered, however, it became second nature. A veteran soldier could fire two to three shots a minute from a standing position. Generally the men went through the motions without using real or even blank cartridges. But whenever an officer could procure blanks he did; one Ohio colonel issued 18,000 rounds to his men for the "firings."[9] In squad drill the recruit also got his first taste of the intricate movements which Civil War armies employed to move to battle and to move in battle, and he received increasingly larger doses of these in the next two stages to which he progressed, the "school of the company" and the "school of the regiment." Now the recruits learned to move from a column of fours, the marching formation, to a line of battle consisting of men in two ranks, one behind the other, and to change from the line back to the column. These movements as described in the manuals seem incredibly involved and they were. But they were the only means by which an army could place itself in a position where it could fight.

---

[8] Jacob Ammen, MS. Diary, July 24, 1861, in Illinois State Historical Library, Springfield.
[9] J. W. Kiefer to Mrs. Kiefer, November 2, 1862, Kiefer Papers.

The practical problem was immense. For example, a division of three brigades of twelve regiments marching along a narrow road might stretch out for a mile and be only eight feet wide. As it approached the battlefield, it had to swing into a completely different formation, throwing itself forward in a series of movements over all kinds of terrain to form a line. But it might sometimes happen that after engaging in battle an army had to maneuver on the field, had, for example, to roll forward to another position. Then its units had to shift from the line to a column of fours again. This was accomplished by the elaborate "marching by the flank," one of the most difficult movements for recruits to master. At the command to march to the right or the left, depending on the situation, the two lines faced in the indicated direction. The men in the rear rank sidestepped one pace and each even-numbered man advanced to the right or left of the man in front of him to make a column of four. If each soldier remembered his number, which was not always the case, the unit moved off smoothly. In the school of the regiment, companies learned to execute these and other movements as part of the regiment. Training beyond the regimental level was relatively rare and seems to have been limited to the brigade. One brigade commander who did drill his regiments described the process in a passage that shows how generals hoped to move their units in battle: "Would you not like to see four or five regiments closing up into mass, then deploying into line of battle, then moving rapidly to the front in 'echelons' forming squares all in one grand oblong parallelogram, then separating into squares of single regiments, oblique and direct; in short, taking all manner of offensive and defensive positions and all moved without confusion or disorder and controlled as by a single thought to the same end?"[1]

All moved and controlled by a single mind to the same end

---

[1] Quaife (ed.), *From the Cannon's Mouth*, 34–5.

—that was the grand purpose of the ceaseless drill in tactics. And the end was to place men where they could fight, to place them there in such a way that their commander could move them as he desired and have them perform as he directed. The evolutions of the manuals may seem complex and merely ceremonial to the modern mind, but they had definitely a combat mission. They were the only method that Civil War commanders knew to position and move men in battle while maintaining one of the immutable principles of war—control or unity of command. A regiment in line of battle formed in two ranks, one behind the other. The men stood side by side with an interval of approximately twenty-four inches between them; the distance between the men in the front and rear ranks was thirty-two inches. If its ten companies were at full strength, a regiment, with an interval of three yards between each company, would take up a space of 300 yards. A brigade would occupy 1,300 yards, and a division attacking in a column of brigades, a common assault formation, would advance on a front three quarters of a mile wide.[2] In short, Civil War units and armies fought in close order (a relatively compact or massed formation) rather than extended order (a loose or spread-out formation), although some of the prewar manuals had hinted at increased use of the wider arrangement. Close order was resorted to because, for one thing, it seemed the easiest way to instruct quickly the hosts of volunteers. For another, it promised to accomplish most readily one of the great objectives of a Civil War army, the delivery of mass firepower. Massed men would produce mass fire—it seemed as simple as that. But above all, close order was employed because it would provide control by a single mind, the mind of a general over an army, the mind of a corps or a division or a brigade commander over his unit,

---

[2] John K. Mahon, "Civil War Infantry Assault Tactics," in *Military Affairs*, XXV (1961), 61–3.

and finally, down where the whole chain ended, the mind of a colonel over a regiment.

It did not work out that way at all. If there is one thing that was characteristic of Civil War battles, it is that nobody, from the commanding general through every grade to the colonels, had anything like full control of what happened. In fact, in many engagements the opposite of control seems to prevail—armies break apart in the hands of their commanders and operate on their own or not at all. The tactical system failed to function as it was supposed to for three big reasons. First, it was adopted from a European school of warfare and could not be readily adapted to the American scene. The Europeans who wrote the drillbook from which the Americans drew their tactics envisioned a battlefield as a gigantic chessboard. The regiments and the larger units and possibly even the whole army would be drawn up on a flat and open space. Every soldier in a regiment would be under the visual control of his colonel, every regiment under its brigadier, and every brigade under its divisional commander. And they would remain under sight and under control in battle. The system broke down, and control along with it, in the American terrain. A commander lined his men up and sent them plunging ahead into woods, gullies, and ravines, and that was the last he saw of them as a unit. Second, the formations in the drillbooks did not allow for the advance in weapons and firepower. A defending force could pour out a greater fire than in any previous war. Yet infantry assaults continued to be made much in the old storybook style of the eighteenth century, with the attackers moving forward in a succession of rigid lines that were supposed to remain parallel until the very moment they hit the enemy. That was the way it was supposed to be, but it hardly ever was. As the attackers approached the defenders and came under heavier fire, they lost their formation. The lines ran together and became finally a bunched mass. At best, a frontal assault would shock the defenders and perhaps dislodge them. More often, it was repulsed or contained.[3] Third, and perhaps most important, the one factor that might have enabled the attackers to overcome the handicap of terrain and possibly that of firepower was lacking. The communications system was inadequate even for as close and small a unit as a regiment.

The problem of tactical communications is an old one in warfare, and in modern times was not satisfactorily solved until World War II and the advent of field radio. After the Civil War, as the firepower of armies grew even greater, the tactical formations became more and more dispersed. Dispersion evaded some of the impact of firepower but increased the difficulties of command and control. All kinds of liaison devices to enable an officer to keep in touch with his men were tried out and were in use by the time of World War I. Communications were improved in that conflict but were not really effective except in static situations. Control of fluid situations became possible only in World War II, when every company and platoon leader might carry a radio, and even then it did not always work. By the time of the Civil War technology had augmented the fire capacity of armies with better weapons, but it had made no contribution to tactical communications. Commanders still had to try to control their units or men with traditional methods. It is commonly said that the close attack formations of the war represent a lag of tactics behind technology—that military conservatism prevented a shift to looser arrangements—and this is in part true. It is also true, however, that the communications lag made any change looking to dispersion utterly impractical. The commander of so small a unit as a regiment had trouble

---

[3] As the war progressed, new assault methods were developed. These looked to a more extended tactical formation. Infantry advanced in a succession of rushes. The skirmish line was strengthened and given a larger combat mission.

controlling his men in a compact formation. He would have had no control at all if the formation was extended. With the crude communications system at their disposal, it was remarkable that the Civil War colonels did as good a control job as they did.

A regiment in line of battle would be drawn up in two ranks as shown on the chart on the facing page. Two paces behind the rear rank stood the "file closers," a thin line of lieutenants and sergeants whose function was to direct the men and to restrain any of them who later might break for a place of greater safety. To ensure that the line of battle and the alignment of the regiment were absolutely straight, men bearing staffs and flags and known as "markers" took up prescribed positions. The field officers—colonel, lieutenant colonel, and majors—were supposed to be on horseback in battle. The colonel took a position thirty-five paces behind the file closers and opposite the center of the regiment. The other field officers took posts farther to the front and to the right and left. Nearest to the colonel was the junior major, who directed the skirmishers moving out ahead of the main attack. The adjutant and the sergeant major, posted on the respective flanks, assisted the lieutenant colonel and the senior major. When all was ready or when the orders came down from above, the regiment stepped off, in the phrase of the drill books, "with life." As the line advanced into battle, the colonel was supposed to remain thirty paces to the rear of the regiment, but as a matter of fact he was likely to be anywhere and everywhere, leading charges, exhorting the men, and giving orders directly instead of through his officers.[4]

When the regiment was standing in line and as it moved off, it was under comparatively good control. Even a full-strength unit drawn up in two ranks could not take up very much space, and it was possible for the colonel, unless there

[4] Casey, *Infantry Tactics*, I, 14, II, 104–5, 148–9, 153–6, 177–8.

REGIMENT IN LINE OF BATTLE

Left guide

Sgt. Major

Senior Major

National and regimental colors

Colonel

Field music

Junior Major

Riflemen (in two ranks, by companies)

Lieutenant Colonel

"File closers" (four sergeants, three lieutenants per company)

Adjutant

Right guide

First Sergeant

Captain

was a lot of competition from artillery fire, to address his orders by voice command. But this phase was only momentary. As the men drove into woods and gullies and the racket of battle swelled in volume and the lines ran together or the companies became separated, voice control was lost. A colonel or another field officer acting for him could, of course, issue orders to knots of men, and if the regiment happened to be halted by fire in a sheltered area the colonel might be able to make himself heard by all the men. But as a rule, once battle was joined, unit control by voice was impossible. The only way that the colonel could exercise any kind of direction of the whole regiment was through the "field music," composed of the company buglers and drummers who for battle were assembled in a special group and posted near the colonel. The field music, not to be confused with the regimental bands, which existed for ceremonial purposes and were discontinued in July, 1862, was the field radio of the Civil War. By bugle call or drumbeat the colonel might make his orders known to his men scattered all over a field and beyond his sight. Casey's *Tactics* prescribed twenty-six general bugle calls for all troops and twenty-three special calls for skirmishers and fifteen drumbeats for all troops and twenty for skirmishers. These signals included such general orders as the "long roll," to assemble for action; "come for orders," to summon sergeants and corporals; "double quick time"; and "retreat"; and such special instructions as "change direction to the right" or "left" and "rise up" and "lie down." Sometimes the calls could not be heard amidst the din, and sometimes a call for one unit might be heard and obeyed by another. Still they worked surprisingly well and offered a colonel his best medium of communication.[5] The system

---

[5] Casey, *Tactics*, I, 15, 228–30. The chain of order transmission in an army, according to the manuals, worked as follows. The commanding general made his wishes known to division commanders by means of staff officers or the telegraph. The division general in turn passed the orders on to the brigade

would not work unless everybody knew what was expected of him. Indeed, the whole business of a Civil War regiment—battles, marches, administration—would not work unless everybody knew his particular business: the colonel, the regimental officers, the company commanders, and the enlisted men. As a part of the learning process, all the parties concerned had to develop a certain trust in the competence of the others. That was what the members of the Twenty-third Ohio were doing in the summer of 1861—learning about the business of war and each other. There was no more eager educator and student than Major Hayes.

---

commanders through staff officers. The brigade commander notified the regimental commanders by "word of command," which presumably meant in person. Casey, *Tactics,* III, 6, 89, 158. The whole subject of how in a Civil War army orders were actually sent down the line and how messages and information were sent up is one that needs investigation.

Chapter 3

The Road to West Virginia

THE OHIO volunteer regiments marched off to war in 1861 amidst scenes of mass emotion that were repeated all over the North. Whenever the units appeared—as they left their home towns, as they assembled in cities like Cleveland or Cincinnati for departure to camp, as they arrived at camps of instruction—they were showered with tokens of affection and hailed as heroes going forth to save the Union. People could not do enough for the young warriors, but few in the applauding crowds believed that this thrilling martial adventure was going to have any serious outcome. When the South saw the might being mobilized against her she would back down, and in the meantime hurrah for the boys and hang Jeff Davis to a sour apple tree and enjoy the whole gorgeous spectacle. One regiment, moving from its first camp to another by rail, was almost mobbed at Cincinnati by relatives, sweethearts, and friends. "Each, anxious to see his own particular loved ones, pushed, crowded, and elbowed about, regardless of the rights, liberties, and corns of his neighbors," wrote an appreciative reporter. "In the general squabble, coats were torn, trousers fractured, and hoops crushed like egg-shells." A bevy of young ladies became so entranced with the wholesale kissing going on that they managed to remain on the cars as the strange procession pulled out of the station. Even after the regiments reached their camps, the holiday atmosphere continued to reign. At a camp near Cincinnati, noted another reporter, the soldiers enjoyed a kind of protracted picnic. "We found the road to camp dotted with carriages protruding from which might be seen baskets and bottles, all fitted with the good things of this life. . . . Indeed, we fear that, while our volunteers are stationed so near the metropolis . . . they will not be permitted to experience much of real camp life, except so far as drills and orders are concerned. There is considerable patriotism shown in refusing to eat mess pork at the expense of Uncle Sam, when Davis' sugar-cured is furnished in abundance by the plethoric purses of loyal citizens, not to mention the enthusiasm excited by the fact that the gambrel of the deceased quadruped . . . is handsomely bedecked with tri-colored ribbons, attached by the dainty fingers of loved ones." When the novelty of camp life wore off, as it soon did, the volunteers relieved their boredom with all kinds of improvised recreations—boxing, fencing, baseball, minstrel shows, and readings and recitations. At one camp the men devoted their efforts to constructing museums featuring such exhibits as a piece of government bacon preserved in spirits and an army biscuit placed under glass to retain its natural toughness; and at night they relaxed from their scientific observations by dancing with each other "into the still, small hours." Officers as well as men contributed to the spirit of fun and frolic. A surgeon at one camp sent up through channels a certificate recommending the discharge of a soldier afflicted with chronic rheumatism caused by his limbs having been broken in a "railroad collision." The document received the approval of officers above him, including his comanding general, and came back with the notation: "This department is not informed that railroads ever collide."[1]

---

[1] Cincinnati *Commercial* and Cincinnati *Gazette,* quoted in E. Hannaford, *The Story of a Regiment* (Cincinnati, 1868), 34–41; Cleveland *Leader,* quoted in Wilson, *Seventh Ohio,* 34; New York *Tribune,* quoted in Frank Moore (ed.), *The Rebellion Record* (New York, 1862–8), II, 52; J. E. D. Ward,

Much of the amateur aura surrounding the muster of 1861 reflected the amateur way in which Ohio and other states, in fact the whole American democracy, lumbered into war. In the first frenzy of excitement regiments were called up for three months to protect the state against a feared Southern invasion. Volunteers came forward faster than the state's inadequate and improvised military department could absorb them. The units were literally poured into hastily designated centers of assembly: Camp Chase near Columbus, the location of Hayes and the Twenty-third; Camp Taylor near Cleveland; and Camps Harrison and Dennison near Cincinnati. Ten thousand men descended on Dennison, which received the largest concentration, and five thousand on Taylor. At Chase the regiments apparently lived under tents from the beginning. At the other camps most, if not all, of the officers and men were quartered in hastily constructed wooden barracks. Many an arriving regiment at these sites found to its disgust that its first duty was to locate lumber and put up its own shelters. But the defenders of the Union had to be not only housed but fed and, because they had left home in whatever costume they were wearing or could procure, uniformed. The state hurriedly arranged with private contractors to supply all these items—for example, contractors agreed to furnish food at the price of fifty cents a man per day—and just as hurriedly sought in domestic and foreign quarters to procure arms of any kind. These and other supplies arrived late or in small numbers or not at all, and the volunteers complained loudly and publicly. Particularly irritating to them after the comforts of home was the inadequacy of the rations. Many attempted to remedy the deficiency by relieving the countryside of surplus chickens and cows and experienced their first taste of enemy fire from farmers' shotguns. Newspapers which circulated in

---

Twelfth Ohio Volunteer Inf. (Ripley, 1864), 18–20; Bates, "Ohio's Preparations for the War," in *Sketches of War History, Ohio Commandery,* I, 133–5.

the camps fanned the discontent by printing stories of the
privations endured by the men, and visiting relatives raised it
still higher by professing shock at the conditions they saw. In
the midst of the turmoil it became apparent that the war was
going to be more than a brief affair, and the state made
strenuous efforts to induce the three-months men to enlist for
the three-year period stipulated in national law. Camp conditions were not conducive to continued sacrifice, and some of
the units went home in disgust at the end of their hitch. But
most of them signed up for the longer service with a great
show of grumbling that hardly masked their underlying purpose to see this war through. It was a combination of re-enlisted and newly enlisted companies that made up the
Twenty-third Ohio, one of the first three-year regiments in
the state.[2]

At Camp Chase the Twenty-third was in a more sober and
businesslike atmosphere than prevailed in the other training
centers. The concentration of men at Chase, three thousand,
was smaller than in such hives as Dennison, and the volunteer
officers had more opportunity to learn their trade. Possibly
the difference was also due to the presence of a number of
professionally educated officers. Certainly the Twenty-third
profited from having professional leadership from the beginning. Rosecrans, its first commander, departed for a higher
assignment during the second week of encampment, but he
left something of a stamp on the regiment. Somewhat above
average height and thin, Rosecrans was a warm, affable man,
incisive in manner and confusingly rapid in speech. Energetic
and impulsive, he did not betray as yet the lack of balance
that would eventually destroy him. He obviously knew his

---

[2] Reid, *Ohio in the War*, I, 28–9, 43, 55–6; Wilson, *Seventh Ohio*, 29–30, 32–4;
Hannaford, *Story of a Regiment*, 41–2; Joseph A. Saunier, *A History of the
Forty-seventh Regiment Ohio Veteran Volunteer Infantry* (Hillsboro, 1903),
10–11; George L. Wood, *The Seventh Regiment: A Record* (New York,
1865), 23–4; Ward, *Twelfth Ohio*, 19.

business, and if others did not know that he knew it, he told them in great detail and with learned allusions to military history. Whatever personal defects he later demonstrated, he was a skilled and trained soldier, and he impressed the officers of the Twenty-third with the idea that war was a serious business to be carried on by serious men.[3] Hayes saw him go with genuine regret. Matthews, as the second ranking officer, could have had the command; but both he and Hayes thought the regiment should have a more experienced leader, and they exerted their influence to get such a man named. But when Colonel Eliakim P. Scammon appeared in late June to take over the regiment, Hayes and other officers were somewhat shocked at what they saw and wondered if they had been right in seeking the service of a professional. Some of the doubters never made up their minds about the new commander.

Scammon, a native of Maine, was a West Pointer, graduating with high honors in 1837. He accepted a commission in the corps of topographical engineers and saw varied service at West Point, in Florida and Mexico, and in the far Southwest. He won advancement, going up to captain; but along with some obvious ability, he exhibited a certain unreliability of character. Assigned to direct road projects in New Mexico Territory, he spent a large sum of money without doing any actual construction, and in 1856 he was dismissed from the service because he could not explain a small shortage in his accounts. He became a professor at a Catholic college in Cincinnati, and when the war started he offered his talents to Ohio. Governor Dennison appointed him colonel of the Twenty-fourth Regiment and then transferred him to the vacancy in the Twenty-third. Scammon's army troubles undoubtedly could be attributed more to carelessness and ineffi-

---

[3] Cox, *Military Reminiscences*, I, 111-12; Reid, *Ohio in the War*, I, 314; Charles Leib, *Nine Months in the Quartermaster's Department* (Cincinnati, 1862), 137.

ciency than anything else, but he came back into the service under something of a cloud. Perhaps because of his reputation, he was especially military, ostentatiously spit-and-polish. But it was in his personality to be that way. A relatively small man, he was inclined to strut and bluster to make his presence felt. He could be friendly and gracious one moment and impatient and insulting the next. An exaggerated preciseness of speech and manner, accompanied by a habit of delicately taking snuff, made him seem ridiculous to the enlisted men, who called him "old granny." They told and retold true or exaggerated tales of his egotism, the favorite being that he had once demanded a private railroad car because he was too good to ride with common soldiers. He was undeniably a character, almost a caricature of the natural and complete martinet. He was fussy about everything and especially detail. Hayes at first acquaintance measured him as being irritating but interesting, intelligent and educated but lacking in "vigor of nerve," and on the whole not fitted for volunteer command. Later Hayes and other critics would have cause to revise their judgments somewhat. For all his faults, Scammon knew his trade thoroughly, and he put the regiment on a rigorous routine of training that transformed it from a raw mass into a disciplined outfit. And in battle he shed his nervous excitability and became a cool and courageous leader.[4]

When Scammon reviewed the regiment for the first time, he had some reason to rant at the peculiarities of volunteer soldiers. The men of the Twenty-third, like those in many other outfits, came to camp in civilian clothes. They hoped to be provided almost immediately with uniforms, but, as was the case with most units, they received nothing. Days and

---

[4] Reid, *Ohio in the War*, I, 915–16; William H. Goetzmann, *Army Exploration in the Far West, 1803–1863* (New Haven, 1959), 361–2; Ward, *Twelfth Ohio*, 56–7; 59; Cox, *Military Reminiscences*, I, 110–11; Hastings, MS. Autobiography; Hayes, MS. Diary, July 12, 1861; Hayes to Mrs. Hayes, June 20, 22, 30, July 2, Hayes MS. Letters.

weeks went by, and their original apparel became ragged and dingy. Then, just as Colonel Scammon appeared, the first clothes issue came through—undershirts and drawers but no blouses and trousers. At the evening parade on the day of issue the regiment turned out before its new commander, the men, either because they had nothing else to wear or because they thought it proper, clad only in their official shirts and drawers. Scammon, in the words of one observer, "simply wilted" and dismissed the parade. But later in his quarters he summoned the officers and gave them a lashing lecture on the importance of correct form in military ritual. Shortly the missing blouses and trousers arrived, and then the men at least looked like soldiers. Other and more serious shortages existed, however, and one of these created a bad situation that Scammon the professional did not know how to meet. It became so grave that had his volunteer officers not intervened he would have lost control of the regiment.

Ohio, like every other state, was practically without weapons to arm its troops, and with the same frenzy that marked all preparations it bought, begged, and distributed whatever small arms it could locate. The Twenty-third, in common with most units, received an issue of old flintlock muskets converted into "percussion locks," that is, equipped with percussion caps, one of which was to be fitted onto the nipple of the gun before firing and when struck by the hammer would ignite a spark to detonate the powder charge. This was too much for the young heroes. They had come forth to save the nation, and they expected to be given proper weapons to do the job. They refused to accept the guns. Some companies stuck the muskets in the ground by the bayonet and marched back to quarters; others simply stacked them in piles. Scammon, who had not thought it necessary to explain to the men why such guns had to be issued, now flew into a rage and ordered some of the company commanders arrested. His conduct only increased the tension, because these officers could not be fairly blamed for failing to control the situation. In some way the men themselves had to be reached and persuaded to accept the muskets, and this result could not be achieved by a ramrod colonel or by such junior leaders as captains. It could be done only by officers of some rank who were from civilian life and could speak the language of the men, who could, in the bluntest terms, appeal to the citizens in uniform on the level of a stump speech.

Hayes and Matthews recognized their role and accepted it. They went from company to company, pleading with the men to take the guns. Hayes did most of the talking. The weapons were the only ones available to the state, he said. They would do for temporary use, to practice the manual of arms, and later better models would be provided. Besides, he went on, the man was more important than the weapon. The ancestors of the men listening to him had won the jewel of American freedom in the Revolution with muskets even poorer than these. Would their descendants then refuse any weapons in an hour of greater peril? It was exactly the kind of exhortation calculated to move the impressionable boys, and they responded as Hayes must have known they would. Somebody yelled: "Bully for Hayes . . . let's get our guns," and the crisis was passed. From the affair Scammon apparently learned a lesson, that in certain situations he would have to rely on his volunteer officers. At a Fourth of July ceremony shortly thereafter he put the regiment through its evolutions, but he remained in the background when Matthews and Hayes orated on the meaning of the day and its relation to the purpose of the war.[5]

---

[5] Hastings, MS. Autobiography; William McKinley, *Rutherford B. Hayes* (New York, 1893), 3–4; McKinley, in an address, *Proceedings . . . Twenty-seventh Annual Encampment, Grand Army of the Republic,* 237–8; H. Wayne Morgan (ed.), "A Civil War Diary of William McKinley," in *Ohio Historical Quarterly,* LXVI (1960), 279. The episode of the guns was McKinley's first meeting with Hayes.

Now the regiment settled down to a routine of training—going through the various schools of drill and mastering the manual of arms—and, profiting from the expert knowledge of Scammon and the tact and inspiration of Hayes and Matthews, it gradually shook down to the shape of a seasoned outfit. Supplies of all sorts arrived in numbers, and the men moved with the satisfaction of pride of soldiers properly sustained. Hayes came to cherish more respect for Scammon and decided that with proper assistance the colonel could get along with volunteers. Eager to learn the military art from any source, Hayes picked up valuable knowledge from Scammon and also from Colonel Jacob Ammen, the West Point-trained commander of the Twenty-fourth Ohio, with whom he had many conversations. The appointment of his wife's brother, Dr. Joseph Webb, as regimental surgeon gave him a feeling of security; with "Dr. Joe" at hand he had someone to turn to who would understand all his problems.[6]

It was well that both Hayes and the regiment were growing in confidence, for late in July, after approximately five weeks of training, the rumor spread through camp that the Twenty-third and other regiments would soon move out— to where nobody knew but certainly to a theater where there would be serious fighting. The news of the Federal defeat at Manassas shook Hayes and other volunteer officers. He and Matthews thought the regiment might be ordered to Washington, and they spent most of one night superintending the opening and distribution of cartridge boxes so that the regiment could march at instant notice.[7] Finally on July 24 the awaited orders came down the line: the Twenty-third would be ready to march at five the next morning with cooked rations for three days and compact baggage. Other regiments were to follow in sequence. As far as anybody knew, the

[6] Hayes to Sardis Birchard, July 21, 1861, Hayes MS. Letters.
[7] Hayes, MS. Diary, July 23, 1861.

movement was to be from Columbus to Zanesville by rail, down the Muskingum River by steamboat to Marietta on the Ohio River, and down the Ohio to Ripley Landing in western Virginia, the region that the Ohio troops already were calling West Virginia. Presumably the ultimate objective of the movement was the occupation of the Kanawha Valley. It looked like business at last.[8]

When the orders were announced, Hayes went in to Columbus to say goodbye to his family. He found, apparently to his surprise, that Lucy was upset by the news. She "showed more emotion at my departure than she has hitherto exhibited," Hayes recorded in his diary. She insisted on spending the night with him at Camp Chase, and together they spent the evening "going around among the men gathered in picturesque groups, cooking rations for three days at the camp fires." The next morning, the twenty-fifth, Lucy took a hack into town to bring her mother back to camp. She was determined to see her husband and his regiment leave camp and to see them off at the railroad station. Hayes remembered well the scene that followed. "I marched in with the men afoot—a gallant show they made as they marched up High Street to the Depot." As the cars pulled out, he kept his eyes on Lucy and her mother. "I saw them watching me as I stood on the platform at the rear of the last car as long as they could see me. Their eyes swam. I kept my emotion under control enough not to melt into tears."[9] Hayes too had been affected by the parting, more than he thought he would be. The great

---

[8] Hayes to Sardis Birchard, July 24, 1861, Hayes MS. Letters; Ammen, MS. Diary, July 24, 25; Regimental Order Book, Twenty-third Ohio, July 24. Again it is stressed that the part of western Virginia that was a distinct military theater and that became in 1863 the state of West Virginia will be referred to in these pages as West Virginia. Significantly, this nomenclature was widely employed by the Federals about to move into the region. Colonel Ammen, for example, wrote in his diary that his regiment would follow the Twenty-third to Ripley Landing, West Virginia.

[9] Hayes, MS. Diary, July 25, 1861.

experience of the war was catching up both him and Lucy, as it was doing with countless others, and was molding them, as it would the whole nation, to its own form. With the Hayeses, the effect was like a release, a response to emotions hitherto restrained by the demands of a formalized society.

At Zanesville the orders were changed. The troops were to continue on to Bellaire on the Ohio and there take the Baltimore & Ohio Railroad to Grafton in West Virginia. At Grafton they changed to a branch of the Baltimore & Ohio and proceeded to Clarksburg, the Twenty-third as the vanguard unit reaching that point on July 27. The Ohio troops, although little more than a hundred miles from the border of their own state and in the midst of a Union-sympathizing population that welcomed them as protectors, felt that they were in the presence of the enemy. The Twenty-third, at least, had made the trip in good shape. Equipped with ample wagons and supplies, the men had not suffered for want of food. Other units were not so fortunate. Colonel Ammen's Twenty-fourth, for example, had no wagons or horses and its cooked rations were carried in the baggage car. Ammen asked a commissary officer at Bellaire to provide him with food, and this functionary coolly suggested the colonel take his 1,000 men to a country grocery and buy some crackers and cheese. When Ammen had the baggage taken out, he found that the cooked meat and the bread had spoiled. The hungry men could do nothing but eat them.[1]

Hardly had the Twenty-third laid out its camp at Clarksburg when General Rosecrans, now commander of all troops in West Virginia, appeared and ordered an advance the next day to Weston, about twenty-three miles to the south. The move was to start at an early hour in the morning, but the task

---

[1] Hayes to W. A. Platt, July 26, 1861, and to Mrs. Hayes, July 27, in Hayes MS. Letters; Hayes, MS. Diary, July 27; Ammen, MS. Diary, July 26.

of organizing the heavy baggage trains was too much for the inexperienced regimental staff. Not until eleven did the march begin and then in a heavy rainstorm. Soon the rain ceased and a scorching sun bore down on the green troops. It was hard, but they were in high spirits. The scenery was fine and not without unexpected delights. "Blackberries beyond all description," in Hayes's phrase, lined the road. Most stimulating of all, they were approaching contact with the enemy, and the enemy was suspected of being all around them. When they stopped for the night, a broken limb in a treetop was thought to be a spy peering down into the camp, and mysterious fires, undoubtedly warming Confederate troops, were detected in the distance. Because of the delay in starting and perhaps because of the blackberries and the need for caution in the presence of the enemy, the regiment made only fourteen miles on the first day. Scammon was outraged and blistered the company officers in an official order. The march of a regiment, he said, "must not be allowed to become the straggling journey of a mob." If a repetition occurred, no excuses would be accepted—it was the fault of the officers and not the men. Even after this admonition, it took the regiment until shortly after noon on July 29 to complete the nine miles into Weston.[2]

Scammon rode at the head as the regiment toiled into town, a long line of men stretching behind him on the Clarksburg Pike, with stragglers even farther back and equip-

---

[2] Hayes, MS. Diary, July 28, 29, 1861; Regimental Order Book, Twenty-third Ohio, July 29; John M. Clugston, MS. Diary, July 28, 29, in Hayes Library; Clugston was a sergeant in the Twenty-third. Actually, the first day's march, fourteen miles, was not bad for a volunteer regiment, especially when the late start is considered. Practically every volunteer unit in the service had march troubles early in the war. Not only were the officers inexperienced and the men green, but many regiments were slowed down by the abundance of their supplies—both in the baggage wagons and in the haversack of every soldier. Wilson, *Seventh Ohio*, 39.

ment scattered along the route of march as far as a village with the fascinating name of Jane Lew. Weston was a typical small West Virginia town of the period. Located in a basin between commanding hills, it boasted beautiful scenery and a population of slightly more than 800. The army correspondent of the New York *Times* found it and the smaller places nearby depressing. Weston, he wrote, was "finished and fenced in by the inertia" of its people; the principal employment in Jane Lew was the sale of applejack; and Jacksonville was noted for its "abominable, anti-abdominable green apple pies." But Hayes, who would be stationed in Weston until August 20, thought it and the whole countryside delightfully unlike anything he had ever seen. Nothing in Ohio could equal it, he told Lucy. The town's inhabitants were divided between the Union and the Confederacy in their sympathies and regardless of their loyalties did not take kindly to the presence of so many strangers. They assured Hayes that the troop concentration was responsible in some way for a spell of heavy rains, and when Hayes accidentally killed a valuable dog belonging to an influential citizen feelings were aroused that survived his election to the presidency. Whatever its aesthetic merits or shortcomings, Weston was an important strategic center. Federal forces were in the area before the Twenty-third arrived, and the regiment had been moved to Weston to strengthen the Federal hold on the front of which the town was the center. Standing astride the Staunton and Parkersburg and the Weston and Gauley Bridge turnpikes, Weston was like a gate commanding the entrance to other and vital areas of West Virginia. It constituted a defensive screen for the Baltimore & Ohio line to the north and an offensive base against Confederate-held territory to the northwest. Similarly, it was a shield against Confederate moves to the south toward the Kanawha Valley, which a Federal force

had occupied in July, and a jumping-off place for advances
into Confederate territory to the south.[3]

As if to herald that the Twenty-third was now in for more
serious work, half of the regiment under Matthews was detached for scouting service around Bulltown and Sutton,
about fifty miles to the south. The other half remained at
Weston under Scammon, with Hayes acting as the next senior
officer. The function of the Weston force was to build up a
large supply depot and to scour the country for guerrillas who
attacked small parties of troops and intimidated Union sympathizers. The guerrilla-hunting expeditions went out almost
daily; they numbered from ten to one hundred men and
sometimes went into the hills as far as forty miles from Weston. Hayes accompanied at least one of them and took a real
zest in the work. The secession supporters, he decided, were
the wealthy classes and the ignorant, and the sound middle
class stood for the Union. Like many other officers of a previously moderate temperament, his attitude toward the war and
the South was hardening. He could be shocked when he
heard that Matthews's men at Sutton had destroyed some
legal records in the courthouse, but two days later he could
write without emotion of the fate of a huge guerrilla of 230
pounds and "long hooked toes, fitted to climb" who had shot
at a squad of the Tenth Ohio: "They probably killed him,
after taking him prisoner, in cold blood—perhaps after a sort
of trial."[4]

The business of rounding up guerrillas was not exactly
enough to occupy all the energies of Scammon. Hayes thought
Scammon had been improving in his knowledge of how to

---

[3] Roy Bird Cook, *Lewis County in the Civil War* (Charleston, 1924), 20, 48,
50–1, 149–50; Hayes to Mrs. Hayes, July 30, 1861, Hayes MS. Letters; Hayes,
MS. Diary, August 1; Edward Conrad Smith, *A History of Lewis County,
West Virginia* (Weston, 1920), 301–2.

[4] Hayes to Sardis Birchard, August 8, 12, 17, 1861, and to Mrs. Hayes, August
15, 17, Hayes MS. Letters; Hayes, MS. Diary, August 10, 12.

Theater Map of
WEST VIRGINIA

deal with volunteers, but now at Weston, in the atmosphere of camp life again, the colonel reverted to his old martinet ways. A series of scolding orders issued from headquarters. Officers and men were not performing their duties with alacrity. Officers, noncommissioned officers, and enlisted men were absent from their posts or asleep on duty, and the penalty for sleeping on duty, to officers as well as to ordinary soldiers, was death. Men were discharging their firearms without orders and unless the practice was stopped the officers would be placed in arrest. Officer resentment against Scammon rose to a new high when he dressed down a lieutenant in front of his men for permitting some of them on guard duty to go to their tents to sleep. But the wrath of the whole regiment was aroused by an order forbidding gambling in camp. Instead of employing themselves in mastering the military art, the directive ran, the men were "sneaking" around to play at cards and dice. Gaming not only engendered a disregard for duty, Scammon said in language calculated to stir soldier scorn, it ruined character: "It makes men *bad* and bad men cannot be good soldiers." Hayes tried to stand between the men and their irascible commander but without much success. The regiment needed more instruction and less grumbling, he noted in his diary: "The men are disconcerted whenever the Col approaches; they expect to be pitched into about something. . . . He gives no instruction either in drill or military duties but fritters away his time on little details which properly belong to clerks and inferior officers."[5]

Suddenly the gloom caused by Scammon's behavior and a series of rainy days lifted—the Twenty-third, or the Weston half of it, heard that it was to move out again, with three days' rations, forty rounds of ammunition to a man, and no tents or cooking utensils. Rumors said that a strong Confederate force was approaching from the southeast, possibly in the Rich Mountain area, where hard fighting had occurred earlier in the summer, and that the Twenty-third was to be part of a rapid concentration to meet the threat. "All is war," Hayes wrote with hopeful excitement in his diary. At daylight on August 19 the regiment was ordered to move to Buckhannon, some sixteen miles to the east. Again the marching performance was not too good, Buckhannon not being reached until the afternoon of the twentieth.[6] Portions of five other regiments were camped here, but they were hardly settled when orders from Rosecrans directed a continuance of the

[5] Hayes, MS. Diary, August 6, 9, 1861; Hayes to Mrs. Hayes, August 9, Hayes MS. Letters; Regimental Order Book, Twenty-third Ohio, August 2, 15.
[6] Hayes, MS. Diary, August 18–20, 1861; Hayes to Mrs. Hayes, August 17, and to Mrs. Sophia Hayes, his mother, August 21, Hayes MS. Letters; Clugston, MS. Diary, August 20.

march to Beverly, almost forty miles to the southeast. Tired but in good spirits, the men of the Twenty-third turned in a creditable march performance, making Beverly in about a day and a half. They were still moving on the Staunton and Parkersburg Pike, but they were in mountain country now and the going was rougher. Yet they stepped along briskly in the bracing air—the rains had suddenly ceased—and thrilled to the sweeping panorama of peaks and valleys as they passed over Rich Mountain. "I never enjoyed any business or mode of life as much as I do this," Hayes wrote Lucy. "I really feel badly when I think of several of my intimate friends who are compelled to stay at home." More than ever he was convinced that his decision to become a soldier was the right one. "I know we are in frequent perils—that we may never return and all that, but the feeling that I am where I ought to be is a full compensation for all that is sinister. . . ."[7]

The Twenty-third and other units at Beverly were getting a real baptism in marching, and more was to come as the Union command tried to decide from which direction the expected Confederate blow would fall. On August 26 the "half" Twenty-third and the Ninth Ohio moved still farther south, to below Huttonsville in the lovely Tygart Valley between Rich and Cheat mountains. Here they joined the command of General J. J. Reynolds, holding the northeastern passes, and here they expected to stay for weeks.[8] They were immediately and cruelly disappointed. On the twenty-seventh orders came to make a forced march to French Creek, a short distance south of Buckhannon, leaving tents and supplies to be sent on later. This was to be no jaunt over a turnpike but a toiling crawl over mountain paths. The move began in the afternoon, with Hayes leading the column over Rich

[7] Hayes, MS. Diary, August 21, 23, 24, 1861; Hayes to Mrs. Hayes, August 22, 24, 25, Hayes MS. Letters; Hannaford, *Story of a Regiment*, 99.

[8] Hayes, MS. Diary, August 26, 1861; Hayes to Sardis Birchard, August 26, Hayes MS. Letters; John Beatty, *Memoirs of a Volunteer, 1861–1863*, ed. by Harvey S. Ford (New York, 1946), 57.

Mountain. Hayes pushed the men as hard as he could, marching them in the dark and not halting until after nine that
night. After the thirteen-mile trek, the men slept on the
ground wherever they dropped. The next day Hayes and 300
of them made the thirty miles to French Creek after thirteen
hours of actual marching. Some companies of the regiment
and of other units and the train did not arrive until August
30. All in all, it was a fine performance, and well might Hayes
say: "We obeyed, and are yet alive."[9]

In its frantic march to French Creek the Twenty-third had
practically doubled back on its original line of march. It had
returned, although not by the same route, to a position on
the Weston-Buckhannon front. The reason for the seemingly
erratic movement was simple. General Rosecrans had decided
that the main Confederate blow would fall on the Kanawha
Valley to the south. He thought he could fortify and hold the
northeastern passes at Cheat Mountain and Huttonsville with
a comparatively small force, and he was concentrating the
bulk of his army to operate in the Kanawha. The Twenty-
third had been brought back to be a part of the concentration.
From Weston, Rosecrans would eventually march by way of
Bulltown, Sutton, and Summersville to reinforce the Federal
forces already in the Kanawha at Gauley Bridge. Early in
September the "half" Twenty-third moved to Bulltown and
was at last reunited with its other wing. The whole regiment
would shortly advance into the Kanawha, and here it would
meet its first test of shooting war. Here too Hayes and its
other officers would first see the big strategic picture of the
West Virginia theater and would come to a sharper appreciation of the character of the region in which they would spend
most of the war.

---

[9] Hayes, MS. Diary, August 27, 28, 1861; Hayes to Mrs. Hayes, August 30, Hayes
MS. Letters; Clugston, MS. Diary, August 27–30.

Chapter 4

The Enchanted Land

THE WESTERN FARM BOYS who marched over the Ohio River in 1861 had never seen anything higher than a big hill. Then they beheld West Virginia—its mountains rolling endlessly to a horizon misted in blue, its rugged cliffs and shaded coves and dark ravines, its forests of spruce and pine and laurel, and over it all the shadows always shifting to reveal a new delight. They were impressed then, and for the rest of their lives they could never quite forget the weird and wild panorama. One among them was an especially sensitive observer, and even after half a century he still envisioned West Virginia and its mountains as an "enchanted land." Ambrose Bierce recalled: "I note again their dim, blue billows, ridge after ridge interminable, beyond purple valleys full of sleep. . . . How we reveled in its savage beauties!" Other military sojourners in West Virginia could not say it in Bierce's wonderful words, but whether they were officers or enlisted men they tried their best, in contemporary lettters and diaries and in postwar reminiscences. Perhaps the one who came closest to Bierce was an Ohio colonel with a strong poetic streak and a real literary flair, John Beatty. In his diary Beatty reverted to the scenery in passage after passage in words like these: "Nests of hills, appearing like eggs of the mountain; ravines so dark that one could not guess their depth; openings, the ends of which seemed lost in a blue mist; broken-backed

[57]

mountains sloping gently to the summit; others so steep a
squirrel could hardly climb them; fatherly mountains, with
their children clustered about them . . . ; mountain streams,
sparkling now in the sunlight, then dashing down into apparently fathomless abysses."[1]

This was the lovely, the best side of West Virginia, the
aspect that the men who fought there liked to recall in after
years. But any realistic checking of memories would have
stripped away some of the romance and revealed another and
less attractive West Virginia, one that in the war was undeniably moist, especially in the mountains, where on occasion the rain fell in sheets for days and even weeks. The occasions were frequent when the first Federal troops entered
the area in the summer and autumn of 1861. "Mud is shoetop
deep," reported a disgusted Indiana soldier. "This week only
3 hours of dry weather. Only 5 days of no rain since we
entered W. Va." To the men of one Ohio regiment on the
march in a steady downfall it seemed that every hair on their
heads was "a safe conduit for the descending bounty of
Jupiter Pluvious" and that the mire, like "thick tar," was
tugging at their heels to pull off their shoes. Sudden storms
would inundate valleys between mountains where camps
were located and blot out entire sites and sweep surprised
soldiers to their death.[2] Often the expeditions hunting guerrillas, such as the ones Hayes and the Twenty-third participated in at Weston, had to travel in rain and mud, and even
in good weather the experience of crawling over mountain

---

[1] *The Collected Works of Ambrose Bierce* (New York, 1909), I, 225, 227–8;
Beatty, *Memoirs*, 31, 33. See also Saunier, *Forty-seventh Ohio*, 17; E. C.
Arthur, "The Dublin Raid," in *The Ohio Soldier*, II (January 5, 1889), 3;
Albert D. Richardson, *The Secret Service, the Field* . . . (Hartford, 1865),
178–9.

[2] Augustus M. Van Dyke to family, August 12, 23, 1861, in Van Dyke MS.
Letters, Indiana Historical Society Library, Indianapolis; Cincinnati *Commercial*, quoted in Moore (ed.), *Rebellion Record*, II, 291–2; Beatty, *Memoirs*,
60.

paths and boulders and through laurel brakes and gullies was enough to give the most ardent warrior a new sense of the beauties of the West Virginia terrain. Subjected to an unaccustomed climate and unaccustomed hardships and often lacking proper shelter, uniforms, and medical care, many of the first regiments were laid low by typhoid, malaria, and diarrhea.[3] Later better facilities would be provided and the health of the men would improve, but the rains never ceased. "Naught but rain and mud," wrote an Ohio soldier in 1863. "The same misty enveloping clouds dragged their way around the hills, deluging the whole surface of the country." And another Ohioan, transferred to West Virginia in 1864, wailed to his probably wet journal: "Want to go home worse than any time since I have been in the service."[4]

The three-year troops who entered the mountain fortress in 1861 would not return to their homes until the end of the war, and within its rocky borders they would spend most of their war career. Although it touched on Ohio, from which most of the Federals came, the troops from that state knew almost nothing about the region. For that matter, the forty-six counties that made up western or West Virginia were pretty much of a mystery to the whole outside world, even to Virginia, of which before the war they were an uneasy and unhappy part. Locked behind its lofty parapets, West Virginia lacked adequate transportation connections with its closest neighbors. The primary mode of travel was a system of turnpikes linked by a set of country roads, most of which were unsurfaced and in bad weather impassable. The major turnpikes, three in number, ran in an east-west direction.

[3] Saunier, *Forty-seventh Ohio*, 43; Wilson, *Seventh Ohio*, 45, 103–4; Hannaford, *Story of a Regiment*, 539; Alexis Cope, *The Fifteenth Ohio Volunteers* (Columbus, 1916), 15–16.

[4] Ward, *Twelfth Ohio*, 65–6; George W. Baggs, MS. Journal, owned by Mrs. J. W. Myers, copy provided by the late Roy Bird Cook, Charleston, West Virginia.

The Northwestern Turnpike extended from Winchester to Parkersburg on the Ohio River. The Staunton and Parkersburg Turnpike, over which Hayes and the Twenty-third trudged on their first long march, linked the two towns that bore its name. Farther south was the James River and Kanawha Turnpike, running from Covington to Charleston and connecting on the Ohio with Guyandotte (present Huntington). Floods and traffic had weakened the pikes, and in 1861 they were not in a state of good repair. Only one major railroad crossed the region to give access to the east and west. From Baltimore the Baltimore & Ohio ran to Grafton and on up to Wheeling, and a branch that was really a main extension reached from Grafton to Parkersburg.[5]

Even before the war this western or, strictly speaking, northwestern part of Virginia had been so distinct from the rest of the Old Dominion as to constitute almost a separate state. Geographical isolation alone was not responsible for its sense of difference. It was a rural region of small farms and small population centers. Only one town boasted of more than 10,000 people—Wheeling with 14,000—and there were only six others that exceeded the 1,000 mark. The white population was 355,000, approximately a fourth of the state's total. What set the area apart from Virginia proper in both human composition and social structure was the absence of slavery and a plantation economy. The number of slaves was only 18,000, less than one twenty-fifth of the whole slave population of Virginia.[6] It was not that the people of the western counties were in any way antislavery. Indeed, like

[5] Robert Blair Boehm, "The Civil War in Western Virginia: The Decisive Campaign of 1861" (unpublished doctoral dissertation, Ohio State University, 1957), 1–2; George Ellis Moore, "West Virginia and the Civil War, 1861–1863" (unpublished doctoral dissertation, West Virginia University, 1957), 22–4. A somewhat shortened version of Moore's work is *Banner in the Hills* (New York, 1963).

[6] Moore, "West Virginia and the Civil War," 8, 10. In addition, there were 2,700 free Negroes, making a total population of about 376,000.

other non-slaveholding Southern whites, they supported the peculiar institution, but in some indefinable way they felt they were different from the rich people to the east who owned slaves. They nourished a dislike and a distrust of those more fortunate folk who, it was bitterly believed, denied the western section a fair share of representation in the legislature and a fair share of appropriations for internal improvements. In sum, the people of the western region were, as were the inhabitants of other mountain areas in the South, outside the mainstream of Southern life and had little sympathy with Southern ideals and aspirations. The mountain counties opposed the secession of Virginia, and even after the act was consummated they refused to accept the result. Two successive conventions of Union men met at Wheeling and established what purported to be the "loyal" government of Virginia. This creation was recognized by the Federal authorities, and in part the sending of Federal troops into the region was prompted by a desire to sustain it. The presence of the troops gave the loyal government whatever real being it had and enabled it in 1863 to bring into existence the new state of West Virginia.[7]

When the Federals first came into West Virginia, they were welcomed as deliverers. But if they thought that all the mountaineers were Union lovers, they soon received a rude and sometimes lethal disillusionment. In many areas the inhabitants either sympathized with the Southern cause or, if not animated by any ideological attachment, resented the presence of the invaders. Operating in small groups or as individuals, they stalked Union lines of communications,

---

[7] C. H. Ambler, *The Makers of West Virginia* (Huntington, 1942), 7–31. Previous efforts to achieve statehood had been hopeless because of the provision in the national Constitution that no state could be divided without its consent—Virginia would not agree to losing any of its territory. But now the loyal government in the western counties permitted these counties to form a new state.

shooting at parties of soldiers and trying to run off cattle, horses, and other supplies. They were called guerrillas or bushwackers by the Federals, who conducted constant expeditions to round them up. If arrested for carrying arms, their invariable excuse was: "We were only hunting squirrels." A typical bushwhacker was thus described by an outraged Federal witness: "Imagine a stolid, vicious-looking countenance, an ungainly figure, and an awkward, if not ungraceful, spinal curve in the dorsal region, acquired by laziness and indifference to maintaining an erect posture; a garb of the coarsest texture of home-spun linen . . . and so covered with dirt as not to enable one to guess its original color; a dilapidated, rimless hat, or cap of some wild animal's skin, covering his head, the hair on which had not been combed for months; his feet covered with moccasins, and a rifle by his side, a powder-horn and shot-pouch slung around his neck, and you have the beau ideal of the West Virginia bushwhacker." The Federals came to hate them passionately and to hunt them without pity. Even as gentle and moderate a man as Hayes could hear of their being killed without a flicker of regret. Eventually many officers sent out to catch bushwhackers would come in without any prisoners. They would merely report that they had arrested So-and-so but that in bringing him in he had slipped off a log while crossing a stream and broken his neck or that he had been killed by an accidental discharge of one of the men's guns. There were also Union bushwhackers or irregulars, who fought their Confederate competitors and plundered Confederate sympathizers, and sometimes the disagreeable job of the Federals was simply to prevent collisions between the two groups, to stifle a West Virginia civil war.[8]

---

[8] Leib, *Nine Months*, 89–90, 93–4, 126–7; Martin F. Schmitt (ed.), *General George Crook: His Autobiography* (Norman, 1946), 86–7; Smith, *Lewis County*, 305–6. For the troubles of a Confederate leader with Union sympathizers, see Thomas L. Brown to Annie Brown, May 15, July 10, 1861,

Most Federal soldiers soon developed feelings of contempt and distaste for all West Virginians, loyal and disloyal alike. In part this was an inevitable reaction of an occupying and homesick soldiery, and in part it was a revulsion against that which was different. The natives were undeniably different. Poor, uneducated, deprived of contacts with the larger world beyond the ranges, they were unlike anything in the prosperous farmlands of Ohio and Indiana, were, in fact, very like the frontier people of the previous century. "These western Virginians eat and sleep like pigs," reported a soldier who had to spend a night in a small mountain cabin where everybody slept in the same room. Even when the inhabitants tried to perform acts of kindness for their military visitors, they aroused irritation by their blundering procedure. One soldier who was wounded in a brush with the enemy sought refuge in a cabin. The woman there willingly took him in and cared for him. A portion of his skull had been shot away, and the wound became infected with vermin. On it she poured liberal doses of the only remedy she could think of—turpentine! When his comrades found him, most of his mental faculties were gone. The soldiers had not the least compunction about taking advantage of the simple mountain folk. One group purchased some food from an old woman at an isolated farm and offered her Federal greenbacks in payment. Being familiar only with Confederate money, she demanded notes of that vintage. One of the men offered a counterfeit Confederate twenty-dollar bill, which the poor creature not only took but returned sixteen dollars in change. And like all delivering armies in the history of war, the Federals conceived that they had an inalienable right to prey on and steal from the people they were protecting. The sheep which grazed on many hill farms were especially favored for

MS. letters in possession of E. B. Fred, Madison, Wisconsin, copies provided by Roy Bird Cook.

confiscation. These creatures, the soldiers claimed, were un-
failingly hostile, shaking their heads menacingly and showing
their teeth as if to bite, and had to be shot in self-defense.
Sometimes the stealers suffered unexpected punishment. Some
men of the Twenty-third made off with a jug of whiskey from
a farmer's house and consumed it. Later the farmer came into
headquarters to complain of the loss of a jug of medicine his
daughter had concocted to treat a skin disease—a mixture
of "chamber lye" and whiskey.[9]

If the Federals were repelled by the people of West Virginia and alternately impressed and oppressed by the scenery,
they were for long periods downright bored with the kind of
war they had to conduct. It was dull, languid, and overwhelm-
ingly inconsequential. Typical entries in the diaries of two
soldiers of the Twenty-third indicate perfectly the tempo of
military life: "Scouting party of eighteen men. Went out
about ten miles where we burned a school house and a still-
house and captured fifty chickens and a number of turkies."
"Went to Piatt with Jenk took four prisoners two male & 2
Female. . . . Jenk went to Charleston got gall of cider to go
back on. . . . Hitch up and start Back   Stop at night where
we did going down   Had a good time with some Gals."[1] Even
when an actual enemy was encountered nothing much was
likely to happen. On the Greenbrier River two parties of
Federals and Confederates contested spiritedly to see which
would get possession of a blackberry patch, with the bluecoats
winning the prize. An officer in one Ohio regiment out on a

---

[9] Wilson, *Seventh Ohio*, 56–7; Hannaford, *Story of a Regiment*, 128–9; Joseph
B. Foraker, in *Tenth Reunion of the Society of the Army of West Virginia,*
1886 (Portsmouth, 1887), 127; Horton and Teverbaugh, *Eleventh Regiment,*
33; Michael Egan, *The Flying, Gray Haired Yank* (Philadelphia, 1888), 37–8;
J. M. Comly to R. B. Hayes, no date, MS. letter in Hayes Library.
[1] Clugston, MS. Diary, January 7, 1862; Michael Deady, MS. Diary, January
24–26, 1863, typed copy in Hayes Library.

scout was shot by a Rebel. Grasping that he was the first man in the regiment to be wounded, he sent a message back to camp with the great news. Dutifully the whole outfit turned out to hunt the assassin but without success. The smallest engagements were reported in the greatest detail and even a rumor of casualties was treated as a major event. One official report solemnly described an affair in which one man was killed and eight taken prisoners as a "disaster." A noncommissioned officer wrote elatedly of a skirmish: "It is reported that we wounded four rebels." He added hopefully: "We are sure of hitting one in the shoulder."[2] Denied the excitement of many or large battles, the soldiers in West Virginia had to spend long periods of inactivity in camp. To relieve their boredom, they resorted to every imaginable kind of recreation. The men of one regiment concentrated on making laurel pipes, carving out several hundred and practically denuding the countryside. Others turned to private study, outdoor games, and, of course, gambling. Some regiments published their own newspapers, the stories in them emphasizing a common conviction that the army in the mountains was being shut out from the big war.[3]

The war in West Virginia might seem trifling, but it had its unusual and even comic aspects. Indeed, at times it became weirdly unreal, as if the environment itself, the hazy, misty,

---

[2] Schmitt (ed.), *General Crook*, 91; Wilson, *Seventh Ohio*, 51; *War of the Rebellion: A Compilation of the Official Records of the Union and Confederate Armies* (Washington, 1880–1901), Ser. 1, XII, pt. 2, p. 116 (hereinafter cited as *Official Records* and unless noted all citations to Ser. 1); Clugston, MS. Diary, August 6, 1862.

[3] Hannaford, *Story of a Regiment*, 144–6; Ward, *Twelfth Ohio*, 68; Wilson, *Seventh Ohio*, 48; Cook, *Lewis County*, 38; Moore (ed.), *Rebellion Record*, II, 99. Actually, the army in West Virginia received excellent outside newspaper coverage. A number of soldier correspondents wrote regularly for the Cincinnati press, and the newspapers of that city and even of New York had their own reporters in the mountains. Many of their news stories are reprinted in Moore's *Rebellion Record*.

and enchanted land, was creating a grotesque parody of the military art. People did strange things. A captain about to lead his men into battle halted them at a farm and rushed into the yard to sharpen his sword on a grindstone. At Gauley Mountain, guarded by a ring of fortifications and batteries of heavy guns, a colonel placed his main reliance for defense on a "Devil's Trap" he constructed—a large log suspended over a road by a cable which when cut would drop the log and annihilate an approaching enemy column. Never having occasion to use it, he was convinced that it alone had held the Rebels at a distance. A regiment moving toward Philippi heard artillery firing in the distance, and its officers concluded a battle was in progress. Assured that such was the case by a cavalryman who chanced by, the men emptied their knapsacks of superfluous articles and began a forced march. Hundreds fell out by the road as heat and fatigue took their toll, but the remnant pushed on to the front. Panting into Philippi, they discovered that the firing was a salute in honor of the Fourth of July.[4]

There must have been more cases of mistaken identity of people and places in West Virginia than in any other theater. An artillery battery at Philippi, under orders to fire at any body of men approaching, detected a line of troops moving toward the town and got ready to blast them. Just in the nick of time the enemy was found to be an Indiana regiment engaged in drill. But the worst confusion occurred in the mountains. Here the net of circling little roads, the tangle of woods, and the always present mist of rain produced many ludicrous episodes. The Ohio troops never forgot the "Battle of Bontecou." A wagon master out looking for forage came

---

[4] Augustus M. Van Dyke, "Early Days; or, the School of the Soldier," in *Sketches of War History, Ohio Commandery*, V, 22–3; Saunier, *Forty-seventh Ohio*, 60; Hannaford, *Story of a Regiment*, 61.

in to General Jacob D. Cox's headquarters to report that he had stumbled upon a Confederate regiment encamped in rear of the Federal camp. Somewhat skeptical, Cox sent out an officer with a scouting party to investigate. The story was confirmed. Still unconvinced, Cox directed a Lieutenant Bontecou, known as an excellent woodsman, to check again. Bontecou came back at nightfall with unimpeachable evidence. He had crept close to the enemy camp, had counted the tents, and on being challenged by the guard had escaped by running through the woods. Cox now resolved on an attack at dawn. A brigade under Colonel Robert L. McCook was to pass beyond the Confederates and drive them toward Cox's troops, who would intercept and envelop them. McCook duly moved out, his guides taking him over many devious roads and finally to a thicket from where he could see the enemy. His suspicions aroused, McCook nevertheless crawled through the woods and looked out at what he thought he would see—the rear of his own camp! All the scouts had been misled into thinking they had gone miles from their starting point. In the meantime, the Eleventh Ohio of the intercepting force was waiting to trap the Rebels. Its colonel, hearing the clatter of approaching horsemen, yelled: "Here they come, boys. Give them hell as they pass." Rifles were cocked to fire when McCook and his staff, convulsed with laughter over the misadventure, rode out of the woods. It was some minutes before McCook could collect himself sufficiently to explain that he had come out to attack his own brigade. The mountain terrain was such that even experienced officers could lose their way a short distance from camp. But mistakes could be made even in relatively flat country. The most embarrassing error of all was committed by Hayes's Twenty-third Ohio. At Weston it heard that a Confederate regiment was encamped twenty miles distant at Walkersville.

Making a hurried night march, the men surrounded the town and waited till morning—when they found that they had captured the camp of the Tenth Ohio.[5]

But the war in West Virginia was not all monotonous routine and comic-opera skirmishes. The region was an important if not a major theater, and both sides recognized immediately the advantage of holding it and moved forces in. Brisk fighting had occurred before the Twenty-third had arrived on the scene, and tougher battles would lie ahead. West Virginia was important for many reasons. It was potentially a source of substantial manpower for the side that could occupy it. It also offered weighty political and psychological advantages to both contestants, more to the North than to the South. If the North could "liberate" this Union-leaning area, it would demonstrate that the boast of Southern solidarity was a myth; West Virginia could be made into a showpiece of Unionism in the midst of secessionism. Conversely, if the South could retain the region, it would deprive the North of a propaganda weapon and strengthen its own position as a united nation; the border of slavery would be the Ohio River, the traditional dividing line between the sections. But primarily West Virginia was important as a military theater, and this significance derived from its location. In the largest strategic sense, West Virginia, with its panhandle jutting up between Ohio and Pennsylvania, was an area dividing the North and the South. Southern possession of it would split the eastern and western parts of the Union, would push the Southern frontier to the Ohio and the Potomac, would, in effect, force the North to fight two separate wars. If the South could do no more than hold the Baltimore & Ohio Railroad or a vital stretch of the line, it could break the North's east-

---

[5] Andrew J. Grayson, *The Spirit of 1861 . . . the Sixth Indiana* (Madison, 1875), 30–1; Cox, *Military Reminiscences,* I, 115–16; Horton and Teverbaugh, *Eleventh Ohio,* 212–14; Ammen, MS. Diary, September 10, 1861; Clugston, MS. Diary, August 16, 1861.

west communications and interrupt the easy flow of troops and supplies from one theater to another. Nor were the Southern possibilities only defensive. It might be within the capacity of the South to mount from West Virginia offensives into Ohio or Pennsylvania, to bring the war right to the heart of the North.

The possibilities for the North, if it could grasp West Virginia, were even more lustrous. Not only would the Federals prevent their own war effort from being divided and deny the South the opportunity for an offensive, they would open up for themselves several inviting avenues of invasion into the Confederacy. They could move with relative ease to turn the Confederate position at Harper's Ferry. Holding the Baltimore & Ohio and using the railroad as a supply line, they could advance from Grafton or some other base southeastward to Staunton in the upper Shenandoah Valley and strike Confederate Virginia on the flank. Or, operating from the Kanawha Valley, they could march southward and deliver a crippling blow at the Virginia & Tennessee Railroad, thus interrupting communications between Virginia and the states to the west. Of the various strategic possibilities available to both sides, those before the Federals were easier to achieve. West Virginia was more "open" to the North than to the South. The blue forces had only to cross the Ohio and move up the river valleys, whereas those in gray had to overcome the Allegheny ranges. For the Confederates there were two routes of entrance to West Virginia: one, the Parkersburg and Staunton Turnpike leading to the Baltimore & Ohio; the other, the Kanawha Valley leading to the Ohio River. In the summer of 1861 the Confederate command decided to direct its main effort at the vital railroad line.[6]

---

[6] It will occur to the reader that the various strategic possibilities sketched above were not achieved by either side. The reasons were two. First, the terrain in West Virginia and the absence of adequate transportation facilities prevented rapid or sweeping movements. Second, neither side was able

The framing of Southern strategy for West Virginia was in the hands of General Robert E. Lee, acting first as commander of Virginia's military forces and then of Confederate forces in Virginia. On May 4 Lee appointed Colonel George A. Porterfield to command in West Virginia and ordered him to proceed to Grafton. Porterfield was a native of the region who was expected to rally Southern supporters to the cause. He understood that he would find bodies of local troops already assembled and that he would have no trouble raising all the men he needed. Lee did not feel it was safe to detach troops from eastern Virginia to accompany Porterfield, and he feared that the presence of such aliens might irritate the mountain inhabitants. When Porterfield stepped off the train at Grafton on May 14, he received a bad shock. Instead of the thousands of volunteers with whom he was to occupy the line of the Baltimore & Ohio he found nobody—he alone constituted the Confederate force in Grafton. Eventually some units came in from counties with Southern sympathies, but the number was small. Late in May, as Federal forces were moving out along the railroad, Porterfield retired southward a short distance to Philippi, where he hoped to effect a concentration. He was able to bring together only 775 men.

The Federals who menaced Porterfield and occupied Grafton after he left were the first contingent of troops from Ohio and Indiana. They were under the command of General George B. McClellan, whose Department of the Ohio included West Virginia. At the moment McClellan was not on the scene. He remained in Ohio to direct the forward movement of his army, making skillful use of the railroad line, and the 3,000 Federals at Grafton were under the direction of General Thomas Morris. Adopting a plan devised by one of his sub-

---

to put in the field large enough forces to attain its objectives. In comparison with other theaters, the armies in West Virginia were pitifully small. It is suggested that the failure of the North, with its larger resources, to commit more strength in West Virginia was a mistake.

ordinates, Morris decided to deliver a surprise attack at Philippi. The blow fell on June 3 and exceeded the rosiest Federal expectations. The Confederates, surprised and out-numbered, put up little resistance and fled all the way to Huttonsville. Philippi was a small engagement, but it was the first land battle of the war and as such it was duly cele-brated in the Northern press. And it was undeniably a Union victory. The rapid retreat of the Confederates became famous as the "Philippi races."[7]

Back in Richmond, Lee moved to bolster the sagging Confederate position in the mountains. He relieved Porter-field, who had not shown the ability expected of him, and named as his successor General Robert S. Garnett, a profes-sional soldier of solid reputation. Lee also reinforced Garnett with troops from eastern Virginia. At the same time he dis-patched to the Kanawha Valley to raise and organize a force there General Henry A. Wise, a former governor. Also directed to move to the Kanawha if necessary was another former governor, John B. Floyd, who was putting together a brigade in southwestern Virginia. Undoubtedly Lee, absorbed with the defense of the whole Virginia frontier, had many problems on his mind, but his dispositions were open to criticism. If it was as vital to hold the western rim as he seemed to think, he should have concentrated his columns, swinging his main blow in one sector, either in the north under Garnett or in the south in the Kanawha Valley.

As a result of the dispersion Garnett lacked the strength to undertake an offensive to regain the Confederate position on the railroad. Arriving at Beverly early in June, he labored to

---

[7] Boehm, "Civil War in Western Virginia," 16–41; Douglas Southall Freeman, *R. E. Lee* (New York, 1945), I, 503–4; Eva Margaret Carnes, "The Battle of Philippi," in *American Heritage*, III (1952), 56–7, and *Centennial History of the Philippi Covered Bridge, 1852–1952* (Philippi, 1952), *passim;* Festus P. Summers, *The Baltimore and Ohio in the Civil War* (New York, 1939), 162–3; Grayson, *Spirit of 1861*, 24.

augment his force but could not bring it up above the 5,000 mark. In the face of a developing Federal push southward, he decided that his only course was to hold the mountain passes and prevent the enemy from advancing on the Staunton and Parkersburg Turnpike into the upper Shenandoah Valley. West of Beverly rose the Laurel Hill range, an offshoot of the Alleghenies, and Garnett fixed on it as his line of defense. He placed the bulk of his small army on the eastern slope of Laurel Hill. A few miles to the south he posted a smaller force on Rich Mountain. Now, in a naturally strong position and protected by breastworks of timber and earth, Garnett felt more secure. His line was well chosen, but he did not reflect that in case of disaster he would have only one road of retreat open to the south. Nor did it occur to him that the Federals might turn Rich Mountain instead of attacking Laurel Hill and cut off his escape route.[8]

In the meantime General McClellan himself had entered West Virginia. The total forces under his command—sixteen Ohio regiments, nine Indiana regiments, and two West Virginia regiments—numbered around 20,000 men, but a large portion was detached at key points to guard the Baltimore & Ohio line. At Grafton McClellan had some 9,000 troops available for field operations. With him as his senior subordinate was General Rosecrans, but recently colonel of the Twenty-third Ohio. Determined to clear the Confederates out of the northwestern counties, McClellan in early July moved his army toward Garnett's position in front of Beverly. Accompanying him was the first field telegraph ever to advance with an American army. His march well masked, McClellan arrived in front of Rich Mountain without the Confederates, who lacked any kind of intelligence service, being aware of his

---

[8] Moore, "West Virginia and the Civil War," 271–2; Freeman, *R. E. Lee,* I, 532–3; Theodore F. Lang, *Loyal West Virginia* (Baltimore, 1895), 34–5; Hannaford, *Story of a Regiment,* 65–6.

presence. Now occurred the fatal flank movement that Garnett in his fastness on Laurel Hill might have foreseen but did not. Rosecrans learned of a road leading to the rear of Rich Mountain, and on July 11 forces under his command smashed their way to the crest. The next day McClellan made juncture with Rosecrans and advanced to Beverly. Garnett's left, or southern, flank was turned and his natural escape outlet was closed. When he realized the situation, he retired northward in a confused fashion, but pursuing Federals caught and killed him at Corrick's Ford. The remnants of his army finally made their way to Monterey in Confederate Virginia. Rich Mountain was the first substantial Northern victory of the war, and it made McClellan's reputation. Later in July he would be called to Washington to take over the command of the Union army around the capital and to begin the career that would demonstrate that his victories in West Virginia had been largely undeserved. Rich Mountain intoxicated the Northern public. From the press came elated predictions that all serious Confederate resistance in West Virginia would now end. Just as delirious were the soldiers who had participated in the pursuit of Garnett. "F.F.V.," they gleefully announced, now had a new connotation—it meant "Fleet Footed Virginians."[9]

The victory was genuine enough, but few of the expected large strategic results followed. At Beverly the Federals were only a hundred miles, a five-day march, from Staunton in the Shenandoah, and they would have met no organized Confederate force on the way. But McClellan's innate caution and restraining orders from Washington held him back. The Federals did, however, push troops farther east to occupy the

---

[9] William R. Plum, *The Military Telegraph During the Civil War* (Chicago, 1882), I, 97–8; Boehm, "Civil War in Western Virginia," 58–80, and "The Battle of Rich Mountain, July 11, 1861" in *West Virginia History*, XX (1958), 5–15; Freeman, *R. E. Lee*, I, 534–5; New York *Times* and Cincinnati *Commercial*, quoted in Moore (ed.), *Rebellion Record*, II, 288, 296; Augustus M. Van Dyke to his family, July 23, 1861, Van Dyke MS. Letters.

important pass at Cheat Mountain. Still the outcome of the summer campaign was for the Federals substantial and satisfactory. At the same time that McClellan had advanced from Grafton, he had sent a smaller army under General Jacob D. Cox into the Kanawha Valley. Crossing the Ohio at Point Pleasant, Cox moved up the valley to Charleston against the weak resistance of Wise and all the way to Gauley Bridge, where the rivers New and Gauley met to form the Kanawha. Thus the Federals had driven two deep and strategically potent salients into West Virginia. Holding the passes in the northeastern counties, they were in a position to drive at Staunton or at Millborough or Jackson's River and the Virginia Central Railroad that supplied the Confederates in the Kanawha. Or, if they retained and strengthened their Kanawha base, they could sweep southward against the vital east-west link of the Virginia & Tennessee Railroad.

At the moment the Federals, while fully aware of the possibilities on both fronts, were too apprehensive of a Confederate offensive to think of launching one of their own. Rosecrans, who succeeded McClellan in command when the latter went to Washington, was content to hold the Baltimore & Ohio line. To this end he fortified the passes at Cheat Mountain and at Elkwater between Huttonsville and Huntersville and placed General Reynolds in command of the defending force. It was to support Reynolds, rumored to be the object of a Confederate push, that Hayes and the Twenty-third had made their long march to Huttonsville in late July. Soon Lee himself arrived in West Virginia and spent fruitless weeks trying to devise a move that would take the Confederates past the Cheat Mountain barrier and on to Grafton.[1]

Lee's inability to move convinced Rosecrans that the north-

---

[1] Moore, "West Virginia and the Civil War," 309–10; Reid, *Ohio in the War,* I, 771; Charles Whittlesey, *War Memoranda* (Cleveland, 1884), 24–5; J. T. Peters and H. B. Carden, *History of Fayette County* (Charleston, 1926), 236.

eastern passes were safe and that the fighting here would settle into a holding action. At the same time rumors came that the reinforced Confederates under Floyd and Wise were preparing to move on Cox. To sustain Cox, Rosecrans now decided to shift the bulk of his army south to the Kanawha. He had another motive for making the move. Both he and McClellan had believed from the first that the Kanawha Valley offered the largest offensive possibilities. If he could, while holding the line to the north, crush the forces of Wise and Floyd, he would hold all of West Virginia and would be free to move east or south on vital flanks of the Confederacy. Before turning toward the Kanawha, he had to establish a secure line of communication between his northern sector and Cox's forces at Gauley Bridge. A chain of posts was set up, running from Clarksburg on a line through Weston, Bulltown, Sutton, and Summersville.[2] On the last day of August Rosecrans set his army in motion southward. The Twenty-third Ohio was a part of the movement. Returning from its rugged trek to Cheat Mountain, it joined Rosecrans at French Creek and advanced to Bulltown and Sutton. At Sutton, Rosecrans organized his force in three brigades: the First, under Henry W. Benham; the Second, under Robert L. McCook; and the Third, composed of the Twenty-third and Thirtieth Ohio, under Scammon, who thus temporarily exercised regimental and brigade command. Then the march continued, and on September 9 the army moved to near Summersville, just north of Cox's advanced line.[3] The Confederates were near at hand, and battle was in the air. From now on Hayes and the Twenty-third would know real war, and they would come to know too every part of the Kanawha Valley. In this rich and rolling land they would fight most of their war.

---

[2] Cox, *Military Reminiscences*, I, 105–7; Moore, "West Virginia and the Civil War," 313–14.

[3] *Official Records*, LI, pt. 1, 471, V, 586; Cincinnati *Gazette*, dispatch by "Agate," quoted in Moore (ed.), *Rebellion Record*, III, 44.

Chapter 5

The First Campaign

HAYES AND HIS REGIMENT were about to enter one of the most picturesque regions in all West Virginia. For almost a hundred miles the Kanawha Valley unrolled in scenic splendor, from the junction of the Great Kanawha with the Ohio at Point Pleasant to Gauley Bridge at the confluence of the New and Gauley rivers. Hills and bluffs rose on either side of the river, and at Charleston, about halfway up its course, the mountains began. Charleston, the metropolis of the Valley, counted a population of only 1,500 and appeared to the invading Northerners as no more than a straggling village. Smaller but more charming was the hamlet of Gauley Bridge, the advance post of the Federals, standing astride the eastern entrance to the Valley and shielded by towering Gauley Mount and Cotton Mountain.[1] Gauley Bridge was a natural bastion and the key to the Kanawha, and its importance had been readily apparent to General Jacob D. Cox when he led his little army into the area in July. The Federal commander, a scholarly politician turned soldier, who would show solid aptitude during the war, had immediately seized the place,

---

[1] Wood, *Seventh Regiment*, 63–4; Whittlesey, *War Memoranda*, 17; MS. description of Charleston by Roy Bird Cook, in Hayes Library; Cook, "The Destruction of Gauley Bridge," in *West Virginia Review* (Oct., 1925), 5–7, 36; Benjamin Franklin Stevenson, *Letters from the Army* (Cincinnati, 1884), 131; Cox, *Military Reminiscences*, I, 83–4.

GAULEY BRIDGE

This picturesque spot, the advance base of the Federals in the Kanawha Valley, would charm Hayes and all other officers who saw it. The drawing is by Corporal J. Nep Roesler of the Forty-seventh Ohio.

1

THE BATTLE OF CARNIFIX FERRY

This drawing, showing the Federals attacking the Confederate works, is another product of the soldier-artist Corporal Roesler.

WEST VIRGINIA VIEWS
Big Sewall Mountain (top) and the Hawk's Nest (bottom), both occupied by the Federals early in the war, were typical of the rugged terrain that awed the Northern soldiers.

THE TOMPKINS ESTATE

Hayes was enraged that this property of a wealthy Confederate should be guarded by Federal soldiers.

IV

and as the weeks passed he felt increasingly secure from attack. His forces, which numbered at the most 4,000, were spread along the Gauley Bridge front and all the way back to Charleston.

Cox's belief that he was safe in his mountain fastness was, as he soon apprehensively realized, without foundation. The Kanawha Valley was important to both sides. Its population, divided in sentiment between North and South, offered a fertile recruiting source. It contained valuable natural riches, including one of the largest salt springs in the country. Most significant of all, the Valley apparently offered tempting military possibilities. For the Federals, the James River and Kanawha Turnpike, running in an east-west direction, could become an avenue of invasion leading straight to Confederate Virginia. Cox, a subordinate commander, saw the Valley only in defensive terms, but his superiors, first McClellan and then Rosecrans, envisioned it as an offensive base. Before the Federals could even think about an offensive, however, they had to mobilize their strength to hold the Valley. For in August it became menacingly clear that the Confederates were preparing an offensive of their own.

The Confederates had more incentives than the Federals to secure the Valley. They too needed its human and material resources, and for reasons of morale they wanted to expel the invaders from Southern soil. And like the Federals, they saw the James River and Kanawha Turnpike as an invasion route, one that might carry them right to the Ohio River valley. Or, because the feeder roads from the pike ran north to connect with the Gauley Bridge and Weston Turnpike, the Confederates could veer to threaten the Baltimore & Ohio line. Even if they did no more than hold the Valley, the Southern forces would accomplish an important objective— they would stand between the Federals and the vital railroads linking Virginia to North Carolina and Tennessee. These were the stakes that brought the Confederates back to the Kanawha.

The stakes were high, but the Confederate play for them was wretched. Two separate Southern armies approached the Valley in August. They operated under what was surely one of the weirdest command arrangements in all the history of war. Technically General Lee commanded all Confederate forces in West Virginia. At this time Lee was north in the Cheat Mountain area, but even had he been on the scene he would have had difficulty in controlling the two unusual individuals who led the gray columns. John B. Floyd and Henry A. Wise were politicians. Both had served as governor of Virginia, and Floyd had been Secretary of War in the last national administration before secession. Neither showed much military ability then or later in the war. But even if they had possessed real quality, their flaws of character would have prevented them from achieving any success. Each was extremely bellicose, irritatingly irresponsible, and apparently more intent on destroying the other than hurting the enemy. When Floyd heard that Wise had been ordered to West Virginia, he exploded: "God damn him, why does he come to *my country?* . . . I don't want the damned rascal here. I will not stand it." Wise, for his part, expressed the most biting contempt for Floyd, once referring to him in the presence of troops, after Floyd had been wounded, as a "bullet-hit son of a bitch."[2]

Floyd outranked his rival and commanded the Confederate forces in West Virginia. His authority was meaningless, however, because the two generals by choice operated separately; and on the occasions when they did join, Floyd's orders were so confused and contradictory that Wise could not have

---

[2] James Morrison, Jr. (ed.), "The Memoirs of Henry Heth," in *Civil War History*, VIII (1962), 13, 15.

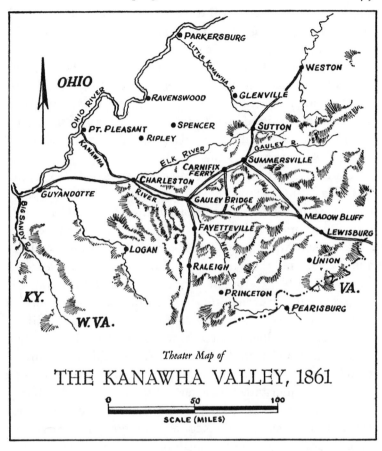

Theater Map of

THE KANAWHA VALLEY, 1861

SCALE (MILES)

obeyed them even if he had been disposed to, which he was not. The Confederate command arrangement augured ill for the success of any offensive. But the situation seemed to threaten real peril to Cox's force at Gauley Bridge. On paper Floyd and Wise had 4,000 men apiece, about twice as many as Cox had. Actually the disparity was not as great as it seemed. Some of the Confederates were local militia and poorly armed, and neither Floyd nor Wise could have put a column of more than 2,000 in the field. Still the danger appeared acute to the Federal high command. If the Confederates could cross the Gauley, they might be able to interpose between Rosecrans to the north and Cox and to cut off Cox if he attempted to retreat down the Kanawha. It was this possibility which led Floyd in late August to approach the Gauley front and probe for a crossing. Wise thought that the Confederates should remain on the south side of the river, and the two generals exchanged sulphurous arguments about strategy.[3]

It was rumors of Floyd's advance that led Rosecrans, McClellan's successor as Federal commander in West Virginia, to prepare to shift his troops southward from the Clarksburg base. By a quick move "Old Rosy" hoped to save Cox from envelopment, to trap the Confederates between his own force and Cox's, and then to organize an offensive to clear the Kanawha Valley. He began to draw together all his available units, bringing in even outfits like the Twenty-third Ohio that had suffered recent hard service. His army, when mobilized, would number close to 8,000 men of all arms. To maintain communications with Cox and to sustain his own line of march south he set up a chain of posts on a line from Weston down to Summersville.[4] The news of the Confederate advance prompted Rosecrans to extend his chain farther south. He ordered the Seventh Ohio Regiment to move from Summersville to Cross Lanes, on the north bank of the Gauley and just a few miles from the important crossing of Carnifix Ferry.[5]

---

[3] Moore, "West Virginia and the Civil War," 317–21; Lang, *Loyal West Virginia*, 43; Freeman, *R. E. Lee*, I, 584–5; Milton W. Humphreys, *Military Operations, 1861–1863, Fayetteville, West Virginia* (Fayetteville, 1926), 2–4. The last item, written by a Confederate participant, contains an inlaid article with no pagination on the campaign of 1861 by Roy Bird Cook, "The Battle of Carnifex Ferry."

[4] Moore, "West Virginia and the Civil War," 324; Cox, *Military Reminiscences*, I, 92–3; Reid, *Ohio in the War*, I, 52–3.

[5] This place, which would have a vital role in ensuing events, had, like so many West Virginia towns, a name of variant spellings. In the official docu-

But suddenly, on August 26 and before Rosecrans had started to march, Floyd struck across the river and routed the Seventh in a surprise attack. The Confederates then retired to a fortified position at Carnifix Ferry.[6]

If Floyd had had a larger force, and some military competence to go along with it, he would have been able to deal the Federals all kinds of trouble. He had interposed between the Federal flanks and could, had he greater strength, have thrust at either. But with only 2,000 men it was the rankest folly for him to stay on the north side of the Gauley, particularly when he knew that Rosecrans's larger army was approaching. Instead of retiring he remained at the Ferry, alternately talking of marching to the Ohio or of being overwhelmed by superior numbers and bickering with Wise, who in the meantime had been skirmishing on the New River front and dispatching his usual quota of insults to his commander. Floyd's location posed both a problem and an opportunity for the Federals. Left alone, he was a potential threat to Cox. If attacked in force, he might be destroyed. In either event, the situation called for quick action from the Federals.

Rosecrans grasped the possibilities open to him. On August 31 he left his headquarters at Clarksburg, and his army swung southward. Making fair time over rugged roads, the troops neared Summersville by September 9. With the blue column came Major Hayes and the Twenty-third Ohio. The regiment, now considering itself something of a veteran unit after its Cheat Mountain experience, joined the line of march at Bulltown, where it had been enjoying a brief rest. Both Hayes and the men were in good condition and stood the march well. It took no great power of analysis to deduce that the army was

---

ments and most contemporary sources it is given as Carnifix but also as Carnifax and Carnifex. The modern version is Carnifex.

[6] Freeman, *R. E. Lee*, I, 583; Moore, "West Virginia and the Civil War," 321; Wood, *Seventh Regiment*, 44–59; Boehm, "Civil War in Western Virginia," 127–31.

moving to some point of decision, and the anticipation of action lifted the feet of the troops. When they reached Summersville, Hayes recorded in his diary: "Enemy near us; a battle to come soon."[7]

His prediction was correct. Rosecrans, aggressive by instinct, was eager to make contact with the enemy. The general knew Floyd must be somewhere in the vicinity of Cross Lanes, but his most assiduous inquiries failed for a time to disclose the whereabouts of the Confederates. But Old Rosy kept his men on the alert. "When you meet the enemy," he proclaimed at a review, "keep close to your ranks and aim at the breast-plates, and keep to your guns. Never fail to face the noise. . . ." Not until he reached Summersville on the morning of September 10 did Rosecrans learn definitely that the Confederates were awaiting him at Carnifix Ferry, supposedly in superior force. "We can not stop to count numbers," he exclaimed; "we must fight and whip him or pass him to join Cox." He ordered the army to move on the Confederate works.[8]

Floyd's position was about eight miles from Summersville and so masked by woods that the Federals could hardly see it until they ran directly into its front. It was really a fortified camp, enclosing almost a square mile of territory, situated on a plateau over 300 feet above the Gauley, which here stretched to a width of 370 feet. A parapet of logs and rails ran across the front and center of the Confederate line for 350 yards, and the flanks were protected by log breastworks curving back to the river. The right was stronger than the left, where the ground was more open and accessible to troops. All in all, it was a site to give the attackers pause. At the same time it was a potential trap for the defenders. Should they be defeated,

---

[7] Hayes to Sardis Birchard, September 3, 1861, and to Mrs. Hayes, September 5, Hayes MS. Letters; Hayes, MS. Diary, September 3, 4, 7, 9.

[8] Cincinnati *Gazette* and New York *Times,* army dispatches, quoted in Moore (ed.), *Rebellion Record,* III, 45–6, 49; Saunier, *Forty-seventh Regiment,* 23; Reid, *Ohio in the War,* I, 317–19.

they would have to make their way down a narrow trail a mile
and a half to the ferry and cross on two flatboats engaged in
service there or on a frail log pontoon bridge.[9]

Nothing seemed to give Rosecrans any reason for pause.
His men had been up since three in the morning and from
their camp above Summersville had marched seventeen
rugged miles. The reports of local citizens, which he apparently credited, placed the Confederate army at 15,000 or
more men. He knew nothing of the Confederate position
until he emerged before it and could see its contours through
his field glasses. Yet he decided to attack. He rode along his
lines crying to the troops: "When we go in, we go in to win."[1]
Old Rosy was displaying a pugnacity all too rare in Northern
generals at this stage of the war, but his decision to assault a
position of undetermined strength could be characterized only
as reckless. Oddly, he later blamed General Henry W. Benham, a professional soldier commanding the First Brigade and
leading the advance, for stumbling rashly against the enemy
works. Benham's handling of his men was undoubtedly inept,
but in plunging on he was only executing the spirit of Rosecrans's orders.

Not until around two in the afternoon did the Federals
deploy before the Confederate line, and it was three before
Benham got his attack going. The First Brigade delivered a
series of pecking pushes at the right center of the enemy position. There was no concert to the assaults, although Rosecrans
later characterized them as "a strong reconnaissance." Coming

---

[9] Roy Bird Cook, "The Battle of Carnifex Ferry," in *West Virginia Review*
(November, 1931), 114–15; Cook, "Battle of Carnifex Ferry," in Humphreys,
Military Operations, n.p.; New York *Times*, army dispatch, quoted in
Moore (ed.), *Rebellion Record*, III, 54–5; Saunier, *Forty-seventh Regiment*,
26.

[1] Harrison Gray Otis, "Personal Recollections of the War," in Santa Barbara
Daily Press, October 19, 1876. Otis, of the Twelfth Ohio, wrote a series of
valuable articles on his war experience. I am grateful to Richard Miller,
biographer of Otis, for calling these pieces to my attention.

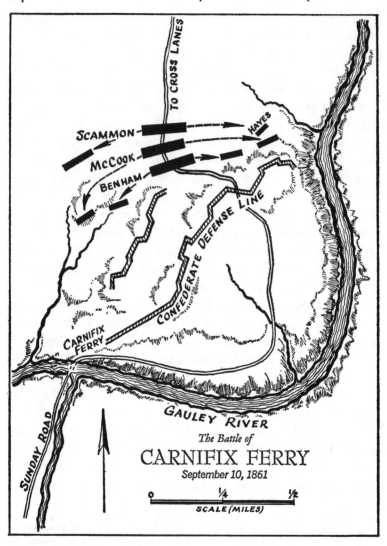

The Battle of
CARNIFIX FERRY
September 10, 1861

up to the front, the general decided to throw Bob McCook's
Second Brigade against the Confederate center, with Scammon's Third Brigade acting as a reserve to follow up whatever
success was achieved. Before this attack got under way Rose-

crans changed his plans. He received information that the enemy right was vulnerable and could be flanked. Hastily he extemporized an assault column consisting of a regiment and a half from the First Brigade, two regiments from the Second, and from the Third four companies of the Twenty-third Ohio under Hayes. The attackers crawled through the woods and ravines and eventually emerged on the Confederate flank. But by now darkness was coming on and the enemy position looked tougher close up than it had at a distance. The two senior colonels decided the movement could not be made and so notified Rosecrans, who readily agreed. In fact, as though recognizing that his attacks had been hopeless all along, he withdrew his whole army a short distance from the field. The tired troops had delivered five assaults, partial in nature it was true, but over four hours. Although many of the men thought they had been through a veritable carnage, Federal casualties were only 17 killed and 141 wounded, one third of whom were in the Tenth Ohio of Benham's brigade; and 32 of the total resulted when the flanking column, retiring in the darkness, got itself in a U formation and the confused men fired on each other. Obviously the effect of the Confederate fire had not been too great.[2]

Obviously, too, the attacking Federals had not done much damage with their fire. Floyd reported his casualties as only twenty wounded, one of whom was himself. Nevertheless, the

---

[2] Summaries of the battle are in Moore, "West Virginia and the Civil War," 326–9; Boehm, "Civil War in West Virginia," 137–48; Cook, "Battle of Carnifex Ferry," in Humphreys, *Military Operations*, n.p.; Boyd B. Stutler, *West Virginia in the Civil War* (Charleston, 1963), 79–83; William Griffee Brown, *History of Nicholas County, West Virginia* (Richmond, 1954), 164–5; and Clarence Shirley Donnelly, *The Battle of Carnifex Ferry* (Fayetteville, 1960), a pamphlet. The source accounts are numerous. The reports of Rosecrans and his officers are in *Official Records*, V, 128–31, 136, 140–6. Rosecrans provided a fuller account in *Reports of the Committee on the Conduct of the War, 1865*, III (Washington, 1865), 9–10. See also the long dispatches from the Cincinnati *Gazette* and the New York *Times* reprinted in Moore (ed.), *Rebellion Record*, III, 46–9, 50, 53.

Confederates were in a perilous position. If they waited to receive another assault and saw their lines broken, they would find it almost impossible to retreat. Wisely Floyd decided to evacuate his army that night. The difficult crossing was made safely, the boats and bridge were destroyed, and Floyd retired twenty miles to Big Sewall Mountain. Wise joined him here, and the two generals happily renewed their feud.[3]

On the morning of September 11 a Negro fugitive came into the Federal camp and reported that the Confederates were gone. Immediately Rosecrans moved into the deserted works and proclaimed the victory for himself. Only in a narrow technical sense was his claim justified. It was true that the enemy had yielded the field and that the Confederate thrust at the Kanawha had been blunted. But the result had not been brought about by any display of generalship by Rosecrans. Rather, Floyd had recognized finally that he was in an untenable spot and had got out. Rosecrans had assaulted a fortified position without attempting to ascertain its strength, and at no stage of the battle had he had his army in hand. With greatly superior numbers, he had failed to hurt the enemy, who had escaped to fight another day. The newspapers puffed up Carnifix Ferry as a victory won by strategic skill. But most of the officers knew better, and none took a more realistic view than Major Hayes, who as something of a veteran was beginning to feel that he could judge military men and events with a new eye.

He penned a full record of his part in the battle in his diary and his letters home. Naturally he was pleased that Rosecrans selected him to lead the four companies of the Twenty-third in the flanking movement. To his surprise he found he was not nervous, as he had supposed he would be, and no more

[3] Cook, "Battle of Carnifex Ferry," in Humphreys, *Military Operations*, n.p., and in *West Virginia Review* (November, 1931), 138; Boehm, "Civil War in Western Virginia," 147–8; Moore, "West Virginia and the Civil War," 329–30.

tense than before an important lawsuit. A staff officer led him
to the brow of a hill and then, Hayes noted with quiet scorn,
said that he had never been over the ground and had no orders
to give, that Hayes was an officer and must use his own judgment. Showing a lingering trace of romanticism about war,
Hayes drew his sword—it impeded his movement in the woods
and could not have been seen by many of his men—and
plowed ahead. The head of his column was fired on and two
of the men were wounded, but most of the enemy bullets
whistled fifty feet overhead. Because of the terrain, he observed
with interest, neither side could see very far and most of the
shooting was done at bushes: "It was a very noisy but not
dangerous affair." Hayes was not surprised when orders came
to fall back. "I doubted the success of the attack," he wrote,
"with good reason and in good company." It was an honest
account, frank in its depiction of the writer and the battle and
revealing an officer rapidly maturing in confidence and competence. Others glimpsed the same quality. Although Hayes
did not figure prominently in the official reports—Scammon
merely summarized his role in the flanking move—the newspaper stories listed him among the officers who had shown
special bravery and dash.[4]

After Carnifix the war in the Kanawha Valley settled into a
rain-soaked and boring stalemate. Floyd and Wise on Big
Sewall Mountain continued to quarrel, Floyd arguing that the
army should retire to Meadow Bluff and Wise contending that
it should stay where it was. On September 21 General Lee
came down from the northeast to take over, hopeful of calm-

<hr>

[4] Hayes, MS. Diary, September 10, 1861; Hayes to Mrs. Hayes, September 11,
15, Hayes MS. Letters; *Official Records*, V, 145; Andrew Stiarwalt, MS. account of military service, in Hayes Library; Judson N. Cross to Hayes, September 13, 1888, in Selected Soldiers' Letters, Hayes Library; New York
Times, army dispatches, in Moore (ed.), *Rebellion Record*, III, 51, 54;
Morgan (ed.), "Civil War Diary of McKinley," *Ohio Historical Quarterly*,
LXIX, 288–9.

ing his balky generals and salvaging some success on the West Virginia front. He soon discovered there was little likelihood of achieving either objective, although he did his best. He had Wise recalled to Richmond, thus removing one of the impediments to action, and he ordered reinforcements in from the quiet Cheat Mountain area, bringing the Confederate strength up to 15,000 men. Rosecrans, in the meantime, had also moved, with 5,200 troops, to Big Sewall, and on the semicircular elevation the two forces confronted each other from opposing crests. Lee was confident that he could hold his line and hoped that Rosecrans would attack him. The Confederate commander toyed with thoughts of an offensive of his own, but he knew the odds were too unfavorable. Drenching rains, impassable roads, and scarce supplies made any advance impossible. The same factors weighed on Rosecrans, and on the night of October 5 he withdrew his army to Gauley Bridge. Lee, who had heard the sounds of the movement and thought it portended an attack, looked out the next morning on an empty Federal camp.[5]

Later in October, Lee did mount an offensive. He moved his army toward Gauley Bridge, hoping to envelop the Federals or at least to push them back to the north. But before contact had been made he called off the movement. He was having his usual transportation troubles in the wet mountains, a large segment of his force was obviously unfit for service, and all in all he despaired of achieving any real success in the limited

---

[5] Freeman, *R. E. Lee,* I, 585–97; Humphreys, *Military Operations,* 5–6; Moore, "West Virginia and the Civil War," 348–50; Lang, *Loyal West Virginia,* 47; Saunier, *Forty-seventh Regiment,* 27–30; *Reports of the Committee on the Conduct of the War, 1865,* III, 10–11, Rosecrans's testimony; *Official Records,* V, 252–3, 615; A. L. Long, "Lee's West Virginia Campaign," in *Annals of the War* (Philadelphia, 1879), 91–2. There is some discrepancy in the numbers of Rosecrans's column. With his own and Cox's army, he had a total force of over 10,000. But having advanced thirty-four miles from Gauley Bridge, he had to leave substantial detachments behind on his line of communications.

time left for campaigning before winter closed in. He returned part of his troops to the northeastern front, and he himself left West Virginia, the scene of his first active assignment and one of his few failures. Only General Floyd remained, his little force perched atop Cotton Mountain.

When Rosecrans ascertained that most of the Confederates had departed and that he had only Floyd to deal with, he developed a counteroffensive. He now had his army organized in four brigades: under Benham, McCook, Cox, and Robert C. Schenck, a political general who took over the Third Brigade. (Thus Scammon, who had temporarily directed the Third, reverted to a purely regimental command.) Old Rosy's plan called for an elaborate flanking movement that would envelop Floyd on all sides. The Third Brigade, and Hayes's Twenty-third Ohio, were to play their part by crossing the New River and attacking the Confederate right. The operation got under way on November 6 and continued until the fourteenth. In briefest summary, it failed to achieve Rosecrans's objectives. Floyd was forced from his position but escaped the trap set for him. The Confederates retreated rapidly, all the way to Dublin on the Virginia & Tennessee Railroad and out of the fighting theater. The Federals followed as far as Fayetteville but never effectively caught up. Hayes and his regiment did not get into the fighting. The Third Brigade could not get over the New at the designated site because of high water and had to return to Gauley Bridge to cross. It did not join Benham's lead brigade at Fayetteville until the movement was virtually ended. Rosecrans blamed his subordinates, and particularly Benham, for Floyd's escape. They may have been culpable, but the truth was that the Federal commander had attempted a plan altogether too complex for his resources. Soon Rosecrans, who in West Virginia had made a reputation not completely deserved, was called to larger responsibilities. Cox assumed the mountain command,

and with active campaigning closed, the army settled into winter quarters.[6]

At Carnifix Ferry, Hayes was flattered that his superiors had thought enough of him to give him an important role in the flanking movement. He received other evidence of their esteem after the battle. Immediately he was placed in command of a column that ranged up the Gauley to head off reinforcements supposedly going to Floyd. Although Hayes doubted that he would find any Confederates—he surmised correctly that Floyd had lost his offensive punch—he was gratified at the size of his force, approximately 700 troopers drawn from his own outfit and the Thirtieth Ohio, "almost a regiment," as he proudly told Lucy. A little later he was appointed judge advocate of the whole army (the prosecutor in courts-martial), a position that gave him all of the privileges of a staff officer. For a period he utilized it to go to the advanced post on Big Sewall, although the Twenty-third was stationed some miles back, and observe events at first hand. He lived in General McCook's tent and saw a great deal of Rosecrans and Cox, liking the latter more every day. "I go with the Generals on all reconnaisances," he wrote home, "see all that is to be seen, and far[e] as well as anybody." Rightly he saw that the army could not supply itself on such a forward line and would soon have to pull back.[7]

Hayes was appointed judge advocate because of his high legal reputation. At first he thought that he would not like the work, and he did not want to be separated from his regiment. But eventually he came to delight in traveling from one

---

[6] Freeman, *R. E. Lee*, I, 599–600; Humphreys, *Military Operations*, 7–8; Boehm, "Civil War in Western Virginia," 159–79; Moore, "West Virginia and the Civil War," 351–4; Saunier, *Forty-seventh Regiment*, 33; Wood, *Seventh Regiment*, 73–5; *Sketches of War History, Ohio Commandery*, VI, 119; *Reports of the Committee on the Conduct of the War, 1865*, III, 11–12; *Official Records*, V, 253, 258–9, 657, and LI, pt. 1, 515.

[7] Hayes to Sardis Birchard, September 14, 1861, and to Mrs. Hayes, September 19, 22, 25, 27, 29, Hayes MS. Letters.

brigade to another and meeting other officers in the comfort of staff headquarters. He liked too the prestige of the position and the extra pay, $96.75 for the months of September and October. And he agreed wholly with Rosecrans that efficient courts-martial could be a potent device to promote discipline. His cases were almost completely concerned with examples of misconduct, of men who had refused to obey orders. One private who was told by his captain to return to his company had answered "he would be damned if he would." Another had said to a corporal: "I will not go for water for your orders, or the orders of any one like you," and thereupon, according to the wording of the charge, "did violently lay hands" on the corporal. Hayes was determined that such men would learn to conform to the rules of the service.[8]

One episode occurring in Hayes's court-martial duties revealed how the war was subtly changing his personality and specifically his attitude toward the enemy. Almost from the day he had arrived at Camp Chase the impact of military life on this previously restrained and solemn man had been exciting. He had become more open and impulsive, much more inclined to let his feelings rule his actions. Now this shift in his nature began to assert itself in his reactions to Southerners. He was hardening, and he was coming to favor a tougher war. In October some units of the army moved to Camp Tompkins near Gauley Bridge. The men spread their tents out on the plantation of Colonel Christopher Tompkins, the richest landowner in the area. His house, Gauley Mount, situated to give a magnificent view of the country for miles around, was reputedly the greatest mansion west of the Allegheny Mountains. Unfortunately for the colonel, a West Point graduate and retired officer, he had let himself be

---

[8] Cox, *Military Reminiscences*, I, 102; Hayes, MS. Diary, September 20, November 2, 1861. The court-martial cases are drawn from the Regimental Order Book of the Twenty-third Ohio for 1861.

persuaded to join the Confederate forces and was, in fact, at that moment in Floyd's lines. Fearful that his home would suffer damage, he wrote to General Cox asking protection for the house and his wife and children. Cox was impressed by the beauty of the estate and more so by Mrs. Tompkins, a Richmond lady of charm and quick cunning, who told the general her husband was a Unionist at heart and had gone with the South against his will. Cox liked to stop at Gauley Mount for a chat and a social hour with its mistress.[9]

Not so impressed was Hayes, who came to the house to hold court-martial sessions in one of the parlors. He was, in fact, enraged at the spectacle of Federal soldiers guarding the property of a rich Rebel when at the same time the homes of humbler men were being burned. He did not seem to be shocked at the destruction he knew was going on; he simply wanted the work to be consistent. "Why devastate the homes and farms of poor deluded privates in the Rebel army and protect this property?" he queried in his diary. "Treat the lady well, as all women ought always to be treated, but put through the man for his great crime." Hayes did not necessarily desire to destroy the house. But he persistently urged that it be turned into a hospital and the family ejected. Whether or not he was responsible, Mrs. Tompkins was finally conveyed into the Confederate lines, and after Hayes left the immediate area the house fell into a state of ruin. Its fate probably would have pleased him. The war was transforming him, as it would transform countless other men in the armies and finally the nation itself. He was losing some of his tolerance and softness, becoming harsher and in an indefinable way stronger.[1]

---

[9] Forrest Hull, "Gauley Mount—The Story of an Old House of Civil War Days," in *West Virginia Review* (February, 1927), 142–57; Whittlesey, *War Memoranda*, 25.

[1] Hayes, MS. Diary, October 14, 1861; Hayes to Mrs. Hayes, October 17, 27, Hayes MS. Letters. At some date after Federal headquarters were trans-

Hayes was on Sewall Mountain when Rosecrans decided to withdraw to a more easily supplied position. He expected Old Rosy to make the move and approved of it. But the action was so obvious—he had several times predicted it—that he was not drawn to surprise or inclined to praise. He was, in truth, the more he saw of war and generals, increasingly critical of professional soldiers. "I am less disposed to think of a West Point education as requisite for this business than I was at first," he confided to Uncle Sardis. "Good sense and energy are the qualities required." With active operations apparently suspended, he had hopes that the Twenty-third— "the crack American Regiment" in West Virginia, he called it with an unconscious contempt of outfits less ethnically pure—would be transferred to Kentucky or some other important theater.[2] But all thoughts of a change in scenery disappeared when he learned that he was in line for a promotion. Stanley Matthews was going to take the colonelcy of a new regiment, and Hayes was slated to become lieutenant colonel of the Twenty-third.

Matthews had never been entirely happy with the regiment, nor the regiment with him. "We honored the man," wrote another officer, "but had no enthusiasm for him, and did not much regret his departure." Matthews and Hayes represented two different types of civilian officers. Matthews was as intelligent as Hayes and a much warmer person, but he could never arouse the respect of troops and hence could not command them, a defect which he eventually realized and which led him to leave the army. Hayes valued Matthews as a man and a friend and was always careful to speak well

---

ferred to Gauley Bridge, soldiers looted the house. At a still later date it was burned, either by Federals or Confederates or passing marauders. According to the Reverend Shirley Donnelly of Fayetteville, the house stood on the present site of the Hawk's Nest Golf Club.

[2] Hayes to Mrs. Hayes, October 3, 7, 1861, and to Sardis Birchard, October 17, Hayes MS. Letters.

of him in his diary and letters. But in everything he wrote there was an undertone of condescension—Matthews could not learn his job and would not do.

Hayes received notification of his promotion on the night of October 31 at Camp Tompkins, where he was in the midst of his court-martial duties. He had expected the news and expressed no gratification, other than to say he was glad to get out of the judge advocate's office and to get rid of the anomalous title of major.[3] He was announced in orders as lieutenant colonel on November 2 and immediately went to join the regiment at Camp Ewing, eight miles from Gauley Bridge on the New River. He was warmed by the welcome of the men, who declared that if he should leave for another theater their interest in the regiment would disappear. Despite his pretended indifference, he was impressed with his new responsibility and resolved to work harder than ever. With the too buoyant assurance he was acquiring, he decided that he would also have to exercise some of Scammon's authority. "I must learn all the duties of Colonel, see that Col S does not forget or omit anything," he wrote in his diary.[4] Immediately he was distressed at the large number of men on the sick list. The regiment had suffered severely during the fall months, from typhus and typhoid and the other ailments that in the army were classified as "camp fever." Hayes inclined to believe that the regimental commanders were to blame if the health of the troops was not good, and he was shaken when he learned that only 750 of the Twenty-third's approximately 950 men were present for duty. "A bad showing," he recorded gloomily. A few days later the number went down to 650, and this at a moment when the regiment was

---

[3] Hastings, MS. Autobiography; Hayes to Mrs. Hayes, October 29, November 2, 1861, Hayes MS. Letters; Hayes, MS. Diary, October 31, November 5.

[4] Regimental Order Book, Twenty-third Ohio, November 2, 1861; Hayes, MS. Diary, November 3.

ordered to cross the New River with the Third Brigade in Rosecrans's complex movement to envelop Floyd.[5]

As soon as Floyd had appeared on Cotton Mountain, Hayes was certain that the Federals would move against him. Apparently he knew of some of the plans being discussed at headquarters and of the preparations being made. He doubted that the crossing could be made in the face of determined opposition. "If it is done," he wrote Uncle Sardis, again expressing that new sense of surety, "I shall do what I can to induce the Genls to see beforehand that we are not caught in any traps." When he saw the place where the brigade was supposed to pass over—he helped to scout it— he was even more skeptical. It was a ferry in the gorge of the New, and the troops would have to descend precipitous rocks 700 feet, cross in four skiffs over a flooded stream, and then ascend equally steep cliffs on the other side against possible enemy fire. He was not surprised and much relieved when orders came for the brigade to proceed to Gauley Bridge and cross there.[6]

Hardly were the troops over when a dispatch arrived from Benham announcing that the Confederates were retreating and urging Schenck to join the pursuit. The men were aroused at midnight and put on the road. Hayes did not like the haste. Night marches did not cover much distance and wore out the troops, he thought. Still, as the brigade labored on to Fayetteville, he was thrilled at the evidences of victory —the road was strewn with equipment dropped by the fleeing Confederates—and by the thought that he and his regiment were in the very forefront of the offensive. At Fayetteville it

---

[5] Hayes to Mrs. Hayes, October 19, 1861, Hayes MS. Letters; Hayes, MS. Diary, October 29, 30, November 4, 5, 8. The Twenty-third had a heavier incidence of sickness than other regiments, a condition which Hayes ascribed to the men coming from comfortable homes and thus being slower to adjust to the hardships of camp life.

[6] Hayes to Sardis Birchard, November 4, 1861, and to Mrs. Hayes, November 10, Hayes MS. Letters; Hayes, MS. Diary, November 8, 9, 12.

was evident that Floyd had gone too far to be caught, and the pursuit was halted. Hayes was naturally disappointed that the operation had not accomplished its full objective. Although he recognized that perhaps the outcome had been unavoidable—high waters had delayed the crossing and the Federals had but a small cavalry force—he also felt that another factor had influenced the results. It was a known fact, he asserted to a friend, that the Cincinnati newspapers had printed accounts of the Federal plans and that these papers had come into Floyd's possession. Colonel Hayes, as a civilian, was quite ready to criticize West Pointers; as a soldier he was just as ready to criticize elements in civilian life that hampered the conduct of military affairs.[7]

It was now mid-November, and the army prepared to go into winter quarters. Brigades and regiments were distributed at strategic points running from the advanced post at Fayetteville to Gauley Bridge and back to Charleston. The men lived in Sibley tents or in hastily built log huts, and those stationed in the highest mountains suffered real hardships from the cold and snow. Cox took over the Kanawha command when Rosecrans departed. At the same time General Schenck left the Third Brigade, and Scammon again took it over. Although Scammon continued as titular commander of the Twenty-third, he necessarily could not give the regiment full attention.[8] Much of his authority descended on Lieutenant Colonel Hayes, who was confident he could exercise it and who was proud that his unit was one of those holding the most southern point of the Federal line. Approximately 1,500 men, from three Ohio regiments, occupied the village.

---

[7] Hayes, MS. Diary, November 13, 14, 16, 1861; Hayes to R. H. Stephenson, November 21, in Nathaniel Wright Family Papers, Division of Manuscripts, Library of Congress, Washington, D.C.

[8] Saunier, *Forty-seventh Regiment*, 34–6; Hannaford, *Story of a Regiment*, 154; Ward, *Twelfth Ohio*, 47–8; Reid, *Ohio in the War*, I, 61; Cox, *Military Reminiscences*, I, 148.

For a short time Hayes acted as post commander, but soon this office went to a senior lieutenant colonel.[9]

The little Fayetteville force settled into relatively easy winter living. With Gauley Bridge only sixteen miles away and with a telegraph line in operation and mail arriving almost daily, the men did not feel isolated. Supplies came over the mountain roads on pack mules and usually in sufficient amounts. Because many of the villagers had decamped at the approach of the Federals, the officers and some of the men were able to find quarters in houses. Hayes, with two other officers, moved into the deserted cottage of a Confederate sympathizer. He had a comfortable room all to himself and wished only that Lucy was there to enjoy it.[1] On some days he rode down to Gauley Bridge to take dinner at army headquarters and stay the night. He indulged himself too much on one visit, eating pickled oysters "immoderately and foolishly," as he put it, and consuming mixed drinks "slightly but foolishly." The penalty was a severe attack of loose bowels that lasted for days. But for the most part he was vigorously healthy—much more so, he noted with interest, than he had been as a civilian—and he reveled in the rides through the snow and rain. He had not shaved since July, had not worn any white shirts or drawers for four months, and for weeks at a stretch had slept in his clothes and sometimes in his boots. He recorded these accomplishments in his diary with an immense sense of satisfaction.[2]

On December 23, while he was at dinner with his messmates, Hayes was handed a telegram. It was from his brother-in-law, Dr. Joe Webb, who was home on leave, and it announced the birth of a baby boy. Hayes was elated. He

[9] Hayes to Mrs. Hayes, November 19, 1861, and to Mrs. Sophia Hayes, his mother, November 25, and to Sardis Birchard, November 29, Hayes MS. Letters; Hayes to R. H. Stephenson, November 21, Wright Family Papers.

[1] Hayes to Mrs. Hayes, December 10, 1861, Hayes MS. Letters; Hayes, MS. Diary, December 10, 11.

[2] Hayes, MS. Diary, November 22, 24, 27, December 13, 1861.

had hoped for a daughter, but as he wrote to Lucy: "it is best . . . these are no times for women." On Christmas Day the regimental band awoke the new father with a serenade. "A fine band and what a life in a Regiment," he wrote happily in his diary. It was for him the best life he had yet found, and although he assured Lucy that he would seek a leave, he cautioned that it might be a month before he could get home. He would come only "if nothing occurs unforeseen."[3]

At the same time he was very much interested in sending some other people back to Ohio. Almost every day a number of runaway slaves came into the regiment's camp, as they did to similar centers all over the South, and asked for haven. Hayes believed that these fugitives, if the property of Rebels, should be given their freedom, and he let them go where they pleased. He picked out one slave, Allen, and sent him and his family to Uncle Sardis with the recommendation that the man be employed as a house servant. The Negroes he saw were more intelligent than most of the native whites, he decided, and deserved a chance. Just as his attitude toward Southerners had hardened, so also were his views on emancipation becoming more extreme. The once moderate lawyer now wanted the army to destroy slavery by its own authority. "I don't want to see Congress meddling with the Slavery question," he exclaimed. He discerned immediately one of the great truths of the time, that whether Congress acted or not the mere fact of the war would abolish slavery. The soldiers would simply not permit the institution of the enemy to continue. What was happening within the lines of the Twenty-third was occurring and would reoccur wherever Union forces appeared in the South. Hayes, an unusually sensitive observer, put the case perfectly: "Time and the

---

[3] *Ibid.*, December 23, 25, 1861; Hayes to Mrs. Hayes, December 23, 25, 29, Hayes MS. Letters. The child was named Joseph after Lucy's brother.

progress of events are solving all the questions arising out [of] slavery in a way consistent with eternal principles of justice. Slavery is getting death-blows. As an institution, it perishes in this war."[4]

But although domestic and political matters might concern Hayes during the quiet winter months, they did not distract him from his main interest, which, as always, was learning his job as a regimental officer. He read what military books he could lay hands on, including General Henry W. Halleck's pedantic *Elements of War and Military Science,* which treated strategy as well as tactics. His verdict on Halleck was indulgent: "Goodish. Youth, health, energy are the qualities for war. West Point good enough, if it did not give us so much of the effete."[5] He took over the instruction of the officers in regulations and himself put the regiment through daily drill evolutions. Of his various subordinates, he was particularly pleased with James M. Comly, an Ohio newspaperman who had come out to take Hayes's place as major.[6]

With his superior, however, he was no more pleased than ever. He admitted Scammon's good personal qualities—"he is best liked when best known"—and tried, as he had before, to stand between the colonel and the men. But he simply could not respect Scammon as a soldier. Late in December, Scammon came to Hayes with a scheme to send a column to Princeton to snap up part of Floyd's force rumored to be in the area. Hayes thought the move might work if properly planned. But whereas the distance to Princeton was sixty-seven miles, Scammon thought it was only forty or fifty and had no notion as to the marching time that would be required. "With proper preparations, the thing is perhaps prac-

---

[4] Hayes to Sardis Birchard, December 19, 23, 1861, Hayes MS. Letters; Hayes, MS. Diary, January 2, 15, 1862.

[5] Hayes, MS. Diary, December 1, 1861; Hayes to Mrs. Hayes, December 2, Hayes MS. Letters.

[6] Hayes, MS. Diary, December 5, 17, 1861.

ticable," Hayes concluded in his diary. "Let me study to aid in arranging it, if it is to be."[7]

It was not to be. Bad weather and the lack of men and transportation prevented the raid. But detachments of the Third Brigade did occupy Raleigh (present Beckley) twenty-five miles to the south, and Major Comly set up a post which he named Camp Hayes. Hayes went down to Raleigh frequently during January, maintaining a headquarters there and sometimes remaining for days, and in March he would establish his command location in the village.[8] But now, when it became obvious that there was no possibility of action, his thoughts turned to home once more. He asked for and received a leave of thirty-one days. He left on February 1 and spent almost the entire month with Lucy and the family in Cincinnati and with Uncle Sardis in Delaware. Then, after picking up some military books and other needed items, he headed back to the mountains. On the twenty-eighth he arrived in Fayetteville. The men of the regiment were glad to see him, and his reaction to them and to the familiar atmosphere of the camp was significant: "felt like getting home."[9] Easily he passed again into the routine of military life and into the planning of new operations. The little army that had seized and saved the Kanawha Valley now had hopes of moving out from its fastness to newer conquests.

---

[7] Ibid., December 6, 26, 1861; Hayes to R. H. Stephenson, December 29, Wright Family Papers.

[8] *Official Records*, V, 495; Hayes to Mrs. Sophia Hayes, January 6, 1862, Hayes MS. Letters; Hayes, MS. Diary, January 4. According to Beckley tradition both Hayes and McKinley spent much of the winter in the town. Hayes had his headquarters in a cottage owned by Mrs. Martha Davis; Harlow Warren, *Beckley U.S.A.* (Charleston, 1955), 18; Hilda Appleton Richardson, "Raleigh County, West Virginia, in the Civil War," in *West Virginia History*, X (1949), 249–53. For information on Hayes's Beckley interlude I am indebted to Harlow Warren of Beckley and the Reverend Shirley Donnelly. The town was originally known as Beckley, but in 1851 the name was changed to Raleigh Court House. Later it became simply Raleigh and in 1896 Beckley once again.

[9] Hayes, MS. Diary, February 2, 3, 19, 25, 28, 1862.

Chapter 6

On to New River

COLONEL HAYES returned to the warm welcome of his men at Fayetteville—and to the icy rigors of a mountain winter. In the first week of March storms of snow, sleet, and rain began sweeping through the hills and continued for most of the month. The weather precluded any significant military action, but it did not hamper Hayes's individual movements. He reveled in the white desolation around him, and on his new horse, Webby, he rode long distances almost every day, covering forty miles in one jaunt. The rides were in part related to his military duties—he gained information about the nature of the country—but essentially they were a reflection of the new Hayes, the strong man who thought he could conquer his environment. "Physical enjoyments of this sort are worth a war," he wrote in a diary passage that revealed an almost primeval zest. "How the manly, generous, brave side of our people is growing. With all its evils war has its glorious compensations."[1]

At the height of the bad weather Hayes learned that he was to take the companies of the Twenty-third then at Fayetteville to join their comrades already at Raleigh, where he would command the post. He sent the troops off first and followed later. When he reached Raleigh, it was dusk, and

[1] Hayes to Mrs. Sophia Hayes, his mother, March 6, 1862, and to Sardis Birchard, March 6, Hayes MS. Letters; Hayes, MS. Diary, March 2–7.

the regiment was forming for dress parade. He immediately experienced one of those bursts of mystic kinship that struck him when he saw the men. "For the first time in months, we are all together," he wrote in a letter home. "Oh! it was a beautiful sight. . . ." "How I love the 23d," he recorded in his diary. "I would rather command it as Lt. Col. than to command another Regt as Col."[2]

His affection for the troops did not lead him to relax the firm discipline he always maintained. Like all the good infantry officers of the volunteer army, he believed in preparing for action in periods of inaction, and so now, whenever the weather permitted, he put the regiment through the routine of drill and instructed the commissioned and noncommissioned officers in such exercises as bayonet practice.[3] And even in these frozen weeks the Raleigh garrison did not go without some action. Its scouting parties suffered frequent attacks from local bushwhackers who sought to escape detection by appearing as peaceable farmers after completing their work. Hayes was infuriated at the forays and struck back savagely. He sent columns of infantry and cavalry to sweep the countryside, authorizing the commanding officers, when they found the hiding places of the guerrillas, to burn all houses and property in the neighborhood "which can be destroyed by fire" and to kill all men identified as bushwhackers "whether found in arms or not." Not certain that Scammon recognized or approved his efforts, he asked for official commendation from headquarters. Scammon fussily answered that the Twenty-third's service was appreciated but that its colonel should not be so eager for the "applause of a Camp."[4]

---

[2] Hayes to Mrs. Hayes, March 13, 23, 30, 1862, Hayes MS. Letters; Hayes, MS. Diary, March 12.

[3] Hayes, MS. Diary, March 18, 27, 28, 31, 1862.

[4] Hayes to E. P. Scammon, March 14, 1862, and to Sardis Birchard, March 16, Hayes MS. Letters; Hayes, MS. Diary, March 14, 15, 19, 24; Hastings, MS.

Actually, the severe orders against the bushwhackers were
never fully executed. The officers in charge of the expeditions
were amenable to pleas not to burn houses, especially when
uttered by weeping women, and Hayes himself did not in-
tend that the destruction should be quite as wholesale as his
orders outlined. He was readily willing to hold out the hand
of forgiveness to any Confederate supporter who would re-
nounce his ways. Thus on one cold March day he received
the interesting news that General Alfred Beckley, the leading
citizen of the area, had resigned his commission in the enemy
army and was in town waiting to see him. Hayes called at
the Beckley mansion and found a man of sixty, old and venerable by the standards of the time, who told Hayes, not quite
accurately, that he had ridden on horseback for weeks to give
himself up. Completely captivated by Beckley's stories of his
acquaintance with Andrew Jackson and by his professions of
loyalty, Hayes agreed to accept his surrender and to let him
stay at home.[5] Hayes could feel kindly toward somebody like
Beckley, but for active and unregenerate Rebels he nourished
a swelling harshness. Already in 1862 he was advocating a
philosophy of war that William T. Sherman would later make
famous. "I am gradually drifting to the opinion that this
Rebellion can only be crushed finally by either the execution
of all the traitors or the abolition of Slavery," he wrote in
his diary. "Crushed, I mean, so as to remove all danger of its
breaking out again in the future."[6]

His desire to strike at the representatives of slavery was
soon to find an outlet. As snowy March broke into warmer

Autobiography; Clugston, MS. Diary, March 17; Scammon to Hayes, March
24, 25, 27, in Hayes Papers, Hayes Library.
[5] Hayes, MS. Diary, March 17, 1862; Richardson, "Raleigh County in the Civil
War," *West Virginia History*, X, 249–50. Later Beckley was arrested on orders
from higher authority and taken to Ohio. After a short captivity he was
returned to his home.
[6] Hayes, MS. Diary, March 27, 1862.

April, the armies stirred in their camps all along the West Virginia front, the sights and sounds of imminent action were everywhere apparent, and at any gathering of officers the talk was of strategy for the spring campaign. The discussions were particularly loud and buoyant at the headquarters of the new commanding general of the department, who had been appointed early in March, John C. Frémont.

No general had entered the war with brighter prospects of a glorious career than Frémont, the former "Pathfinder" and explorer of the West and the Republican party's first presidential candidate in 1856. But in his initial assignment as commander of the huge Western Department, which had its most active theater in Missouri, Frémont had not measured up to expectations. He gave ample evidence that he did not have the administrative ability to run a department or the military capacity to direct an army, and he became embroiled in a political fight with President Lincoln over emancipation. Lincoln finally had to remove him. He would have preferred to let him remain on inactive duty. But powerful elements in the Republican party, who liked Frémont for his antislavery views, demanded another chance for the general, and Lincoln felt constrained to oblige them. He created for Frémont a command called the Mountain Department. It embraced the whole of West Virginia and contained a district east of the Alleghenies as well. Under Frémont were some 35,000 troops, among them Cox's Kanawha force on the southern rim of the department.[7]

Frémont was well aware that he was being given a last chance to prove himself, and he was anxious to produce a plan that would promise large successes. He fixed his eyes on a sound strategic objective—the Virginia & Tennessee Railroad, one of the most vital links between the eastern

---

[7] *Official Records*, V, 54.

and western parts of the Confederacy. Uniting most of his forces in the northern section of his department, he proposed to move up the Shenandoah Valley to a point near or on the railroad line. At the same time Cox was to advance south along the New River and strike the railroad at Dublin Station or Wytheville. Eventually Frémont hoped to combine his columns and, using Gauley Bridge as a base, move westward along the rail line to Knoxville.[8] Like the plans of some other generals in the war, this one was good in theory but defective in detail. It assumed too many things—that Frémont's separate forces could move at their own schedule to the appointed destinations and that the enemy would remain passive while the various movements were in progress. It assumed too that the weather would be favorable in the mountains, a supposition which was always doubtful in West Virginia. The weather would affect particularly the movement of Cox's army, which was in effect a detached right wing of the main Federal force and hence was particularly vulnerable to a counterthrust by the enemy.

Two avenues of advance were open to Cox. At Princeton, forty-three miles from the Raleigh post, a road led south and east to Giles Court House (or Pearisburg) and on to the Virginia & Tennessee line at Dublin. Another road at Princeton would take the Federals to the railroad at Wytheville. Both routes presented forbidding natural barriers to the invaders. The Giles road passed through the New River Narrows, a gorge only two miles wide, breathtaking in its splendor

---

[8] Ibid., XII, pt. 1, 7; Moore, "West Virginia and the Civil War," 422–3, 450–2. The strategic possibilities presented by a strike at the Virginia & Tennessee Railroad were, it may be noted, never adequately developed by the Federal high command. Possession of the road would cut an important transportation link and offer the Federals a back-door approach into either Virginia or East Tennessee. While it may be allowed that the region posed frightful problems in logistics that might give an attacker pause, it is also true that the Federal planners, their attention caught by other theaters, overlooked the significance of this one.

but a military nightmare. The other road ran through a similar declivity at Rocky Gap. If either of these southern routes seemed too difficult, Cox had a third possibility. He could throw a force eastward to Lewisburg, move from there to the Virginia Central Railroad, and turn south toward the Virginia & Tennessee. It was a roundabout way, and Cox did not give it major consideration.

To accomplish his mission Cox had at his disposal 12,000 troops, of whom, however, only 8,500 were present for duty. He organized his force in four brigades. One, consisting of West Virginia units, was to remain as a garrison in the Kanawha Valley. Another, under Colonel George Crook, was to make a minor and diversionary move on Lewisburg. The main effort was to be to the south and by the First Brigade under Scammon and the Second under portly Colonel Augustus Moor. Leading the advance would be the First Brigade, made up of the Twelfth, Twenty-third, and Thirtieth Ohio, and leading the brigade would be Colonel Hayes's Twenty-third. Confronting the Federals was a Confederate force of not more than 1,500 under General Harry Heth. The Southern infantry held the New River Narrows and Rocky Gap, and the gray cavalry was flung forward to guard the pass over Flat Top Mountain in front of Princeton. The defending army was small, but it was so situated that it could make things ugly for the attackers. Cox was not fully apprised of the obstacles he would have to overcome. He did know, however, that he could not move on any route to the south until he had seized Princeton.[9]

On April 6 Cox informed Frémont that Scammon wanted to advance on Princeton at once and had asked permission to undertake the movement. The place could be taken easily,

---

[9] *Official Records*, XII, pt. 3, 10–11; Cox, *Military Reminiscences*, I, 203–4; Moore, "West Virginia and the Civil War," 453–4.

Cox quoted Scammon as saying, and possession would stop enemy recruiting in the area. Frémont, not quite ready to launch his general campaign, agreed to an advance but limited it for the present to the vicinity of Flat Top Mountain. Accordingly Cox directed Scammon to occupy the Flat Top barrier and at the same time prepared to bring up Moor's Second Brigade in support. Scammon seemed to be the advocate of this preliminary episode. But although the brigade commander undoubtedly favored an aggressive push, it is probable that he himself was incited to action by the colonel of his lead regiment. From the moment the campaign was announced Hayes showed a feverish impatience to get on with it and a strong tendency to disregard restraining orders. Twice Scammon had to caution him, once telling him that he could not move the Twenty-third until the brigade was closed up and again that he must not advance the regiment in separate columns. The second dispatch was so incoherent as to indicate that the author, under the strain of responsibility, was approaching a breakdown. If Scammon was not in control of the situation, Hayes, as the campaign developed, would give increasing evidence that he did not want to be controlled.[1]

Immediately there was no movement at all. After the orders to advance were issued, the rains came. They came in sheets and for day after day. The First Brigade, which had assembled at Raleigh, remained there in soggy immobility. Not until April 18 was Hayes able to get the Twenty-third on the march, and even then he was able to move only beyond the camp confines before he had to stop. But in a few days

---

[1] *Official Records*, XII, pt. 3, 42, 53; Cox, *Military Reminiscences*, I, 204; Hayes to Sardis Birchard, April 8, 1862, Hayes MS. Letters; Scammon to Hayes, April 8, 13, Hayes Papers. Scammon was, it should be noted, under limiting orders from Cox not to proceed rashly; *Official Records*, XII, pt. 3, 89–90, 93–4.

the weather cleared, and Hayes pushed on to Shady Spring at the foot of Flat Top Mountain.[2] He was now in the presence of the enemy and eager to go farther. But because of Scammon's orders, he found time to write Lucy, "we are not allowed to push on as fast as we would like." He was not disposed to be bound too much by the orders. He was in his "proper element," as one of his officers later admitted significantly, "in command of a force, near the enemy and cut loose from telegraphic communication with his superior commanders."[3]

On the twenty-ninth Hayes heard that a notorious gang of bushwhackers were supposed to be operating in the vicinity of Camp Creek, about sixteen miles from his camp. He ordered Lieutenant J. L. Botsford of Company C to go after them. Botsford's men scouted the area but found no Rebels. Unknown to them, the guerrilla leader was observing them all the while and had reported their presence to the Confederate commander at Princeton, Colonel Walter H. Jenifer. Jenifer decided to snap up the little Federal column, and, collecting his available force, about 300 troops, he marched toward Camp Creek. Botsford, in the meantime, had taken up quarters in a farmhouse at a place called Clark's Hollow. At daybreak on the morning of May 1, as the company was forming in the yard, shots rang out, and Confederate troops appeared on all sides. Hastily Company C retired into the house and prepared for a desperate defense.

On the same morning Hayes had the regiment up and ready to march at six o'clock. Later, when he was under criticism for sending Botsford so far ahead, he would reply that the lieutenant had quartered only four to six miles from

---

[2] Hayes to Mrs. Hayes, April 17, 20, 1862, Hayes MS. Letters; Hayes, MS. Diary, April 18, 20–22, 24, 25; Clugston, MS. Diary, April 28; *Official Records*, XII, pt. 3, 108, 112, 114.

[3] Hayes to Mrs. Hayes, April 29, 1862, Hayes MS. Letters; Hastings, MS. Autobiography, April 25.

where he knew the regiment would camp. This was all true enough, but the implication was plain. Hayes had from the first meant to follow his advance company, perhaps to support it, more probably in the hope of finding action. Now his desire to fight would be gratified. The firing at Clark's Hollow was loudly audible, and Hayes gave orders to march to the sound. Rain was falling, and the going on the muddy roads was rough. But the men, just as eager as their colonel, plunged forward. When they reached the clearing around the farmhouse, the now outnumbered Confederates broke and fled toward Princeton.

Hayes rode up immediately after the enemy left. He almost dissolved when the men of Company C, some of them wounded, saluted him with presented arms. "My heart choked me," he admitted, and he could not speak. One of the men said: "All right, Colonel, we know what you mean." In a minute he had recovered control and was all the officer again. Confidently he ordered a pursuit. The troops needed no urging. Excited by the prospects of a chase and fired by Hayes's leadership, they swept forward. Soon they caught up to the Confederates, and a running fight, lasting thirteen hours and covering twenty-two miles, ensued. At one stage the cavalry commander asked Hayes if he should attempt another charge. Hayes answered jauntily: "Try them again, if you like to do so." All over the field Hayes rode, constantly crying to the men to "push on." (Curiously, in that same month of May, in the Shenandoah Valley to the east, "Stonewall" Jackson would wreck Frémont's campaign with the same kind of aggressive advance and would make a similar phrase, "press on," a Confederate byword.) Toward nightfall the pursuers burst over the mountain in front of Princeton and saw great clouds of smoke rising to the sky. Jenifer, rattled by the turn of events, had ordered the town fired and had continued his retreat. When Hayes's men entered the town, they tried to put out the flames but could save only a few buildings. A stream of civilian refugees took the road south after the Confederates. "And so ended the first of May," Hayes recorded in his diary. "A good day's work." One of his soldiers, who also kept a diary, was more philosophical. "What a day . . ." this man wrote; "fun for us but terrible fright, destruction and death to the people of this quiet valley."[4]

The day was an undoubted success, and it was so pictured in the press, eager for stories of Northern vigor and victory. One account described Hayes as "a noble, brave officer" and declared that his men would follow him anywhere. Hayes was highly pleased with his work, and he was naturally outraged when he learned that Scammon had censured him in a dispatch to Cox. Scammon praised the gallantry of the Twenty-third, but he condemned Hayes for detaching Botsford and implied that only the behavior of the troops had saved their colonel from a disaster. In a hot reply Hayes denied that he had exceeded orders or had been rash. "This is not a disaster," he protested, "but a fight of a sort which crushes the rebellion." Boldly he demanded praise rather than rebuke. His superiors agreed with him when they came into possession of all the facts. Cox expressed satisfaction at Hayes's promptness in marching on Princeton, and Frémont commended the colonel and his regiment in a dispatch to the War Department.[5]

Hayes had rightly stood his ground in the controversy, and his analysis of the battle was on the whole correct. After all,

---

[4] Hayes, MS. Diary, May 1, 1862; Hayes to Mrs. Hayes, May 2, Hayes MS. Letters; Henry, MS. Diary, May 1; Moore, "West Virginia and the Civil War," 458–60; David E. Johnston, *A History of Middle New River Settlements* (Huntington, 1906), 221–2; Harold R. Saunders, "The Early History and Development of Princeton, West Virginia," in *West Virginia History*, XX (1959), 96–7.

[5] Cincinnati *Commercial*, quoted in Moore (ed.), *Rebellion Record*, V, 3–4; *Official Records*, XII, pt. 1, 449, pt. 3, 129–30, 132–3, LI, pt. 1, 592–4.

it had been a Federal objective to seize Princeton, and Hayes
had done the job. He had, despite his denials, gone somewhat beyond his instructions, and he had been unduly scornful of the wishes of those above him. But at the front he had
been in a better position than officers in the rear to determine
if those instructions needed modifying, and he had not
hesitated to act on his own information. Above all, he had
shown a dash and an aggressive spirit that were sadly lacking
in most Northern officers at this stage of the war.

Even now, after escaping a possible reverse and a reprimand, Hayes was not disposed to rest at Princeton. He
bombarded Scammon with requests to be permitted to go
on to the Narrows and to Giles Court House. The enemy
was in a fright, he argued, and the Federals should press
forward in pursuit. But he assured his superior that this time
he would not violate his instructions: "Rest easy on that
point." He urged Scammon to bring his brigade to Princeton
and, with the condescension he could not resist in addressing
the colonel, penned some lecturing suggestions on strategy:
"A further advance while the panic prevails is a plain duty
and I doubt not you will order it as soon as you arrive. . . .
This you will understand by looking at any map of this
region. . . . I speak of the future in the way of suggestion
that your thoughts may turn towards planning enterprises
before the scare subsides." Scammon, partly because he did
not trust his impetuous subordinate but mainly because he
was inherently fussy, insisted that Hayes send several reports
every day. Hayes, who thought this frequent writing was
foolish, promised to keep his commander informed but contended that one daily dispatch would be sufficient.[6]

Hayes undoubtedly meant to conform to instructions, but
he could not keep himself in leash very long. On May 6 he

---

[6] Hayes to Scammon, May 2, 4, 5 (two dispatches), 1862, *Official Records,*
LI, pt. 1, 594–5, 599–603.

learned from contrabands that the Narrows was held by but
a small enemy force. Immediately he ordered Comly to move
thither with a detachment and authorized the major, if he
found he could, to go on to Giles Court House. Comly encountered no Confederates at the Narrows and proceeded to
Giles Court House, which he occupied without opposition.
The only Confederates on the scene were engaged in trans-
ferring supplies from the village to Dublin, and Comly
captured some of the stores. At midnight Hayes received a
dispatch from the major announcing the success of the movement. "Very lucky!" Hayes admitted in his diary, "and
Colonel S thereupon approved of the whole expedition, although it was irregular and in violation of the letter of
orders." To Lucy he crowed: "Do you know that Giles C. H.
was captured with a large amount of stores & by a party sent
by me from Princton? It was so bold and impudent!"[7]

Impudent it was, and also imprudent. For the second time
Hayes had anticipated a move his superiors should have made,
and probably would have made eventually, and had forced
them to conform their movements to his. Scammon, who
reached Princeton on the sixth, saw the advantage of grasping
Giles Court House and secured from Cox permission to reinforce Comly. He ordered Hayes to march to the town with
the rest of the Twenty-third at daylight on the next day.
Hayes made the move and reported that the advanced detachment was "perfectly safe." Scammon at least acquiesced
in what Hayes had done, and General Cox expressed warm
satisfaction, informing Frémont that the victory at Camp
Creek (Clark's Hollow) was apparently only the harbinger of
greater successes.[8] Both officers might have reflected, however,

---

[7] Ibid., LI, pt. 1, 605; Hayes, MS. Diary, May 6, 1862; Hayes to Mrs. Hayes,
May 11, Hayes MS. Letters; Hastings, MS. Autobiography, May 6.

[8] Hayes, MS. Diary, May 7, 1862; *Official Records*, XII, pt. 3, 137, 140; LI,
pt. 1, 606. Hayes's men were, as before the move on Princeton, aware that
their colonel was likely to interpret his instructions freely. One of them

that they had advanced faster and farther than they intended to and that the commander of their lead regiment was manifesting an increasing tendency to push them into premature action. Shortly they would learn that the situation at Giles Court House was neither as safe nor as promising as Hayes had made them believe.

Hayes himself was the first to wonder if he had gone too far. Although he besought Scammon to bring the brigade on to Giles Court House and organize it there for an offensive, he also reported the presence of gathering Confederate forces and begged his superior for reinforcements of infantry and artillery. When they did not arrive promptly, he became angry as well as alarmed. "It is a great outrage that we are not reinforced," he wrote in his diary. "Shameful. Who is to blame?" If the Confederates attacked at night, he planned a house-to-house defense, and if by day, a retreat to the Narrows. His men were quartered in the courthouse and slept on their guns. They sensed their colonel's anxiety, but knew, as one of them wrote, that he was not going to be "frightened out" by "West Point military rules."[9]

Scammon was quite willing to advance to Giles Court House. But the dangers hinted at in Hayes's reports had the effect of throwing him off balance, as he had been in the move against Princeton. In a long, peevish dispatch to Cox he said that he was going to Hayes's aid. He also complained that the column was getting too long again and suggested that for reasons of morale—an obvious excuse—he should put another regiment in the lead. To Hayes he wrote a chiding note charging his subordinate with rashness, "creating neces-

wrote: "We are glad Colonel Scammon is not along as Colonel Hayes is not hampered and will do something, in scaring up the rebels"; Henry, MS. Diary, May 5, 7.

[9] Hayes to Scammon, May 8, 1862 (two dispatches), *Official Records*, LI, pt. 1, 608–10; Hayes, MS. Diary, May 8, 9; Hastings, MS. Autobiography, May 8; Henry, MS. Diary, May 8.

sities which control my movements," and forbidding any advance beyond Giles Court House. Cox too was beginning to have some worries about his extended line. He ordered Moor's Second Brigade to come on to Raleigh, where he had his headquarters, and prepared to move his whole force toward Princeton. Then, on May 9, as Scammon was preparing to march, Cox received really disquieting news. Frémont reported that his forces in the Shenandoah Valley were under heavy attack by Stonewall Jackson and directed Cox to concentrate his army and suspend for the time his advance. Immediately thereafter Cox learned of a more immediate threat. The Confederates around Giles Court House were preparing to launch an offensive of their own. Colonel Hayes reported in urgent tones that the enemy in his front outnumbered him at least two to one and that without help he could not hold his position.[1]

Hayes's analysis of the numbers of the Confederates was more accurate than he could have known. The Confederate high command, impressed by the danger to the Virginia & Tennessee Railroad, had sent reinforcements to General Heth, and Heth had in addition pulled in troops from adjoining areas. His force, although not operating as a unit, nevertheless totaled close to 5,000.[2] He meant to drive the invaders from their advanced position and, if possible, from their base at Princeton. As a first step, he planned to snap up the Twenty-third at Giles Court House with a surprise attack.

A surprise attack, however, was exactly what Hayes was expecting and was ready to meet. He had pickets posted on every approach to the village, and each morning he rose at dawn and walked out to inspect the lines. As he was making

---

[1] Scammon to Hayes, May 9, 1862, Hayes Papers; *Official Records*, XII, pt. 3, 148–9, 157–9; Hayes to Scammon, May 9 (two dispatches), ibid., LI, pt. 1, 611.

[2] Heth drew in troops from Lewisburg, which enabled Crook, leading another prong of Cox's offensive, to occupy that town.

his rounds at four on the morning of May 10, he heard a blaze of shots. "No mistake this time," he thought, and rushed back to form the regiment in line of battle. In a moment the Confederates were piling into the streets, and the Twenty-third met them with a stiff volley. But Hayes saw, as he had known before the attack came, that his men could not hold out very long. The more numerous Confederates would eventually be able to envelop the defenders and cut off their line of retreat. He ordered the regiment to fall back fighting. One of his soldiers quoted him as shouting: "It's all right, boys, it's all right. We will fall back on something before night so that we can give them hell." The refuge Hayes meant was the New River gorge, some six miles distant, and the withdrawal began. But the eager enemy pressed on so fast that a leisurely movement was impossible. It took six hours of a running fight to reach the gorge. Here Hayes thought he was safe. Heth was able, however, to bring up artillery, and soon he shelled the Federals out. A fragment of one missile struck Hayes on the right knee, inflicting a slight flesh wound. He impressed the men by saying calmly: "Boys, it is getting rather hot here; we had better move down."[3] Back five more miles, to East River, Hayes had to retire. On the following day Scammon moved up to join him, and the danger was over.

Hayes was out of a tight spot, the worst one he had yet been in. He did not admit the narrowness of his escape, and he did not acknowledge any fault in his own conduct. "Masterly" was the exaggerated label he used to describe the retreat. It had been "only exciting fun," he told Lucy, and but three lives had been lost. The regiment had behaved gloriously, and he had never been as thrilled as when the men cheered him at a critical moment in the battle. Yet in this

[3] Hayes, MS. Diary, May 10, 1862; Hayes to Mrs. Hayes, May 11, Hayes MS. Letters; Henry, MS. Diary, May 10; Hastings, MS. Autobiography, May 9, an entry that covers events through the seventeenth; Clugston, MS. Diary, May 11; J. A. Joel in New York *Graphic*, June 23, 1876.

same letter to Lucy he conceded: "We got off as by a miracle";
and to Uncle Sardis he confessed: "Our impudence saved us."[4]
His contradictions were not the product of confused thinking,
but of a defensive sensitivity about his record. He knew that
he was open to criticism for rashness in ever advancing to
Giles Court House, and apparently he entertained some inner
doubts as to the correctness of all his actions.

As if anticipating censure, he took the verbal offensive,
writing in his report to Scammon that it was regrettable he
had not been reinforced before the attack. He deleted this
aspersion at Scammon's request, because, he explained, he
did not want to "embarrass" his superior. It is more probable
that he and Scammon arrived at a tacit understanding not
to embarrass each other. Scammon did not want the issue of
his failure to reinforce Hayes raised, and Hayes did not want
the question of his impetuous movements placed before headquarters. In his reports to Cox, Scammon praised Hayes
mildly and referred only in passing to Hayes's complaints
about not being sustained.[5] Both men soon had larger problems to occupy their energies. The Confederate offensive,
which had stalled after the victory over Hayes, was soon
rolling again. Two enemy columns, one under Heth and
another under Humphrey Marshall, began a drive on
Princeton.

Princeton was the advanced field base of the Federals. General Cox had his headquarters there, but the town was lightly
held. The Second Brigade was still struggling forward to reach
the front, and Scammon's First Brigade was at the mouth of
East River. On May 15 Marshall's advance struck the Federal
picket lines, and on the next day the main Confederate force

---

[4] Hayes, MS. Diary, May 11, 1862; Hayes to Mrs. Hayes, May 11, and to
Sardis Birchard, May 15, Hayes MS. Letters.
[5] Hayes to Scammon, May 11, 1862, Hayes MS. Letters; Scammon to Cox,
May 11, 12, 1862, *Official Records*, XII, pt. 3, 176–7, 182–3.

THE BATTLE OF SOUTH MOUNTAIN

This idealized drawing, made by Joseph A. Joel of the Twenty-third Ohio, shows the wounded Hayes in the left foreground; two soldiers are about to help their commander to an ambulance. The artist depicted the ground as being much more open than it actually was.

v

HAYES'S QUARTERS IN RALEIGH

According to local tradition in Beckley, the Raleigh of the Civil War, Hayes and William McKinley spent part of the winter of 1861–62 in these cottages.

HAYES IN 1861
*In this photograph Hayes appears as a typical fledgling officer, fired with
romantic notions about the glories of war and quite ready to strike a pose.*

R B Hayes
Col 23 Ohio

COLONEL HAYES OF THE TWENTY-
THIRD IN 1862

It was a very serious Hayes, beginning to show some signs
of the strain of command, who sat for this photograph.

broke into the town. Cox hastily departed, riding to French-ville to urge the Second Brigade on and sending orders to Scammon to push for Princeton immediately. Now ensued a series of odd events not creditable to the leadership on either side. Marshall, hearing of Cox's rumored return and not hearing anything from Heth, decided to evacuate Princeton. As his men were marching out on the morning of the seventeenth, Cox and the Second Brigade suddenly appeared and attacked. After some sharp fighting the Federals secured the town. A lull followed, as both commanders waited—Cox for Scammon, and Marshall for Heth. Scammon arrived late in the afternoon. Heth, following Scammon's route, came to within a few miles of the scene but did not get into the action. He heard that Marshall had retreated and, interpreting the information to mean that his colleague had engaged in a full withdrawal, retraced his steps. Cox, learning of Heth's approach and believing that he faced a superior force, also decided to retire. On May 18 the Federals pulled back to Flat Top Mountain, the barrier that guarded Raleigh.[6]

Colonel Hayes was at East River when the orders came for the brigade to march to Princeton. This time Scammon took no chances with his impulsive subordinate. He put Hayes in command of the rear guard. It was, however, as Hayes correctly understood, a post of honor. Although the brigade was moving on Princeton in an ostensibly offensive action, Heth was known to be following its line of march, and Hayes was covering what was also a retreat. He was assigned to the same position when the whole army left Princeton. If he felt any chagrin at the kind of work he had to do, he did not reveal it. He expressed disappointment only that the withdrawal

---

[6] This four-day action from May 15 to May 18, small in the numbers of men engaged but complicated in detail, is treated at length in the documents. The Federal reports are in *Official Records*, XII, pt. 1, 504–9; pt. 3, 176, 183–5, 188–90, 193, 198, 209, 217, 227–8. The Confederate reports are in ibid., pt. 1, 513–17.

had to be all the way back to Flat Top.[7] In fact, in camp on the crest of the mountain, Hayes, as he reviewed the campaign in his mind, came to some chastening conclusions. He voiced them in letters to Uncle Sardis and Lucy. He had been irritated when he was not reinforced at Giles Court House but now: "Perhaps I was wrong." He had thought that Cox should have stood and fought at Princeton: "but it is not quite certain." Thankfully he noted that he had come through the whole operation with no censure on his record. "I am glad to know that no body blames me with anything," he exclaimed. He added thoughtfully that if the reported numbers of the enemy were correct no person on the Federal side should be blamed for the collapse of the offensive that had begun with such bright auguries.[8] The strains of that offensive had made Hayes a humbler and a better man. He had tasted the sweets of success and applause and the bitters of controversy and criticism, he had encountered danger and touched death, and finally he had experienced the frustration of failure. He still valued energy and dash, but he knew now that a subordinate officer could not act entirely on his own initiative. He was still inclined to condemn shortcomings in his superiors, but with a larger appreciation of the problems of command he had become more tolerant. He was willing to admit that anybody could make mistakes, even that he himself had perhaps erred.

He confessed to Lucy that his experience in the retreat from Giles Court House had made him realize that death was a real possibility. But "I still feel just as I told you, that I shall come safely out of this war. I felt so the other day when danger was near." An odd event in the camp on Flat Top impressed on him that the end could come in any way. A

---

[7] Hayes, MS. Diary, May 17, 18, 1862.
[8] Hayes to Sardis Birchard, May 20, 1862, and to Mrs. Hayes, June 3, Hayes MS. Letters.

violent thunderstorm broke one evening while Hayes and his staff were eating supper. Two of the officers got in a discussion as to the length of time between the flash of lightning and the sound of the thunder. As the storm seemed to be subsiding, the group stepped outside, and one of them took out a watch to time the next reverberation. Suddenly there was a flash and a deafening roar. Hayes felt as though a stone had hit him on the top of the head. His horse Webby was nearly knocked down, and a sentinel near him staggered. Over a hundred men in the regiment were in a state of shock for several minutes.[9]

Although Hayes was able to rationalize the outcome of the recent campaign, he and everybody else connected with it had to admit that it had been a failure. The Federals had not been able to reach the Virginia & Tennessee Railroad line, and they had lost their base at Princeton. Nobody was justly to blame for the result, although the army's leadership had not been of the best. The offensive had simply bogged down in the extent and ruggedness of the West Virginia terrain. On Flat Top, Cox organized his forces in three brigades, the First under Scammon, the Second under Moor, and the Third under Crook. A fourth brigade of West Virginia troops, mostly cavalry, brought the army up to only 10,000. It was a good army, Hayes thought, but too small to operate in the "magnificent distances" before it.[1] For long months it would remain inactive on its lonely mountain bastion.

---

[9] Hayes to Mrs. Hayes, May 26, June 3, 1862, ibid.; Hayes, MS. Diary, May 30.
[1] *Official Records*, XII, pt. 3, 308–9; Hayes to Mrs. Hayes, May 22, 25, 1862, Hayes MS. Letters.

Chapter 7

Into the Big Picture

FROM HIS HEADQUARTERS on Flat Top Mountain, General Cox directed the defense of a broad front. The bulk of his army was on or around Flat Top, and this was where the Twenty-third Ohio rested. But his patrols ranged as far north as Summersville and probed southward toward the New River Narrows and the Confederate lines. In addition, his Third Brigade under Crook was thrown far to the east, to Meadow Bluff guarding the James River and Kanawha Turnpike. Cox had some 12,000 infantry under his command, and he heavily outnumbered the enemy in his immediate presence. But he believed that the Confederates could reinforce easily if he advanced, and he was content to stand on the defensive. There was some basis for his analysis of Confederate capabilities, but essentially the reason for the general's inaction lay with himself. He was intelligent and competent, and he never made a bad mistake. He never accomplished a great success, either. He lacked the dash and imagination to raise himself above the average level. Tall and graceful in appearance, he was elegant and coldly restrained in manner. Although he had been a politician, he did not speak the common tongue and did not know how to fire the hearts of the citizen soldiery. He won the respect of his men, but he could not arouse them to that enthusiasm which carried impossible fields. Whatever his shortcomings, the soldiers appreciated that he would not misuse them in wasteful endeavors. The morale in his army was always good.[1] It was good now, as the first hint of summer touched Flat Top and the other mountains of West Virginia.

Hayes and his regiment welcomed the respite from campaigning, but for different reasons. The colonel seized on the time as an opportunity to put the men through the evolutions of the drill process again, to reinstill in them that sense of group cohesion which all field commanders prized. "They take it with much spirit and improve rapidly," he noted with satisfaction. Soon after going into camp, the regiment received an issue of new rifled muskets, many of them actually old flintlocks altered to percussion use. Hayes carefully tested the guns in target practice and calculated that at 200 yards one shot in eight would have hit a man, at 400 yards one shot in ten, and at 700 yards one shot in eighty. Despite these rather dubious results, he pronounced the arms to be excellent.[2]

For the men the camp on Flat Top was a delightful interlude. The air was clear and bracing, and even in late June, while the days might be warm, the nights were cool and called for fires and winter blankets. The officers had the protection of tents, but the men had to construct shelters of bark and rails, their efforts leading Hayes to christen the site "Wood chuck Camp." Although Hayes drilled the men, he also gave them plenty of time for recreation and participated in some of their frolics. Over the company streets the soldiers built large and leafy bowers, under which they drilled by day and danced by night. Hayes took particular pleasure in watching the buffoonery of the men during the dancing. "Occasionally the boys who play the female partners in the dances exercise their in-

---

[1] Whittlesey, *War Memoranda*, 77–8; Reid, *Ohio in the War*, I, 777.
[2] Hayes, MS. Diary, June 1, 13–15, 18, 1862; Hayes to Mrs. Hayes, June 12, Hayes MS. Letters.

genuity in dressing to look as girlish as possible," he wrote his mother. "In the absence of lady duds they use leaves, and the leaf clad beauties often look very pretty and always bold enough."[3]

An end to this idyllic existence came on July 12 when orders arrived to proceed to a camp at Green Meadows. The new site was fifteen miles down Flat Top and over 1,000 feet lower and hence much warmer. It was also much nearer the enemy, and four companies under Major Comly were pushed forward as pickets to Pack's Ferry, where the Blue Stone River entered the New. Hayes, with the other six companies, remained at Green Meadows. The two detachments were approximately eight miles apart.[4]

At first Green Meadows promised to be as quiet and pleasant as Flat Top. The weather was warm but not oppressive, and most of the men found the change welcome. The area abounded in wild pigs and blackberries, both of which the soldiers hunted mercilessly. So common did the consumption of these items become that one captain felt constrained to issue a warning at company parade: "Gentlemen, gentlemen, this eating blackberry pie and roast pigs in July makes men mutinous; we must come down to *first principles,* hard tack and bacon." Hayes thought the camp was as nice a one as he had yet seen, but he did not want to stay there. New troops could hold the present line, he opined, and Cox's best regiments could be sent to a theater where more important work waited to be done.[5]

He meant, of course, where the chances of promotion would

---

[3] Hayes, MS. Diary, June 6, 27, July 7, 1862; Hayes to Sardis Birchard, June 21, and to Mrs. Sophia Hayes, July 10, Hayes MS. Letters.

[4] Hayes, MS. Diary, July 12, 13, 1862; Hayes to Mrs. Hayes, July 14, Hayes MS. Letters; James Webb to his sister, July 21, in Webb Family Correspondence, Rutherford B. Hayes Library.

[5] Henry, MS. Diary, July 25, 27–30, 1862; Hayes, MS. Diary, July 16; Hayes to Sardis Birchard, July 17, Hayes MS. Letters.

be brighter. Like most officers in West Virginia, Hayes at times became oppressed with the nature of the fighting in the theater, with the small engagements that offered little opportunity to win distinction. In addition, he had a peculiar personal problem. Although he was in actual command of the Twenty-third, he had only the grade of lieutenant colonel. Scammon was titular commander of the regiment and would remain as such until he attained permanent promotion to brigadier. Hayes doubted that Scammon would demonstrate enough ability to make the jump, and even if he did the situation would be bleak—the regiment would be retained in Scammon's brigade and indirectly would still be under his control.

After musing over his problem, Hayes decided to apply for command of one of the new regiments being raised back in Ohio. By a curious coincidence, on the very day that he arrived at his resolve he received notification that he could have the direction of one of the new units, the Seventy-ninth. He was pleased but was immediately beset by doubts and hesitations. The appointment was not yet official. Would it go through? If it did, could he leave the Twenty-third? "I shall never like another Regt so well," he wrote in his diary. "Another Regt is not likely to think as much of me." If he could get any hint that he would become its commander, he would stay. He decided to postpone "the evil day of decision" as long as he could.[6]

In the midst of his deliberations an incident occurred that determined him to get out from under Scammon's control. A loyalist from Monroe County, across New River in enemy-held territory, asked Hayes to spirit his wife and four children to safety. Hayes was eager to undertake the rescue and pro-

---

[6] Hayes, MS. Diary, July 23, 1862; Hayes to Mrs. Hayes, July 23, Hayes MS. Letters.

posed to Scammon that a small expedition be sent at night to pick up the family. He received from his superior what he called "a lame, halting permission," an "*if* and *if*" directive, and he exploded in his diary: "It is ridiculous in *war* to talk this way. If a thing ought to be done according to the lights we have, let us go and do it, leaving events to take care of themselves. This half-and-half policy; this do-less waiting for certainties before action is contemptible." Putting his bold words into action, he took six companies of infantry and one of cavalry over the river one night and brought the family to safety. Although the enemy was all around him, the party was never in much real danger. Hayes had demonstrated again what a little daring, along with careful planning, could do. He dismissed the project in his diary as "a pretty jolly expedition! ... All sorts of incidents;—funny good time."[7]

Determined now to seek another command, he requested leave of absence to go to Ohio to assist in raising the Seventy-ninth Regiment. To his disappointment, he was informed that no leaves were being granted to officers seeking appointments in new regiments. Cox took something off the edge of the refusal by telling him that he was certain to get the colonelcy of the Twenty-third when Scammon moved up to brigadier. Perhaps Hayes was not as cast down as he seemed. He admitted to Lucy that he would be a "great fool" to leave a veteran regiment to take over "a mob of raw recruits—dirty, sickly, lawless and complaining."[8] Still—he wanted action and a chance to gain a reputation.

Unexpectedly he got action, or at least a touch of it. Early on the morning of August 6 a courier aroused him to say that firing had been heard at Pack's Ferry. Hayes decided that a small Confederate party was annoying Comly and ordered two

[7] Hayes, MS. Diary, July 24–26, 1862.
[8] Ibid., July 29, August 2, 1862; Hayes to Adjutant General C. W. Hill, July 31, and to Mrs. Hayes, August 6, Hayes MS. Letters.

companies to proceed to the Ferry. Before they could move off, other reports came in, conflicting reports that stated that the enemy was attacking in force, that the enemy was not attacking in force. Somewhat puzzled, Hayes nevertheless did the right thing. He acted on the assumption that the worst of the news might be true. Dispatching Scammon on Flat Top for help, he prepared to support Comly with greater strength.

As he put his men on the march, he placed the band in front of them and spoke some unusual instructions. For some time he had been impressing on his officers the value of deception in war, teaching them the art of making a small body of men appear larger than it was. He told one small-unit commander about to venture into enemy lines to lie like an official bulletin about the size of his force. It was a venerable and respected doctrine, well known to the ancient Chinese military thinkers and not unknown to men on the early American frontier. But deception was rarely practiced in mid-nineteenth-century warfare and was practically unheard of in the Federal armies, whose officers preferred to rely on the big build-up rather than on their imaginations. Where Hayes got the principle cannot be determined, but he employed it well. So now he said to his men about to start for Pack's Ferry: "Fighting battles is like courting the girls: those who make most pretension and are boldest usually win. So, go ahead, give good hearty yells as you approach the ferry, let the band play. But don't expose yourselves, keep together and keep under cover. It is a bushwhacking fight across the River. Don't expose yourself to show bravery; we know you are all brave."[9]

The ruse worked. At least, the Confederates retreated at the approach of Hayes's column, although they may have already been discouraged by the stiff resistance put up by

---

[9] Hayes, MS. Diary, August 6, 1862; Hayes to Mrs. Hayes, August 7, Hayes MS. Letters.

Comly's men. Meanwhile, Hayes's dispatch to Scammon had started other wheels in motion. Scammon reported the news to Cox, who ordered the First Brigade commander to march to Pack's Ferry. Scammon did not reach the Green Meadows camp until four in the afternoon, and here he learned that the battle was over. Hayes thought that his superior had been inexcusably slow and, as usual, nervous and fussy. "He cut around like a hen with one chicken," Hayes wrote in his diary. Scammon for his part, was not inclined to give Hayes much credit for saving the day. In the official reports the strongest commendation went to Comly. The major, intellectual and impassive in appearance, was steadily rising in the estimation of the regiment, although the men would never feel as close to him as they did to Hayes. He had undoubtedly handled himself well in the engagement. Hayes continued to like him, although he thought his subordinate had erred in too hastily burning the largest ferryboat, thereby, as Hayes put it, doing the Confederates' work for them.[1]

Although he expressed no bitterness at the neglect of his work, Hayes was obviously hurt by the Pack's Ferry incident and confirmed in his desire to be transferred elsewhere. At any rate, a few days later he came to a decision. He would accept the colonelcy of the Seventy-ninth. As he wrote Lucy, he was not sure even now of his motives. Maybe it was just that he wanted to get out of the dreary mountains . . . or to secure a leave to visit her. But then was it not his duty to volunteer his service to an untried regiment? Even as he poured out these thoughts in a letter, trying to get the thing straight in his own mind, a messenger arrived from general

---

[1] Hayes, MS. Diary, August 7, 1862; *Official Records*, XII, pt. 2, 127–8; pt. 3, 541–2. The characterization of Comly is in Henry, MS. Diary, July 25. Hayes voiced the criticism of Comly in his diary, August 6.

headquarters with an order that would change all his plans. The order was marked secret, and it directed Hayes to have his regiment ready to march at instant notice. He could only speculate as to his possible destination. It would turn out to be better than he dreamed.[2] The West Virginia army was going to move to eastern Virginia and at last into the big war.

The directive to transfer the mountain army came from the highest army level. Behind the decision was a complex command situation and some confused military planning. When Stonewall Jackson had driven northward through the Shenandoah Valley earlier in the summer, he had forced the change of many plans. Frémont, with most of his force, had to move eastward to meet him and could give no central direction to his command. Cox, during the Valley campaign, operated virtually on his own. Then, after the Jackson threat had subsided, President Lincoln installed a new command arrangement. The Mountain Department was abolished, and all the troops in and around Washington and in the Valley were combined in a new army, the Army of Virginia under General John Pope, just brought in from the West. (Frémont refused to serve under Pope and took his departure.) Cox's army, for no logical reason, was included in Pope's command. Pope's mission was to advance southward toward the Rappahannock River and to distract Confederate attention from the army of General McClellan, then bogged down before the eastern gates of Richmond. The high command hoped, although it would not turn out that way at all, that Pope eventually could reach Richmond from the west and together with McClellan pinch the city into submission.

Almost immediately Cox besought Pope for permission to bring his army to the Virginia theater. His troops were veterans, Cox wheedled, and would furnish a seasoned strength

---

[2] Hayes to Mrs. Hayes, August 10, 1862, Hayes MS. Letters.

to Pope's column. Pope, eager to add to his strength, readily consented. But in a casual way that indicated he had little conception of the difficulties involved, he advised Cox to march to the Valley and on to Charlottesville, where contact could be made with the main army. He was asking Cox to traverse 200 miles of rough terrain, through enemy country, and with an uncertain line of communications. Cox agreed, probably just to keep the project going, but then he suggested a counter plan. He would march his troops to Camp Piatt near Charleston and at the head of navigation on the Kanawha River, a distance of almost 100 miles. Here steamers would pick them up and convey them down the Kanawha and up the Ohio, another 150 miles, to Parkersburg, the Ohio River terminus of the Baltimore & Ohio Railroad. From the latter place the railroad would carry them the 400 miles to Washington, where they could easily join Pope. As the proposed movement involved large strategic considerations and required, for its water and rail facilities, War Department co-operation, it had to be decided by the highest authority, General Henry W. Halleck, the President's military adviser, and the Secretary of War. The permission came through on August 11, and on that same day Pope wired Cox to hurry on his movement. The secret order which Hayes received was drafted when Cox thought he might advance through the Valley, but it held also for the second route.[3]

As the details of the project were finally worked out, Cox was to leave behind him 5,000 troops to hold the Kanawha Valley. He would make his move with over 5,000 men, 1,100 horses, 270 wagons, and two artillery batteries of six guns each. The troops he took with him he considered his best: the First Brigade under Scammon, the Twelfth, Twenty-third, and

---

[3] Moore, "West Virginia and the Civil War," 508–10; Summers, *Baltimore and Ohio in the Civil War*, 163–4. The official correspondence is in *Official Records*, XII, pt. 3, 451, 460, 551, 560–1, 570

Thirtieth Ohio, and the Second Brigade under Moor. In the East the browned, hard-bitten mountain force would be known as the Kanawha Division. The command of the troops left to guard the Kanawha line devolved on Colonel J. A. J. Lightburn.[4]

The movement began on August 14, the regiments moving out on systematic schedules. The Twenty-third did not leave camp until the next day. It took three and a half days of hard, hot marching to cover the ninety-seven miles to Camp Piatt. Hayes was elated at the prospect of action. "This means to Gen. Pope in Eastern Virginia!" he exclaimed in his diary. "All hail!" At a halt after the march began, he made the men a speech: "Men of the Twenty-third—I congratulate you on being together again, that we are going to a place where we shall have plenty of work to do, and I hope no one will do an act but what we can always take each other by the hand and say Comrade." An appreciative soldier who recorded the address added that Hayes could beat any Methodist minister he had ever heard. The men, unaccustomed to heat or exertion, found the march increasingly onerous, and Hayes had to exert himself to keep them going. Constantly he rode up and down the line, exhorting and comforting the men and sometimes dismounting to let a tired soldier ride. When his efforts seemed to lose effect, he would cry out: "Let us hear from the band." The musicians would break into "We are so glad to get out of the wilderness," and the men would step out again. It was the kind of stern yet fatherly treatment that inspired soldiers to make one more effort and that the good infantry officer instinctively knew how to use. The regiment stumbled into Camp Piatt before noon on the eighteenth.[5]

---

[4] Cox, *Military Reminiscences*, I, 225–6.

[5] Hayes, MS. Diary, August 14–18, 1862; Henry, MS. Diary, August 15; J. A. Joel, in New York *Graphic*, June 23, 1876; John S. Ellen, "Battle South Mountain, Md., Sept. 14, 1862," six-page manuscript in Rutherford B. Hayes Library, hereinafter cited as Ellen, "South Mountain."

As each unit arrived, it was loaded onto one of the waiting steamers, and the transfer to Parkersburg began. The trip down the Kanawha was uneventful, but the Ohio was at low stage and the ships could navigate it only with the greatest difficulty. At various shoals and bars the troops had to land and march around the barriers. Still the lead units of the army reached Parkersburg on August 21, and others, including the Twenty-third, on the next day.[6] The movement so far had shown what careful planning could do to expedite the transportation of a large force over a long distance. But ahead was the most intricate part of the operation, the railroad phase, and now the most skilled planning of all would come into play.

At Parkersburg railroad and War Department officials were waiting with 400 cars and sufficient locomotives and a schedule of departures for Washington. The first regiments moved out on the twenty-first, and others followed at frequent intervals. Because of the heavy traffic, every train had to slow its speed. Nevertheless, each one made the trip in about forty hours. The lead units passed through Washington on the twenty-third and continued on to Warrenton, Virginia, where Pope had his headquarters. The others stopped in Washington or Alexandria. By August 26 the whole force had reached the capital, although the horses and wagons were still on the way.[7]

In all, Cox's army had traveled 650 miles, 250 by land and water and 400 by rail. It was one of the first great mass transportations of the war. Earlier, before the battle of First Bull Run, the Confederates had moved 11,000 men from the Valley to Manassas, but only thirty-four miles of the journey was made by rail. In that same summer of 1862 the Confederates would, however, give a striking demonstration of the use to

---

[6] Hayes, MS. Diary, August 19–22, 1862; Hayes to Mrs. Hayes, August 19, Hayes MS. Letters.

[7] Moore, "West Virginia and the Civil War," 510–11; Summers, *Baltimore and Ohio in the Civil War,* 164–5; Cox, *Military Reminiscences,* I, 226–9.

which railroads could be put in war. They moved 25,000 troops from Tupelo, Mississippi, via Mobile, to Chattanooga, a distance of 776 miles. The Federals would surpass this feat in 1863, shifting 23,000 men 1,200 miles from Virginia to near Chattanooga. Some of the logistical lessons learned in the transfer of Cox's force were put into use in the 1863 operation. The little Kanawha army had something to do with pointing military thinking along modern lines.

Hayes and the Twenty-third reached Washington on the morning of August 26. Hayes thought that in due time the Kanawha Division would move to join Pope at Warrenton or wherever the main army was. He anticipated he would see some fighting, but he looked for nothing serious. McClellan's army, which had failed before Richmond, was being brought back to the Washington area, and as its units arrived they were ordered forward to join Pope, who was known to be facing increasing numbers of Confederates. With all these reinforcements pouring in, Hayes believed Pope was in no danger. He rather expected that Pope would defeat the enemy before the mountain troops could get to the scene.[8]

On the twenty-seventh the division moved across the Potomac and took position on Upton's Hill, one of the key points in the western line of the Washington fortifications. The whole division was not present. The first two regiments to arrive, the Thirtieth and Thirty-sixth Ohio, had pushed on to join Pope, and now Cox ordered Scammon to take two more, the Eleventh and Twelfth Ohio, to hold the bridge over Bull Run. Soon word came that Scammon had had a sharp fight at the bridge; Hayes was surprised that his superior was supposed to have behaved with "coolness and skill." Rumors flew apace through the camp. Heavy fighting was said to be taking place to the west, probably at Manassas Junction, and on the

---

[8] Hayes, MS. Diary, August 25, 26, 1862; Hayes to Mrs. Hayes, August 25, and to Sardis Birchard, August 25, Hayes MS. Letters.

twenty-ninth and thirtieth Hayes could distinctly hear the booming of artillery. The news was conflicting, but Hayes was not too disturbed. He expected a victory or, at the worst, a drawn battle. Whatever the result, he assured Lucy, he was glad he was in a place where decisive actions were going on rather than in West Virginia, where success or failure hardly affected the general cause. And he was going to stay with the Twenty-third. Although he was prouder than ever of the regiment, he candidly admitted that Scammon's increased chances for promotion had influenced his decision.[9]

Although Hayes was slow to realize it, the main army had suffered a near disaster. On those last hot days of August, General Robert E. Lee, Hayes's old antagonist in West Virginia and now commander of the Confederate field army in Virginia, had prepared one of the most cunning traps of the war for Pope. Lee sprung the trap at the battle of Second Bull Run, and although the Federal army escaped, it had to retreat to the Washington defenses. Hayes saw the battered troops march past his lines. He did not think they were demoralized, but he was certain the Eastern troops could not fight as well as those from the West. The defeat he ascribed to poor Northern generalship, a quality that he feared was all too pervasive. "The result is we must conquer in land warfare by superior numbers," he confided to Uncle Sardis. His opinion of Federal leadership sharpened in the next few days when the Kanawha Division was assigned the task of guarding the western fortifications against a possible enemy attack. On September 4 a Confederate reconnaissance party probed at the Upton's Hill position. A lieutenant who came to Hayes to ask what were the orders to meet an emergency remembered that the colonel answered with deep feeling "that there were no orders, or

---

[9] Hayes, MS. Diary, August 27, 28, 30, 31, September 1, 1862; Hayes to Mrs. Hayes, August 30, September 1 (two letters), Hayes MS. Letters; *Official Records*, XII, pt. 2, 405–6.

directions from head quarters, that the army was floundering without a head." Hayes resigned himself to the prospect that the army would remain inactive within its lines until the Confederates made a move in another direction that would force it to come out.[1]

His analysis was partly right and partly wrong. The army did have a head, but that general was devoting his main energies to reorganizing the beaten army. McClellan, who had first risen to fame in West Virginia and who had been largely a passive bystander during the recent battle, had been given the command of all the troops around Washington, his own Army of the Potomac, some of whose units had participated in the battle, and Pope's force as well. McClellan was rapidly whipping the whole mass into shape, but he was not going to have the time to rest within fortifications as Hayes had envisioned. Lee, eager to exploit his success, suddenly crossed the Potomac above Washington and drove into western Maryland. McClellan's army had to move out to meet him.

On the morning of September 5 the army broke camp and, skirting Washington, headed into Maryland, its first march objective being the town of Frederick. The Kanawha Division, possibly because it was known as a good marching outfit, headed the advance of the right wing. It was attached to the Ninth Corps, which was temporarily under the command of Jesse L. Reno, an aggressive bantam of a man rising fast in the estimation of his superiors. The division made good time, reaching Ridgeville on the eleventh, a day's march ahead of the rest of the corps. Here it was learned that Lee had evacuated Frederick, and Cox was directed to hasten his advance to the town.[2]

---

[1] Hayes, MS. Diary, September 2–4, 1862; Hayes to Mrs. Hayes, September 3, and to Sardis Birchard, September 4, Hayes MS. Letters; Ellen, "South Mountain."

[2] Cox, *Military Reminiscences*, I, 263–8; Hayes, MS. Diary, September 5, 6, 1862; Hayes to Sardis Birchard, September 6, Hayes MS. Letters.

On the march Hayes was delighted with the performance of his men—they kept up the pace and did not straggle. The Eastern soldiers looked pretty sorry in comparison, he thought. Because he was so proud of the regiment, he would not allow criticism of it from any source, and his feeling involved him in a controversy always remembered by men who witnessed it. On the night of the seventh, the Twenty-third made camp near a stubble field. The men helped themselves to straw from a stack, some taking it for forage for the horses, some for bedding to lie on. Hayes noticed them but made no objection. If the owner was loyal, he would not care. If he was disloyal, Hayes did not care. Suddenly General Reno galloped up. The corps commander was in an obvious passion at what he saw. He began to berate the men, addressing them as "You damned black sons of bitches," and demanded to know who was their colonel. Scammon, who was standing nearby, characteristically remained silent.

Not so Hayes. He stepped forward and said he had the honor to command these troops, and he defended their conduct. Reno calmed down a bit and asked Hayes for his name. Hayes complied respectfully, but then, although he knew whom he was addressing, asked Reno for his. Reno said that they were in a loyal state and that he would not tolerate pilfering. This was the play-by-the-old-rules psychology of so many West Pointers that Hayes regarded as soft-minded sentiment, and the colonel bridled up again. "Well," he said, "I trust our generals will exhibit the same energy in dealing with our foes that they do in the treatment of their friends." Naturally offended, Reno asked what the remark meant. Nothing in particular, Hayes answered, at least nothing disrespectful. Reno was not completely mollified, and his anger was heightened by the cheer the men raised for Hayes as he rode off. Later Reno spoke of putting Hayes in irons. Hayes did not worry about being arrested. Scammon and Cox sustained him, and, whatever the outcome, the regiment would support him. He was convinced that he had acted correctly. It had been a classic encounter between the professional and the citizen soldier.[3]

From Ridgeville the army marched toward Frederick on three roads, the Kanawha Division still leading the Ninth Corps. Not until near the town did opposition, in the form of gray cavalry, appear. Hayes and the Twenty-third deployed across the fields, while a detachment of cavalry and a battery of artillery dashed ahead on the road. The Confederates put up only token resistance and went out one end of the town as the Federals came in the other. The Twenty-third led the march down the main street, the men responding gaily to the cheers of the townspeople. Chief among the Union casualties was Colonel Moor, who had entered with the cavalry and was captured. George Crook was elevated to command of the Second Brigade, and the division pushed on immediately to Middletown, a few miles to the west, and made camp on the thirteenth. Just beyond frowned the rampart of South Mountain.

Hayes, as a regimental commander, was naturally not aware of the complex strategic situation around him that was about to come to a blazing climax. Lee, after concentrating his army at Frederick, had evacuated the town for what he considered good reasons. The Confederate commander learned that a Federal garrison had been left at Harper's Ferry in the Valley, to the south and in his rear. Unable to resist the lure of its capture, he sent one corps of his army under Stonewall Jack-

---

[3] Hayes, MS. Diary, September 7, 1862; Hayes to Sardis Birchard, September 8, Hayes MS. Letters; Cox, *Military Reminiscences*, I, 268–9, 547–8. Cox in his account stated that Reno was angry for the additional reason that the regiment was not bivouacked in close mass. He got this impression from Reno, who brought the controversy to Hayes's immediate commander. But it is clear from Hayes's diary record that the only issue was the straw. Both Reno and Hayes soon quieted down, and both expressed regret for the incident.

son racing southward, and with the other, under James Long-
street, retired behind South Mountain. Lee thought that
Jackson could gobble up the Harper's Ferry troops and return
to join him for a slash into Pennsylvania—before the slow-
moving McClellan realized what had happened. It might well
have developed exactly that way but for one of those accidents
that often happen in war to confound the best of plans. A
copy of Lee's march order fell into McClellan's hands, and the
Federal commander, realizing the opportunity presented to
him, had pressed his army forward, right up to South Mountain. Lee, to his surprise, saw a strangely alert McClellan
almost upon him. He knew that he would have to fight a
defensive battle, and he fixed on the little town of Sharpsburg
behind Antietam Creek as the place to make a stand. But
meanwhile he had to have time—to recall Jackson and to
concentrate his scattered units. Hurriedly he rushed all available troops to contest the passes over South Mountain. McClellan would have to fight to cross the barrier.

Three gaps opened through South Mountain, from north
to south: Turner's, Fox's, and Crampton's. McClellan was
close enough to have carried them on September 13, but his
fatal caution came into play and restrained him. He did,
however, order a general advance for the next day. The
Kanawha Division stood before the second opening, Fox's
Gap. Cox did not understand that he was to bring on a battle
but only to support a reconnaissance by the army's cavalry.
Studying the situation a little more, he decided that he would
have to move with both his brigades, Scammon's First in advance and Crook's Second in reserve. He so informed Reno,
who answered to go ahead and promised that the whole corps
would soon be up. Scammon's troops went forward at seven in
the morning, and Crook's followed half an hour later. The
scene before them recalled West Virginia—a mountain which
they would have to ascend for two miles, its side covered with

trees and laurel thickets broken here and there by fields. The defending Confederate force at the crest was small, but in this terrain it could put up a murderous resistance. The attackers did not know what opposition they would meet, and they were prepared for the worst. Cox's plan called for his column to overlap the enemy right. In the key position on the Federal left was Hayes and the Twenty-third. Hayes was directed to keep in the woods as much as possible until he struck the Confederate flank.[4]

Hayes received his instructions from Scammon, who added that a battery of two guns on the Confederate right would have to be taken. What if he found six guns with a strong support? Hayes asked. "Take them anyhow," Scammon replied. So Hayes recorded the conversation in his diary. Another source recounts that he then turned to his men and shouted: "All right then, we'll take it."[5] He said other things that in the excitement of the moment he could not recall. Later he was told that, his eyes shining like a cat's, he cried: "Now, boys, remember you are the 23d, and give them Hell. In these woods the rebels don't know but we are 10,000; and if we fight, and when we charge yell, we are as good as 10,000 by ——." He most certainly yelled: "Give them hell! Give the sons of bitches Hell." He spurred up the slope, and the regiment plunged after him.[6]

Keeping to the cover of the woods, the attackers came almost to the crest before they ran into opposition. But here a Confederate force in the woods met them with a heavy volley. Hayes, now dismounted, feared that his men would not stand under the fire too long and ordered a charge. The regiment surged forward and forced the enemy back. The decimating

---

[4] Hayes, MS. Diary, September 10, 12, 1862; Hayes to Mrs. Hayes, September 10, 13, Hayes MS. Letters; Ellen, "South Mountain"; Cox, *Military Reminiscences,* I, 271–5.

[5] Hayes, MS. Diary, September 14, 1862; Joel and Stegman, *Rifle Shots,* 501.

[6] Hayes, MS. Diary, December 8, 1862; Barnard, *Hayes,* 221.

fire continued, however, and Hayes ordered another charge. This time the Confederates were driven clear from the woods and had to take shelter behind a stone wall. The battle was going well for the Federals along the whole line, and Hayes, sensing victory in his sector, shouted for another advance. Just as he gave the command, he felt a stunning blow on his left arm and found that a musket ball had struck him right above the elbow.[7]

His first thought was that an artery might be cut, and he asked one of the soldiers to tie his handkerchief above the wound. Then, feeling faint and sick, he lay down on the ground. He was about twenty feet behind the line of his men and was still able to give directions. Seeing some of them retire to the cover of the woods, he thought they might be giving way. He forced himself to his feet and ordered them to hold. A sergeant approached him and said: "I am played out; please, sir, let me leave." Hayes pointed with his sword to his helpless arm and replied: "Look at this. Don't talk about being played out. There is your place in the line." But soon he had to sink to the ground again. A wounded Confederate lay near him, and Hayes and this man engaged in a friendly conversation. "You came a good ways to fight us," Hayes remarked. The Confederate asked where Hayes was from. "I am from Ohio" was the answer. "Well," said the graycoat, "you came a good ways to fight us." Hayes finally gave his new acquaintance a message for Lucy if he should die there.

At this point somebody told Hayes that there was danger the enemy might be able to flank his left. He ordered the companies on the left to wheel backward so that they could

---

[7] Cox, *Military Reminiscences*, I, 282–3; Joel and Stegman, *Rifle Shots*, 501; Clugston, MS. Diary, September 14, 1862; Horton and Teverbaugh, *Eleventh Regiment*, 71–2; Schmitt (ed.), *George Crook*, 96; Ellen, "South Mountain"; Hayes, MS. Diary, September 14. Although the lengthy entry on South Mountain in Hayes's diary is dated the fourteenth, it seems certain that most of it, if not all, was written at a later time; the major section is in Mrs. Hayes's writing.

face the threatened attack. The whole line followed the movement, with the result that Hayes was left between his men and
the Confederates. Comly, who had taken over command of the
regiment, came up and asked if he had meant to retire all the
line. Hayes answered no, just the left companies, but to let
the arrangement stand. He evidently lost consciousness for a
short time, and when he revived he could see neither friends
nor foes. He called out: "Hello 23d men, are you going to
leave your Colonel here for the enemy?" A half dozen soldiers
sprang forward and offered to carry him anywhere he wanted.
Their appearance drew a hot fire, and Hayes ordered them to
return to cover. But soon Lieutenant B. W. Jackson of Company C arrived and insisted on taking Hayes out of the range
of enemy fire. He led the colonel back and laid him down
behind a big log. Soon the fire slackened all along the line,
and Jackson returned. He conducted Hayes to a field hospital,
where Dr. Joe Webb dressed the wound. Hayes felt well
enough to walk half a mile to the house of a Mrs. Kugler. He
remained there several hours, and then an ambulance took
him to Middletown, where he went to the home of a Jacob
Rudy.[8]

While Hayes was going to the rear, his regiment and others
in the division continued the battle. Late in the afternoon a
final charge broke the Confederate line, and the Federals had
Fox's Gap. At Turner's and Crampton's also the bluecoats
had won, and McClellan was free to advance beyond South
Mountain. The Twenty-third, which bore the brunt of the
fighting at Fox's Gap, suffered the heaviest casualties in the
Kanawha Division, a total of 130, including 32 killed. Hayes

---

[8] Hayes, MS. Diary, September 14, 1862; J. A. Joel, in New York *Graphic*,
June 23, 1876; Hayes, three-page manuscript on South Mountain in Rutherford B. Hayes Library, hereinafter cited as Hayes, "South Mountain." This
last source differs in minor detail from the diary. The scene as here recon-
structed follows in the main the diary. In some cases the quotations have
been altered slightly to eliminate abbreviations.

was prouder than ever of the regiment, and he glowed at the references to it and to himself in the reports. Both Cox and Scammon singled out the Twenty-third and its colonel for special mention, Scammon writing that Hayes had "gallantly and skillfully brought his men into action." Hayes prized also personal letters from Cox and Scammon praising his conduct and wishing him a speedy recovery. Hayes was at Middletown when the army pressed on and fought on the seventeenth the battle of Antietam, technically a draw, although Lee retreated at its close. Eager to learn the outcome, he paid two boys a dollar each to stand at the window of his room all day and retail to him news from passers-by. It was probably later that he learned with regret that his recent adversary Reno had been killed in the fighting.[9]

Hayes was not going to have a speedy recovery. The ball that struck him broke the bone of the arm, causing a painful fracture. As Dr. Webb informed the family, it was not a dangerous wound, but it would keep Hayes inactive for a long period. Hayes himself was aware of the nature of the wound and resigned to weeks of convalescence. He was comfortable and well cared for at the Rudy home and longed only for Lucy to come. He feared that she had not heard of his mishap or, that if she had, she would not be able to locate him in the chaos surrounding the battle area. On a day when she failed to arrive as expected he scribbled in his diary: "This hurts me worse than the bullet did."[1] He had small cause for worry. Lucy had heard and was on the way. She did not know, however, despite all the telegrams Hayes and Dr. Webb had sent

---

[9] *Official Records*, XIX, pt. 1, 187, 459–61, 466–7; Joel and Stegman, *Rifle Shots*, 502; Hayes, "South Mountain." The Twenty-third fought at Antietam but not as prominently as at South Mountain, incurring casualties of 69; *Official Records*, XIX, pt. 1, 198, 426.

[1] J. T. Webb to Sardis Birchard, September 15, 19, 1862, Webb Family Correspondence; Hayes to Mrs. Sophia Hayes, September 15, 16, 18, and to Sardis Birchard, September 22, Hayes MS. Letters; Hayes, MS. Diary, September 16–20.

home, exactly where her husband was. She searched vainly the hospitals at Washington and Frederick. Finally she ran onto a wounded soldier from the Twenty-third, who told her to go to Middletown. She found Hayes pathetically delighted to see her and almost himself again.[2]

He was, in fact, well enough to go home to complete his recovery. Granted a leave, he returned with Lucy and spent all of October and most of November in Columbus and Cincinnati. His greatest anxiety now was not his arm but a command problem. During the South Mountain campaign some of his friends, thinking to help him secure the command of the Seventy-ninth, had induced the War Department to issue an order relieving him of service with the Twenty-third. He was free to accept the commission he had once desired, but now he did not want it. He had determined to stay with his regiment, his resolve strengthened by the certain prospect that Scammon would be promoted to brigadier and perhaps also by gossip that Scammon hoped his subordinate would take another appointment. Through the influence of Cox and others he was able to get the War Department order revoked. Shortly thereafter Scammon received his promotion, and new orders announced Hayes as a full colonel. On November 21 Hayes left for West Virginia to resume command of his regiment. He went with the assurance that he deserved his rank.[3]

Hayes traveled by river steamer up the Ohio and the Kanawha to Charleston. At the latter place an ambulance met him and carried him to the regiment at Camp Haskell near Gauley Bridge. He stepped out to look on a familiar West Virginia winter scene—a cold, damp landscape, a camp of wooden huts, some of them in process of construction, and

[2] Williams, *Hayes*, I, 201; Hayes to Mrs. Sophia Hayes, September 26, 1862, Hayes MS. Letters.

[3] Hayes to Sardis Birchard, September 26, October 23, 1862, and to Mrs. Sophia Hayes, November 19, Hayes MS. Letters; J. T. Webb to Hayes, September 28, Webb Family Correspondence.

the grim mountains frowning above, promising even worse
weather yet to come. Still he was glad to be back, back with
the men and officers, who rushed forward to greet him, back
with the mountain army, which was free of alien Eastern associations and by itself again. "It was like getting home after
a long absence," he admitted to Lucy.[4]

He found too a strategic situation virtually unchanged from
the one he had left in August. While the division had been in
the East, a Confederate column had swept down the Kanawha
Valley, defeating Colonel Lightburn's defending forces, capturing Charleston, and sending cavalry raiders clear to the
Ohio. But the success was only temporary. In October the
division, no longer needed in Virginia, was returned to West
Virginia, and it easily reoccupied most of the lost territory.
Cox became commander of all West Virginia as a separate
department, and he proceeded to establish a string of defensive
posts to hold the most vital areas. In the north two divisions
guarded the Baltimore & Ohio Railroad and the Cheat Mountain region. In the south two divisions of approximately 6,000
men each protected the Kanawha Valley, the First under
Crook and the Second under Scammon. Most of these troops
were concentrated around Gauley Bridge, with a detachment
thrown forward to Fayetteville. Hayes was in the Second Division and again under Scammon's command.[5]

But for the moment at least Hayes was happy with all his
associations, even with Scammon. He enjoyed particularly the
comradeship at his mess, the food and wine and the good talk
before a roaring fireplace at night. With him were Dr. Webb,
Comly, now a lieutenant colonel, and his new major, J. P.
McIlraith. He was becoming especially fond of another new

---

[4] Hayes, MS. Diary, December 1, 1862; Hayes to Mrs. Hayes, December 1,
Hayes MS. Letters; J. T. Webb to Mrs. Hayes, December 1, Webb Family
Correspondence; Conrad Doup to Hayes, March 16, 1887, Selected Soldiers'
Letters.

[5] *Official Records,* XXI, 940.

officer, a second lieutenant, William McKinley, whom he described as "a handsome bright, gallant boy."[6] And his affection for his men mounted ever higher. On Christmas Day the regiment engaged in volley practice, and Hayes handed out prizes of a turkey and bottles of wine to the best marksmen. As he looked at the regiment, he thought that the companies were smaller than in the summer but that the men were healthy and in good fighting shape.[7]

He did not, however, expect much fighting in the immediate future, either in his own theater or in others. The war was in a state of lull, he told Uncle Sardis. But this would not last. When Lincoln issued his promised emancipation proclamation the nation would take on a new purpose. And eventually the right military leadership would emerge. He who had been so impatient now counseled patience in the press and among the people. "It is a virtue much needed in so equal a struggle as this. If the people can hold out we shall find the right man after while." He issued a proclamation to the regiment reviewing its deeds of the past year and congratulating the men on their achievements. They were entering on a period of repose, he said, but they should use it to prepare for continued calls and greater sacrifices in the future.[8]

---

[6] Hayes, MS. Diary, December 3, 13, 1862; Hayes to Mrs. Hayes, December 14, Hayes MS. Letters.

[7] Hayes, MS. Diary, December 28, 1862; Hayes to Mrs. Hayes, December 28, Hayes MS. Letters; Clugston, MS. Diary, December 26.

[8] Hayes to Sardis Birchard, December 20, 1862, and proclamation to regiment, January 4, 1863, Hayes MS. Letters.

Chapter 8

A Year of Repose

THE FIRST MONTH of 1863 broke in West Virginia with characteristic weather—cold, wet, some snow and the threat of more to come. Hayes was busy and happy at Camp Haskell, shortly to be renamed Camp Reynolds. He put the men to work making the site livable and preparing it for winter quarters, digging drainage ditches, laying out a parade ground, and constructing log huts. He ordered an ample habitation built for himself, a double cabin of two rooms eighteen by twenty feet each. When he moved in, he was somewhat disappointed to find it less comfortable than he had anticipated. It had a "shake roof" (shingled with large openings between the shingles), and the snow came through in clouds. He said he felt that he should sit before his fire with an umbrella over him.[1]

But despite such creature discomforts, he was satisfied and relaxed, more so than he had been since the opening days of his service. He was resigned to a period of inactivity. Campaigning in the winter in the mountains was almost impossible, and anyway the Union forces in West Virginia were not large enough to undertake an advance that would get anywhere. Their available strength was diminished still more in January when Crook's division was sent to reinforce the

[1] Hayes to Sardis Birchard, January 4, 1863, Hayes MS. Letters; Hayes, MS. Diary, January 11, 17.

Federal field army in Tennessee. Crook would later return, but in the meanwhile the command of all the troops around Gauley Bridge and at Fayette devolved upon Scammon. Although Hayes did not know it, General Cox and other high command officials were coming to the conclusion that West Virginia was not a very promising base for offensive operations. They were content to hold their present territory, which embraced the most valuable areas and which in June of 1863 would become the new state of West Virginia. The Confederates too had about written off any hope of recovering the region. They were determined to maintain their position along the New River Narrows to forestall a Federal thrust at the Virginia & Tennessee Railroad, but hereafter their offensive activities would be restricted to stabbing raids behind the Union lines.[2]

Hayes could accept the situation with relative grace because he was coming to see that promotion was possible even in this immobile war. He received notification in the first week of January that he had been named commander of the First Brigade of the Second Division. His command was, as he noted in his diary, "a small affair," for the brigade was not a full-sized unit. It consisted of but two regiments, his own Twenty-third, now under Comly, who had the same anomalous command position that Hayes had previously had and disliked, and the Eighty-ninth Ohio, plus a couple of cavalry detachments. Nor were the regiments at anywhere near full strength. Only 600 of the 799 men in the Twenty-third were effectives and only 650 of the 950 in the Eighty-ninth. His own regiment illustrated what the attrition of war was doing to most units. During the past year it had received 68 recruits. But it had discharged 66 men for various reasons and suffered 82 deaths, for a net loss of 80. On paper Hayes

---

[2] *Official Records*, XXI, 992–3; Moore, "West Virginia and the Civil War," 553–6.

commanded 1,859 troops; actually present he estimated were 1,350.[3]

The promotion pleased one part of the inner Hayes, the part that yearned for recognition and prestige. Balm for another inner area also came in this long span of military quiet. Lucy announced that she was coming for an extended visit and bringing with her the two oldest boys, Birchard and Webb. Even for so resolute a woman who was also the wife of a colonel and hence entitled to some official courtesy, a winter journey that far into the West Virginia mountains was a difficult venture. As far as Charleston she could travel by water, but from there on she had to ride a jolting coach. She felt better when Dr. Webb, who was in Ohio, decided to return with her. Between Charleston and Gauley Bridge, the party stopped overnight at a tavern called the White House. The surviving register bears the notation: "Mrs. Hayes, two sons, Dr. Webb, and dinners. $7.50." For some unexplained reason the innkeeper added after the entry: "Les Dishabille."[4]

The family arrived at Camp Reynolds on January 24 and would stay with Hayes for approximately two months. He settled them comfortably in his cabin. The boys rowed, fished, rode horseback, and enjoyed all the varied activities of an army camp. Mrs. Hayes, gracious and tactful and obviously aware of her obligations as an officer's wife, made a special effort to impress the regiment. She visited the hospital and the quarters and won the affection of the officers and the positive worship of the enlisted men. A favorite camp tale was of the recruit who asked a comrade: "Where is the woman who sews on buttons?" The friend mischievously directed him to the house of the colonel's lady. Proceeding thither, the soldier accosted Lucy and inquired if she was the female

[3] Hayes, MS. Diary, January 6–8, 1863; Hayes to Sardis Birchard, January 12, Hayes MS. Letters.
[4] Forrest Hull, in Charleston *Daily Mail,* February 2, 1958.

who fixed the buttons of the regiment. Mrs. Hayes took in the situation and accepted the blouse the man offered. "I will be glad to do the work," she said, "leave it with me and I will see it is done." By the time he was to recover the garment the poor innocent had discovered the truth, and he was in a horrible state of embarrassment when he returned. Mrs. Hayes assured him that it was all right, that she and he had turned the trick on the perpetrator.[5]

In the middle of March orders came for Hayes to garrison Charleston. He moved thither with the Twenty-third and went into quarters at Camp White across the river from the town. The other regiments of his brigade were strung out at posts from, as he put it, Gauley Bridge to the Kentucky line. His superiors had pulled him back to provide a stronger protection for the most important base on the Kanawha. Shortly they would augment his force with the Fifth and Thirteenth Virginia regiments, really composed of West Virginia loyalists. Hayes had little confidence in the capacities of the local soldiery and was not reassured by his reinforcements. "I am in command of some of the best and some of the poorest troops in service," he observed. He did not think that he could hold his position against a formidable attack.

At higher command levels the same kind of doubts were felt about the whole West Virginia line. The transfer of Hayes to Charleston represented a Federal apprehension that consolidation, a drawing in of strength, was necessary to retain control of the mountain region. It was also a reflection of the confused command arrangements to which the mountain department was generally subjected. At this time another shift was made. All of West Virginia was placed in the Middle Department, whose commander, Robert C.

[5] Hayes to Mrs. Sophia Hayes, February 8, 1863, and to Sardis Birchard, March 9, Hayes MS. Letters; Hayes, MS. Diary, March 15; Hastings, MS. Autobiography, January 24.

Schenck, had his headquarters at Baltimore. Cox received orders to report elsewhere and left the West Virginia scene permanently. To his place Schenck named no one commander but divided the authority among four officers in separate theaters, one of whom was Scammon on the Kanawha. Scammon's troops were designated as the Third Division. Necessarily Schenck would exercise but little supervision over this distant department, and each local commander proceeded pretty much on his own.[6]

The move to Charleston was hard on the men of the Twenty-third. From warm huts they had to go into tents which at first had no facilities for fires. Many were stricken with severe colds and pneumonia. Lucy and the boys had accompanied the regiment, and for them Hayes took possession of a nearby house, although he knew that his duty was to live like the men. Possibly because the situation bothered him, more probably because the visit had been unusually extended for an officer's wife, Lucy and the sons left for home on March 21. Right after she departed, Hayes felt constrained to write her a tender note saying that already he was lonely. But he took occasion to point out that tonight he would sleep in a tent, for the first time since before South Mountain.[7]

A week later he wrote her that apparently she had got out just in time. Rumors reported a general Confederate advance on all the Kanawha posts. Hayes, however, did not think that the enemy was mounting a major thrust. He was scornful of Scammon's frenzied preparations—his superior was in a regular "stew," he noted in his diary—although the Kana-

---

[6] Hayes, MS. Diary, March 22, 1863; Hayes to Mrs. Sophia Hayes, March 22, and to Sardis Birchard, March 22, Hayes MS. Letters; *Official Records*, LI, pt. 1, 994; Cox, *Military Reminiscences*, I, 444–5.

[7] Hastings, MS. Autobiography, March 15, 1863; Hayes to Mrs. Hayes, March 21, Hayes MS. Letters.

wha commander was acting quite properly in readying for
any eventuality. As it turned out, Hayes was right. The great
Rebel offensive materialized as only a cavalry raid behind
the Union lines. Although the raiders reached Point Pleasant
at the mouth of the Kanawha, they had to retreat speedily
and with severe losses. Comly took five companies of the
Twenty-third down the river to try to intercept the graycoats, but the regiment as a whole was a spectator of the
episode. Hayes remained calmly at Camp White and pro-
fessed no surprise at the outcome. He had thought it a "sorry
raid" from the start, and he was a little smug that his judgment had been confirmed.[8]

But when Lucy wrote that she would like to come for another visit and bring the boys and when Uncle Sardis announced that he might come too, Hayes cautioned them to
wait. Confederate raiders were active on all fronts in West
Virginia, he said, and another thrust on the Kanawha might
come at any time. He doubted that Scammon's small force
could repel an attack delivered in strength. By the end of
April, however, he was more optimistic. The posts around
Charleston had been partially fortified, he wrote, and he
did not look for any movement until after the first of June,
when the enemy could live off the country. So if the family
wanted to chance it, all right.[9] Coincidentally, hardly had
he made his decision when rumors started up of another
coming Confederate raid. The news threw Scammon into
a fit of angry excitement. Warning Hayes to be alert, the
general said that he possessed correspondence proving that
many citizens of Charleston had been conspiring with the

---

[8] Hayes to Mrs. Hayes, March 28, April 1, 1863, and to Sardis Birchard,
April 1, Hayes MS. Letters; Hayes, MS. Diary, March 26, 28, 30, 31; *Official
Records*, XXV, pt. 1, 76–7, pt. 2, 165–6.

[9] Hayes to Mrs. Hayes, April 5, 10, 15, May 2, 1863, and to Sardis Birchard,
April 9, 22, 30, Hayes MS. Letters.

Rebels and that if the raiders attempted to enter the town he would destroy it with artillery fire. He directed Hayes to have the guns ready.

Hayes obeyed the order, although he took the whole situation much more calmly than Scammon. The absence of any entries in his diary for weeks may indicate, however, that he was apprehensive and hence unusually busy. This time there was some cause to worry. The Confederates had projected a full-scale attack on the Kanawha posts, with a cavalry column that had been raiding in the north moving down via Summersville and an infantry force coming up from the south. It was a good plan, but the Confederates did not have the resources to execute it. The leaders of the cavalry raiders, John D. Imboden and William E. Jones, finding their men and mounts exhausted, simply pulled out of the operation. The infantry party attacked Fayette on its own and was easily repulsed.[1]

The unexpected outcome cheered Hayes. Writing Lucy in a confident mood, he said that the Kanawha army was now strong enough to hold its line against any threat the Confederates could muster. He was especially pleased that his two West Virginia regiments, showing the results of good training, had developed into crack outfits. The situation was now safe, he promised, and Lucy was to come on, bringing with her as many of the family as she wished.[2] Lucy needed no urging, but she could not start immediately. She intended to travel with her mother and all four of her sons, Webb, Birchard, Rutherford or "Ruddy," and the infant Joseph, who had been born just before Christmas in 1861, and it took some time to arrange transportation for so many people. The party did not arrive at Camp White until June 15. Hayes

---

[1] *Official Records*, XXV, pt. 2, 507, 509, LI, pt. 1, 1039.
[2] Hayes to Mrs. Hayes, May 17, 1863, Hayes MS. Letters. Uncle Sardis, who had hoped to be included, found that his health did not permit travel.

settled them in a cottage near his tent and prepared to enjoy
at least a brief period of family bliss. At first it seemed it
would be that way. But before a week passed little Joseph
fell sick of dysentery and after a few days died. The body
was placed on a table in the bedroom of the cottage—"surrounded by white roses and buds," Hayes recorded in his
diary—and later was sent to Cincinnati in the care of a corporal of the regiment.[3]

Joseph was a handsome boy, resembling his father more
than did his brothers, who took after the Webb side of the
family. Lucy, the grandmother, and the other boys were
struck down with grief. They all had a special feeling for
Joseph, partly because he was the youngest and partly because he was afflicted with some kind of mental disorder.
Hayes, resorting to the curious language that people of the
nineteenth century used to describe such matters, said the
boy's brain was "excessively developed," and he thought that
the death had prevented future greater suffering. His reaction
seems cold and detached. But even if Joseph had been completely normal, Hayes would still have been philosophical.
His response was born of the war, and something like it must
have been felt by countless other soldier-fathers who had
children born and die during the conflict. As Hayes confessed, it was hard for him to realize a sense of loss at the
boy's death. "I have hardly seen him," he mused in a letter to
Uncle Sardis, "and hardly had a fathers feeling for him."[4]

The tragedy took the joy out of the visit for everyone, and
on July 1 Lucy packed up the family and returned home.
Hayes regretted the parting. "You could not have felt the
loss of me more than I did of you," he wrote Lucy. But in
the same letter he proceeded immediately to discuss military

[3] Hayes to Mrs. Sophia Hayes, June 19, 1863, ibid.; Hayes, MS. Diary, June 25.
[4] Hayes to Mrs. Sophia Hayes, June 24, 1863, and to Sardis Birchard, June 25,
Hayes MS. Letters.

matters, by which she might have guessed that he could find solace from almost anything in the business of war. One of his West Virginia regiments had been ordered to Fayetteville, he revealed, and the Twenty-third would probably follow soon. In fact, it looked like the whole division would undertake a forward movement. He would have an important part in anything that developed. Scammon's division counted over 5,000 men present, and Hayes's First Brigade contained 2,700 of them. The brigade was now a full-sized outfit, comprising the Twenty-third and three West Virginia regiments plus two cavalry companies and a battery of artillery. The orders Hayes expected soon came. On July 11 the division left Charleston and two days later was at Fayetteville.[5]

Apparently Scammon had not seen fit to let the commander of his First Brigade in on the details of his proposed advance, for not until they reached Fayetteville did Hayes learn that the objective was Raleigh, once a Federal outpost and now serving the same function for the Confederates. An air of vague mystery surrounded all of Scammon's planning. He hoped to go beyond Raleigh if possible, perhaps to the New River Narrows, which Hayes would shortly figure out, and he intended to throw his cavalry against the Virginia & Tennessee Railroad at Wytheville, which Hayes did not know about until after the operation was over. Hayes did not approve the enterprise. "We are too weak to accomplish much," he put in his diary; "run some risks; and I see no sufficient object to be accomplished." His judgment was again proved correct. The column moved on Raleigh but found the Confederates waiting behind strong fortifications. Scammon, with his of-

---

[5] Hayes to Mrs. Hayes, July 6, 1863, and to Sardis Birchard, July 6, Hayes MS. Letters; Hayes, MS. Diary, July 9–11; *Official Records,* XXVII, pt. 3, 449–50, 664, LI, pt. 1, 1073. At this time West Virginia was again under a departmental commander, General Benjamin F. Kelley, who had his head-quarters in the north, but who exercised only the loosest supervision over Scammon and other subordinates.

ficers' concurrence, decided that it would be too costly to
storm the works and that it would take too long to turn them
and that therefore he had better withdraw. That night, however, the Confederates themselves pulled out. Scammon made
no attempt to follow. Apparently oppressed by the possible
dangers awaiting him, he ordered the works destroyed and
retired, although he did allow the cavalry to continue on to
strike the railroad at Wytheville. By the sixteenth the division was back at Fayetteville.[6]

It arrived just as exciting news was breaking—John Hunt
Morgan, the famous Confederate cavalry raider, was north
of the Ohio and heading for Gallipolis opposite the mouth
of the Kanawha. According to a postwar account by a soldier
in the division, Hayes was the first officer to get the information. He had rushed to the telegraph office to find out what
was happening in other theaters. While he was talking with
the operator, a wire arrived telling of Morgan's raid. Immediately grasping the situation, Hayes sent a dispatch to
Charleston asking whether any steamboats were there. Two
were available, came the answer. Hayes directed that the
vessels be sent at once up Loup Creek, a tributary of the
Kanawha. Then he galloped back to camp to find Scammon.
He explained to the general the opportunity before them—
the troops could march to Loup Creek, board the steamers,
and shortly be on the Ohio and in position to intercept Mor-

---

[6] Hayes, MS. Diary, July 12, 16, 1863; Hayes to Mrs. Hayes, July 16, Hayes
MS. Letters; James M. Comly, MS. Diary, July 16, in Ohio Historical Society
Library, Columbus; the Society kindly furnished a microfilm copy of the
diary, which runs from January, 1863, to December, 1864. In the Hayes
Library there is a typed copy of extracts from the diary for the period
April–December, 1864. Also in the Hayes Library is a document titled
"Journal Compiled Principally from the Diary of Major Comly," which is
based on the diary extracts. In the entry cited above Comly claimed that
he was responsible for the withdrawal, that he convinced Scammon the
division should go back to meet a probable Rebel thrust from the east at
Charleston. The statement is dubious. Hayes, who knew much more about
the situation, records no sense of urgency in the retrograde movement.

gan. Scammon was persuaded, and Hayes, with the Twenty-third and the Thirteenth West Virginia, set out on a difficult night march to meet the steamships.[7]

The story was somewhat dramatized. Hayes had no need to hasten to the telegraph office to check on military news. Even before the division had left Camp White for Fayetteville, he knew about the fall of Vicksburg and had a fairly accurate impression of the Union success at Gettysburg. If he went to the office at all, it was to communicate with his home or Charleston. But it is evident from his diary and letters that he learned from some source in Fayetteville that Morgan was in Ohio and close enough to be struck by forces from Scammon's division. It is also fairly clear that he took the information to Scammon and that he convinced the general to move. Scammon "wisely and promptly" determined to head Morgan off "by sending me," Hayes wrote in the diary. But he added significantly: "This was after a sharp controversy." If Scammon required urging, he acted decisively once he was committed. He followed Hayes in person with two more regiments.[8]

This was no ordinary raid of local partisans and no ordinary raider that Hayes was going to meet. John Morgan was one of the Confederacy's ablest cavalrymen. If he sometimes overestimated what his men and animals could do, if he sometimes got himself in situations from which there was no escape, he was still a daring, dangerous operator, and his troopers had been known to fight as well as raid. He had swung up out of Tennessee and across Kentucky into In-

---

[7] Otis, "Personal Recollections," Santa Barbara *Daily Press*, October 28, 1876. This article contains a number of inaccuracies. It has the expedition to Raleigh leaving in June, earlier than it did, penetrating to the Virginia & Tennessee Railroad, farther than it did, and returning on July 23, later than it did. It also errs in depicting Hayes as being completely ignorant of events occurring in other areas in recent weeks. But the main outlines of the account are probably true, for the reasons given in the text above.

[8] Hayes, MS. Diary, July 22, 1863.

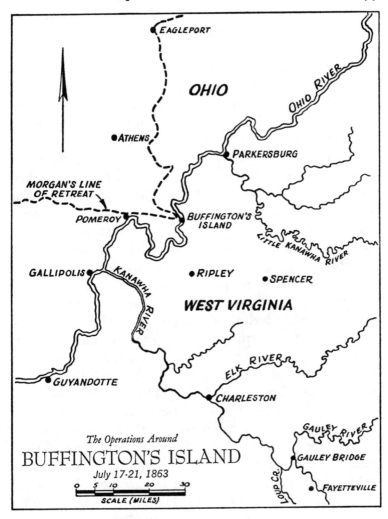

The *Operations Around*
BUFFINGTON'S ISLAND
July 17-21, 1863
0   5   10   20   30
SCALE (MILES)

diana. Then he turned east into Ohio and, skirting the
northern edges of Cincinnati, rode straight across the southern part of the state. But now pursuers began to close in
behind and around him—local militia who offered minor

although irritating opposition and, more formidable, regular
cavalry. Desperately Morgan rode for the Ohio River, seeking a ford to safety. The Federal cavalry was so hot behind
him that he had to go farther upstream than he intended.
He headed for Buffington's Island, above Gallipolis. He did
not know that two gunboats were prowling the river to prevent his crossing. Nor did he realize that infantry from Scammon's division were on the way to head him off.

Hayes and his two regiments made their night march to
Loup Creek and boarded the waiting steamers. They reached
Gallipolis at daylight on July 18. Here Hayes heard that
Morgan was farther up the river, apparently aiming to cross
at Pomeroy. He loaded the men back on the ships and made
for Pomeroy, reaching there the same day. The town was full
of militia, who reported Morgan was coming. The Confederates arrived near noon, and Hayes deployed his troops
to meet them. Morgan dismounted his men and ordered
them forward to feel out the opposition. When he realized
that he was facing army infantry instead of militia, he re-
mounted them and continued his flight. Hayes directed the
Federals, although Scammon was on the scene. The meeting
was no more than a skirmish. Hayes had one man wounded
and claimed he inflicted 21 casualties on the enemy. Although
Hayes thought that he had prevented the Confederates from
crossing the river, it is unlikely that Morgan was seeking a
ford at Pomeroy. The raider, with pursuing cavalry right
behind him, was trying to get to Buffington's Island as fast
as he could. He had confronted Hayes, not to fight him for
a river crossing, but to test if he would have to fight to pass
these troops who could make him real trouble. He must have
been relieved when he was able to break off the action. Hayes,
if he had shown any real aggressiveness, might have bagged
the weary Confederates. But in a rare display of indecision,
he let them escape. It was his worst mistake during the war.

The gray column lurched on to Buffington's Island, reaching there the next day, the nineteenth. Close behind it was the mountain division, which traveled by steamer but arrived too late for the final act. The pursuing cavalry was already on the scene, and the gunboats were watching the ford. Morgan had no hope of crossing and little more of escaping the net being drawn around him. He tried to fight his way out. But his men were too tired to put up much of a scrap, and many surrendered when they saw the odds against them, over 700 laying down their arms. Morgan himself and 1,100 raiders managed to break through, but more of the men fell into Federal hands that day or the next when they tried to cross at other fords. Hayes and his troops, who acted largely as spectators at the fight at Buffington's Island, were deployed on both sides of the river to watch for running Rebels, and they collected over 200 prisoners. Morgan and a small party turned north and after a long chase were captured near Lisbon, the farthest point north reached by any Confederates in the war.[9]

The raid that had terrorized two states for two weeks was now over. Scammon and Hayes assembled their units for the return to Camp White. Traveling by river steamers, as they had come, the mountain troops were back at Charleston by July 22. They were tired men. Since the first part of the month they had marched to Raleigh and returned to Fayette and had chased Morgan up and down the Ohio. They were also very satisfied men. They had participated in a significant operation and had played their role well. It had been a

[9] Hayes describes his part in the raid in his diary, July 19–22, 1863, and in *Official Records*, LI, pt. 1, 207. Reports by other officers are in ibid., XXIII, pt. 1, 677–9. Accounts that stress or mention the activities of the mountain division are Hastings, MS. Autobiography, July 17, 18; Clugston, MS. Diary July 18; Comly, MS. Diary, July 17–21; Moore (ed.), *Rebellion Record*, VII, 263, 264; Charles R. Rector, "Morgan Goes 'A-Raiding' and Views West Virginia," *West Virginia Review* (May, 1929), 310–11; Stutler, *West Virginia in the Civil War*, 231–41.

romantic episode, this cruising on the Kanawha and the Ohio and landing at intervals to confront Rebel raiders. Best of all there never had been much danger, as evidenced by the low casualties in the division, which did not total more than 50. Morgan's men had been pathetically eager to surrender at the last. The Twenty-third cherished the story of one of its sergeants and six men who found 145 Confederates in the woods and marched them in as prisoners. Hayes summarized perfectly the feeling of the men. It had been "the liveliest and jolliest campaign we ever had," he wrote. "It was nothing but fun—no serious fighting at all." The soldiers would remember this time as one of the happiest events of their lives, he ventured, using, interestingly, almost the same words that William T. Sherman would later employ to characterize a similar operation, the march across Georgia. Hayes was also pleased with his own part in this campaign which he had done so much to initiate. If he noted that Scammon gave him scant credit in the official report, he voiced no sentiment of bitterness at a neglect he had come to expect.[1]

At Camp White the two Kanawha brigades, the First under Hayes and the Second under Carr B. White (after whom the camp was named), prepared to enjoy another period of repose and routine.[2] "We are again settled down in our pleasant old camp and feel as if we were home again," Hayes wrote his mother. In other letters he analyzed why the military situation was likely to remain static. The Federals did not have enough strength to undertake an offensive, and neither did the Confederates. Reports that the enemy was building

---

[1] Clugston, MS. Diary, July 19, 1863; Hastings, MS. Autobiography, July 17; Hayes to Mrs. Hayes, July 21, 22, and to Sardis Birchard, July 22, Hayes MS. Letters.

[2] Hayes's brigade at this time included three regiments. A fourth regiment that had been added before the movement to Raleigh was now removed. Ordinarily a brigade contained four regiments, but in West Virginia the brigades were rarely up to size. Colonel White commanded only two regiments. *Official Records*, XXIX, pt. 2, 139.

up his numbers he measured correctly as only added protection against a possible Federal thrust at the Virginia & Tennessee Railroad. Although he would have liked some action, Hayes was quite as ready as his men to savor the delights of inactivity. He rode around the countryside a lot, read much—newspapers, novels, military books—and slept long hours. He and his troops would spend their days in this lazy fashion until near the end of August. Then, with the first breath of autumn chilling the mountains, he resigned himself to the prospect of spending another winter in West Virginia. He promised Lucy that if the division remained at Camp White he would send for her.[3]

Soon he was able to speak more definitely. It was almost certain that the division would go into winter quarters, he wrote, although there was a prospect of a raid against Confederate railroad communications in eastern Tennessee. Therefore Lucy was to start out immediately before bad weather set in and, because the military situation was not yet settled, to come alone. He was watching events in Tennessee closely at this time, probably thinking that he might be sent there, and the news of a severe Federal defeat at Chickamauga struck gloom to his heart. "I suffer from these blows more than I did from the loss of my sweet little boy," he confided to his diary.[4] He could do nothing but study the battles in the larger theaters and try to analyze their results—and wait for Lucy to arrive to relieve the monotony of his own existence. So anxious was he to see his wife that he met her at Gallipolis, and together they returned to Camp White by steamer. Lucy would stay a month on this visit. The wives of several other officers were in camp, including

---

[3] Hayes to Mrs. Sophia Hayes, July 26, August 9, 1863, to Sardis Birchard, August 6, 17, and to Mrs. Hayes, August 15, 30, Hayes MS. Letters; Clugston, MS. Diary, August 21.

[4] Hayes to Mrs. Hayes, September 4, 6, 11, 1863, Hayes MS. Letters; Hayes, MS. Diary, September 21.

Mrs. Comly, and Lucy thoroughly enjoyed the social good times and the trips to Charleston, which under the stimulus of Federal occupation was in the process of becoming something of a war boom town.[5]

No military movements of any kind, no Federal or Confederate offensives, occurred to mar Lucy's stay. Hayes was occupied, however, with a matter that was peculiar to his job as a brigade commander and that was fully as important as any battle activity he could have engaged in. Early in 1864 the terms of enlistment of the three-year men in the regiments raised in the first year of the war would be up. Unless these veterans could be persuaded to re-enlist, the nation would face a real crisis. They were the seasoned soldiers who formed the core of the armies in every theater. No legal power could force them to continue in service; they had done their stint and by law were entitled to return home to enjoy their reward. Their departure would not only take out of the armies a sizable number of good fighters but could wreck the existing regimental organization. By 1863 most of the first regiments had suffered so much attrition that they stood at half or even less of their original strength. The Twenty-third, for instance, was down to about 500 men. Further depletions could cause some regiments to lose their identities. The veterans had to be induced to re-enlist and to come back into their own units.

The national and state governments were apprehensively aware of the problem and were already acting to meet it. From Washington came a promise that every re-enlistee would receive a cash bounty of $400 and a furlough of thirty days and that a regiment signing up three fourths of its present strength could go home as a unit. The state governments offered additional bounties. Hayes was also alert to the prob-

---

[5] Hayes to Sardis Birchard, September 24, 1863, and to Mrs. Sophia Hayes, October 10, Hayes MS. Letters.

lem and was doing something about it as early as October. He had decided to re-enlist himself, and he was determined to keep the Twenty-third in existence. Turning on his considerable oratorical powers, he addressed the men, appealing to their patriotism and emphasizing the pecuniary rewards they would derive by rejoining. He would have to make more of these entreaties before he could achieve his goal, but he had the re-enlistment process under way in the Twenty-third before it was even started in any other of the Ohio regiments. Diverse motives prompted his vigorous action. One of the sources for his pride in the regiment was his conviction that it was the first three-year outfit raised in the state, and now he meant to sustain its high reputation. If enough veterans would re-enlist, the regiment could go home on furlough and by recruiting increase its strength still more. His own career depended on his efforts—unless the regiment was kept up he might lose his colonelcy. And his present rank seemed preferable to anything loftier. It was at this time that he coined an expression he would repeat many times in the future: "My feeling is that I would rather be one of the good colonels than one of the poor generals."[6]

In those same autumn weeks he had to give his attention to still another activity that was distinct from battles and yet in this modern war was as much a part of the military process as a charge on a desperate field. The Civil War, more than any previous American conflict, was a war of ideology, waged for fundamental principles, for, in the highest sense of the words, political objectives. The North was fighting for the preservation of nationalism and, secondarily, for the destruction of slavery. These were the official war aims, but

---

[6] Hayes to Mrs. Sophia Hayes, October 10, 1863, and to Sardis Birchard, October 10, ibid.; Hayes to R. H. Stephenson, October 27, Wright Family Papers; Clugston, MS. Diary, September 30; Hayes, MS. Diary, November 7; Reid, *Ohio in the War,* I, 173-5.

not all people in the North accepted them. A substantial
minority, the Peace Democrats, proposed a cessation of hostilities and a restoration of the Union on its former basis,
with nothing changed. They charged, in the most violent
language, that the central government was using the war as
an excuse to assume dictatorial powers, and they opposed
practically all the measures that the government employed
to prosecute the war. Although most of them were essentially
no more than old-fashioned agrarian sectionalists who could
not adjust to the realities of their time, to Republican supporters of the war and to Hayes they seemed to be traitors.
This opinion would appear extreme in the light of later
knowledge, but it was a natural one for men like Hayes to
hold. It came easily in the fall of 1863 when the state elections fell due in Ohio and other states. If the Peace Democrats won control of the governments of key states, they might
be able to halt the flow of men into the armies and wreck the
war effort.

That was what Hayes feared would happen in his own
state. Ohio, populous and powerful, was a critical state, and
the contest there threatened to be uncomfortably close. John
Brough was the Union Republican candidate for governor,
and he faced the leading Peace Democrat in the country,
Clement L. Vallandigham. The Republican leaders, who
were also the state's officials, felt that it would be necessary
to turn out an almost solid soldier vote for Brough if he was
to win. State law provided that men could vote in the field.
Commissioners would go to the regiments to collect the bal-
lots, but the outcome of the election would be determined
by a variety of factors, the candidates and the issues and the
editorials in home newspapers, but above all by the attitude
of those whom the troops respected most, their regimental
and brigade commanders.

It was here that an officer like Hayes could exercise a dominating influence—a civilian and politician himself, who could appreciate as few West Pointers could the importance of politics in a modern war. Hayes felt that it was vital for Brough to receive a large soldier vote, both to aid the candidate's cause and to rebuke the peace groups supporting Vallandigham. He was careful not to make any speeches or to do anything that could be interpreted as interfering with the right of the men to exercise their own free judgment. But it was easy for him to let his own opinion be known, and the members of the Twenty-third, already disposed to Brough, certainly knew whom their commander was for. The result was certain. On election day the regiment cast 514 unanimous votes for Brough. Its quartermaster, revealing that he at least was not neutral, thereupon issued a ration of whiskey "for the Union." A similar vote in other regiments helped to put Brough in the governor's chair. Hayes recorded the outcome with perceptive satisfaction: "A victory equal to a triumph of arms in an important battle. It shows persistent determination, willingness to pay taxes, to wait, to be patient."[7]

Hardly was the election out of the way when the first chills of autumn turned the thoughts of officers and soldiers to the necessity of preparing winter quarters. Already the men, without waiting for orders, were collecting material for shanties and laying out company streets. A sergeant of the Twenty-third described in his diary the routine of a day that would soon become typical: "No mail. Two members of Co. K had a fight and one bit off the ear of other. Sanitary committee from Cincinnati were here this eve. The bands new instru-

---

[7] Hayes to R. H. Stephenson, October 27, 1863, Wright Family Papers; Clugston, MS. Diary, October 12; Hayes, MS. Diary, October 15. Hayes stated that his brigade cast over 800 votes for Brough. But the *Official Records* show the Twenty-third as the only Ohio unit under his command. Either some other Ohio outfit was temporarily attached to his brigade or some of his West Virginia troops, claiming to be Ohioans, were voting.

ments . . . arr. and were used at dress parade this evening. Col Hayes is exchanging photographs with the boys of the regt." Colonel Hayes was as sure as the boys that operations on the Kanawha were closed out. Anticipating that orders would soon come down authorizing officers to set up winter quarters, he decided that he wanted his family with him in the dreary months ahead. So he sent Lucy home in late October. She was to "gather up the chickens," as he put it, and return as soon as possible.[8]

It took Lucy longer than he expected to do the gathering, but by the last of November she was back. She brought with her Webb and Ruddy—Birchard had decided to stay with Uncle Sardis—and her mother. The little circle had hardly begun to enjoy camp life together when Hayes received orders that would take him away for a ten-day campaign. General Benjamin F. Kelley, who had been commanding the Department of West Virginia since July but not exercising much supervision over his subordinates, suddenly decided to launch a cavalry raid against the Virginia & Tennessee Railroad. The raiders were to move via Monterey and strike the rail line at Salem. They would have to head east and execute a long semicircular loop before turning south toward their destination. For a time they would be operating considerably north of the Kanawha area. To distract Confederate attention from the cavalry column, Kelley directed Scammon to make a diversionary advance on Lewisburg, straight to the east. Scammon was to attack the enemy force there, occupy the town, and manifest every indication that he meant to do more before withdrawing.

Scammon moved out with his two brigades on December

---

[8] Clugston, MS. Diary, October 19, 1863; Hayes to Sardis Birchard, October 21, to Mrs. Hayes, October 25, and to Mrs. Sophia Hayes, November 1, Hayes MS. Letters.

8. He was at Lewisburg by the twelfth and with no trouble drove the Confederates out. But then reports of enemy reinforcements in his front and guerrilla parties in his rear threw him into a fright. He fell back to Meadow Bridge, where he prepared orders for a slow, careful retreat to Charleston. Brigade commanders Hayes and White were instructed not to pass a road intersection without reconnoitering the whole area and to scout every woods before them with skirmishers. With no incident whatsoever the column returned to Charleston. It was a ponderous and painful performance, and Kelley was bluntly scornful of Scammon in his report. Hayes certainly knew that Scammon had done badly, and he must have suspected that a blot had been put on his superior's record. But although ordinarily critical of Scammon, he said little about the episode in his diary or letters. He merely recorded the facts of the expedition and stopped. Perhaps he held his pen out of a sudden hope that Scammon's failure would cause the general to be transferred elsewhere.[9]

Back at Camp White, Hayes was content to resume the easy life of winter quarters. He found new delights in the company of Lucy and the boys. When a cold snap froze the Kanawha over, temporarily isolating the camp from the outside world, he felt a warm sense of satisfaction in being alone with his family. And alone too with his troops and particularly with the men of the Twenty-third. That identification with the regiment would always rise up to compete with any other loyalty. He was still laboring to persuade the veterans to re-enlist, to secure the required three fourths of the present strength so that the regiment could go home to recruit. Right after the first of the year he estimated that

[9] *Official Records,* XXIX, pt. 1, 920–2, 939–40, pt. 2, 550–1, LI, pt. 1, 1134–5; Hayes, MS. Diary, December 18, 1863; Hayes to Mrs. Sophia Hayes, December 18, Hayes MS. Letters.

300 of the old men had signed up. "The 23d may now be counted as a veteran regiment," he wrote proudly.[1]

Now that the magic figure was reached, the regiment was entitled to return to Ohio. It went off, company by company, during January, leaving Hayes without much of a command and feeling, as he confessed, "very lonely." He intended to follow with Lucy and the boys, but various details kept coming up to delay him.[2] Then, as he was at last ready to set out, electrifying news arrived to cause another postponement. General Scammon had been captured by the Rebels! The details of the episode, when they came out, would make the general look pretty ridiculous and add a little more tarnish to his reputation. With two aides, he had gone down the Kanawha on some business to Point Pleasant. Desiring to return quickly to Charleston, he ordered the captain of a river steamer to take him back. The captain demurred, maintaining that a night trip was dangerous, but Scammon insisted that he start at once. Shortly after midnight the vessel tied up at Red House Shoals. It was seen by a company of prowling irregular Virginia cavalry, who proceeded to board it and capture all present in their cabins. The next morning the Rebels put their captives ashore and burned the ship. They offered paroles to the prisoners, most of whom accepted. Scammon refused his parole, however, and the raiders rode away with him. Hayes and 100 of his men and other Federal parties tried to intercept the Confederates on the river without success.[3] Scammon eventually ended up at Richmond, where he remained until he was exchanged in August. He

---

[1] Hayes, MS. Diary, December 30, 1863, January 5, 1864. By another estimate, Reid, *Ohio in the War*, I, 175, the Twenty-third re-enlisted 257 veterans. Either figure would place the regiment around the middle in a listing of veteran re-enlistments in Ohio regiments.

[2] Hayes to Mrs. Sophia Hayes, January 17, 24, 1864, Hayes MS. Letters.

[3] *Official Records*, XXXIII, 109–10; Moore (ed.), *Rebellion Record*, VIII, 495–6; Claude M. Morgan, "Capture of General Scammon," in *West Virginia State Magazine* (July, 1958), 13.

was then assigned to duty in the Southern coastal theater and would never return to West Virginia.

Hayes could feel sorry for Scammon. But like so many officers who had had to serve under the general, he could not resist a sardonic although guarded laugh. He revealed his reactions in a letter to Uncle Sardis: "I must be cautious in what I say, but to you I can write that his capture is the greatest joke of the war. It was sheer carelessness, bad luck and accident. It took a good many chances, all lost, to bring it about. Everybody laughs when he is alone. And very intimate friends laugh in concert when together. General S's great point was his caution. He bored us all terribly with his extreme vigilance. The greatest military crime in his eyes was a surprise. Here he is caught in the greatest and most inexcusable way."[4]

Scammon's departure meant that a new commander had to be named for the Kanawha division. The appointment was made in February, and it went to a man who had been in and out of the West Virginia theater since the beginning of the war, George Crook. Crook was West Point and regular army and, as the troops would immediately realize, a stern, exacting disciplinarian. Of medium height and build, with light hair and a sandy beard, he affected, perhaps because of his experience as an Indian fighter in the West, an informal costume, "half civil and half military" as one observer described it.[5] He was a soldier of solid attainments, one of the better subordinate officers of the war, and the division would come to have a feeling for him that it had never had for Scammon. Hayes, when he came to know Crook better, would develop a tremendous respect for this professional whom he might have been expected to resent.

At the moment Hayes had no opportunity to learn any-

---

[4] Hayes to Sardis Birchard, February 7, 1864, Hayes MS. Letters.
[5] Cox, *Military Reminiscences*, I, 205–6; Horton and Teverbaugh, *Eleventh Regiment*, 261.

thing about the new commander. Early in February he departed for home, and he remained in Ohio the rest of the month resting himself and recruiting his regiment. When his leave was up, he returned to Camp White, reaching there on March 10. Even though Lucy accompanied him, he voiced his usual emotion when he saw the tents and the troops of the Twenty-third: "I certainly never felt a more homelike feeling then I have with my men."[6]

[6] Hayes to Mrs. Sophia Hayes, March 11, 1864, Hayes MS. Letters.

Chapter 9

The Great Dublin Raid

ALL THINGS POINT TO early action," Colonel Hayes wrote in his diary on April 26, 1864. He had been observing the steady flow of troops into Camp White in recent weeks—new Ohio and West Virginia regiments and some Pennsylvania regiments from the Army of the Potomac and finally a cavalry force of 2,000 under General William W. Averell, who also carried with him the aura of a previous Eastern service, although one marred by serious criticisms of his capacity. Among the arrivals was the Thirty-sixth Ohio, a proud unit which had gone through the debacle of Chickamauga; once Crook's old regiment, it was now commanded by Colonel Hiram F. Devol. To Hayes's intense pleasure, it was assigned to his brigade. So also were a part of the Thirty-fourth Ohio, a mounted infantry outfit, and the Fifth and Seventh West Virginia Cavalry. When these last units were ordered to get rid of their animals and to operate as infantry, Hayes knew there was something big afoot. He warned Lucy that she would have to leave for home in a few days and plunged into the job of organizing his command. Hayes was proud that at last he had approximately a full-sized brigade. He commanded, in fact, a third of Crook's total infantry force of 6,100. Colonel White still led the Second Brigade,

[169]

and Colonel Horatio G. Sickel headed the newly created Third Brigade.[1]

Hayes knew that an advance was imminent, and he must have guessed its objective, a strike at the Confederate communications on the Virginia & Tennessee Railroad, the most logical and, indeed, the only feasible movement that the Kanawha army could undertake. He had amused himself back in January by writing out a plan for just such a raid. He would have been flattered if he had known that the present operation would resemble his scheme and that it had come from the brain of the highest Federal planner, Lieutenant General Ulysses S. Grant, commanding all Federal armies and directing strategy for all theaters. Grant's grand plan for 1864 called for a simultaneous advance of Federal armies, large and small, along the whole circumference of the Confederacy. Even if the lesser columns did not accomplish much, they would at least engage the enemy's attention, Grant thought, and thereby contribute to the success of the main armies. He foresaw an important role for the West Virginia force in what he hoped would be the campaign that would break the back of the South.

West Virginia was again a part of a larger territorial command. It was within the jurisdiction of General Franz Sigel, who had his headquarters and some 7,000 troops in the Shenandoah Valley. As Grant envisioned it, the forces of Sigel and Crook could provide valuable support to the Army of the Potomac when it advanced to fight Lee south of the Rapidan-Rappahannock line and at the same time accomplish an independent strategic objective. The supreme commander proposed to send Crook southward to hit the Virginia & Ten-

---

[1] Hayes to Sardis Birchard, March 20, April 3, 20, 24, 1864, Hayes MS. Letters; Hayes, MS. Diary, April 26; *Official Records*, XXXIII, 1007; E. C. Arthur, "The Dublin Raid," in the *Ohio Soldier*, II (January 5, 1899), 1–2. Arthur wrote seven valuable articles on the Dublin campaign; they appeared in issues of the magazine over a span of four months.

nessee road at Dublin and the New River Bridge; if possible, Crook was also to destroy the salt-processing works of the Confederates at Saltville. Simultaneously Sigel was to move up the Valley toward Staunton, distracting attention from Crook and menacing another Confederate communication, the Virginia Central Railroad. If all went well, the two columns could eventually unite around Staunton and move on Lynchburg. Grant summoned Crook to his headquarters to explain the plan, largely because Crook's part in it was the most important, but possibly because the general in chief did not trust Sigel's capacity to organize the expedition. Returning to Charleston, Crook decided he could best execute his mission by operating in two columns. He would send Averell and the cavalry against Saltville, while he and the infantry would go to Dublin. If Averell was successful, he could ride east to join Crook, and the combined force could wreck a long line of the railroad.[2]

It was no easy thing that Crook had been asked to do. He realized the difficulties before him and laid his plans carefully. First, he would have to take his division to Gauley Bridge, which because of its water communications would serve as his advanced field base. But when he turned south from there, he would have to depend on his own horse-and-wagon transportation for supplies. The distance from Gauley Bridge to his destination on the New River was approximately 140 miles, over hills, mountains, and spring-swollen creeks. Crook would have to perform a considerable feat in logistics before he ever got near the enemy. But he was a confident man, and the troops, catching his mood, were confident when they marched out from Camp White on April 28. The weather was fair, and, as regimental bands played martial

---

[2] George E. Pond, *The Shenandoah Valley in 1864* (New York, 1883), 9–10; Schmitt (ed.), *George Crook*, 114; Arthur, "Dublin Raid," *Ohio Soldier*, January 5, 1889, 2; Robert U. Johnson and Clarence C. Buel (eds.), *Battles and Leaders of the Civil War* (New York, 1887–8) IV, 487.

airs and brigade commanders shouted "Forward," the men stepped off briskly. They were not accustomed to marching, however, and soon slowed the pace. The Twenty-third was glad to stop after a march of only fourteen miles. The other units made similar time, and it was not until May 1 that the whole division reached Camp Reynolds near Gauley Bridge, where Hayes had spent part of the winter of the previous year. Lucy, with the boys—Webb and Birchard—followed the troops on a steamer almost to Gauley Bridge to say farewell. Hayes watched them recede down the river, waving their handkerchiefs as long as they were in sight. "Bid Good-Bye to the dear ones!" he wrote in his diary. To Uncle Sardis he penned a terse prediction: "It looks like a Big Raid."[3]

The men too knew that it was a raid when the next morning the line of march took them south on the route leading to the Virginia & Tennessee rail line. They began cheering, for Crook, for themselves, and for the idea that maybe they were going to do something important. Hayes felt the same elation. "At last our work begins," he said to a staff officer, "and with General Crook to lead us we shall surely win." Crook's orders were to set a fast pace—march fifty minutes and rest ten. The troops started willingly enough, but they were still a little soft and could not consistently maintain the schedule. To their discomfort, a cold rain set in at eleven o'clock and soon turned into driving sleet. They made seventeen miles, however, passing through Fayette in the afternoon and camping four miles beyond on the Raleigh road. For the men of the Twenty-third and some other units, memories stirred as they came again to places they had once held but had had to abandon. They would see more familiar sites as they continued the march—Raleigh, Flat Top, Camp Creek, and

[3] Hayes, MS. Diary, April 28–May 1, 1864; Hayes to Sardis Birchard, May 1, and to Mrs. Sophia Hayes, May 1, Hayes MS. Letters; Arthur, "Dublin Raid," *Ohio Soldier*, January 5, 1889, 2.

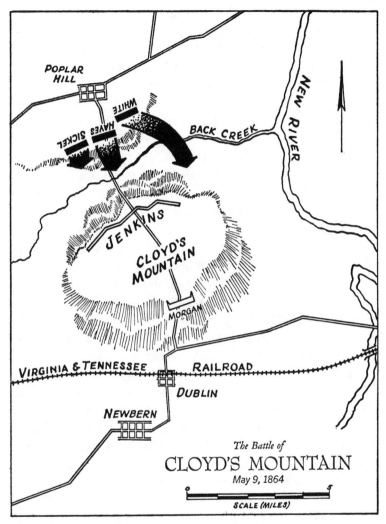

The Battle of
CLOYD'S MOUNTAIN
May 9, 1864

SCALE (MILES)

Princeton, where they encountered their first opposition, a
small Confederate cavalry force that appeared and then disappeared.

Those of them who had been in the spring campaign of
two years before must have wondered if Crook would try

to fight his way through the New River Narrows. The general had no intention of doing anything so foolish. Feinting toward the Narrows, where the Confederates were expecting him, he moved instead through undefended Rocky Gap and by the evening of May 8 was at Shannon's Bridge, only seven miles from Dublin. Here he was informed that the Confederates were waiting for him two miles ahead on Cloyd's Mountain. The next morning he rode out to examine the position. He studied the terrain a few minutes through his field glass. Then, lowering the glass, he said with the assurance his officers had come to accept in him: "The enemy is in force and in a strong position. They may whip us, but I guess not."[4]

Crook's quick diagnosis exaggerated somewhat the capacity of the opposition. The defenders numbered no more than 3,000, and their position, although naturally formidable, had been hastily chosen and hastily fortified. Haste had marked all of the Confederates preparations to meet Crook's sudden appearance near the vital railroad line. General John C. Breckinridge was the gray commander in the area, but he had gone to the Shenandoah Valley to deal with Sigel's offensive. In temporary command was General A. G. Jenkins, who, after some frantic discussions with his subordinates and local citizens who knew the terrain, decided to contest the Federal advance at Cloyd's Mountain. He placed his troops, some of whom were militia and home guards, on a ridge commanding the road over which Crook would have to pass and threw up a line of fortifications of logs, rails, and stumps. Crook's force stood on an opposite ridge, and between the two little

---

[4] Hastings, MS. Autobiography, May 2, 1864; Hayes, MS. Diary, May 2–7; Arthur, "Dublin Raid," *Ohio Soldier*, January 5, 1889, 2; Mary Elizabeth Kincaid, "Fayetteville, West Virginia, During the Civil War," *West Virginia History*, XIV (1935), 364; *Official Records*, XXXVII, pt. 1, 10; Moore (ed.), *Rebellion Record*, XI, 14–15. West Virginia had been admitted as a state in June, 1863, and Crook's troops could feel that as they approached Dublin they were invading Virginia, were definitely on enemy soil.

armies was a beautiful meadow 400 to 500 yards in expanse.[5]

Immediately after inspecting the position, Crook decided on a battle plan. To go on to the railroad, he would have to attack the force in front of him, and he hesitated not an instant in ordering an assault. Bringing up his brigades, he formed them in line, from left to right, White's Second, Hayes First, and Sickel's Third. Quickly he explained the plan to the brigade commanders. White's brigade under cover of the dense woods would secure a position on the enemy right flank and then attack. When Hayes heard the sound of White's guns, he was to charge across the meadow. The Third Brigade would follow and support the First. Although Crook had issued his instructions at an early hour on that May 9 morning, he had to hold up his attack. It took White longer than expected to work his way around the enemy flank, and not until about eleven did Hayes receive orders to move forward.[6]

Up to this time Hayes had been sitting his horse at the head of his brigade. Confederate artillerists could see the bluecoats on the opposite ridge and opened a hot fire on them. The troops were partially sheltered in the woods, but Hayes and his staff were an obvious target. The colonel, knowing the effect any sign of fear on his part would have on the men, smiled and chatted with his officers while the shells burst overhead. Now Crook came to him and said White must

---

[5] *Official Records,* XXXVII, pt. 1, 46–8; Arthur, "Dublin Raid," *Ohio Soldier,* January 5, 1889, 4. Cloyd's Mountain was named for a family who lived on it; also known locally as Big Taylor Mountain, it is approximately 2,500 feet high. For information about the area, I am indebted to Mr. Sam Neal of Chatham, Virginia. Hayes wrote that the meadow was 300 yards across but other sources put it as much wider.

[6] Schmitt (ed.), *George Crook,* 115; Moore (ed.), *Rebellion Record,* XI, 14–16. Participants in Civil War battles usually differed as to the times when movements started, and the men at Cloyd's Mountain were no exception. Various sources state that the frontal assault began at ten, at noon, and at intervals in between. The official reports indicate that eleven was the probable hour.

be ready to strike. Hayes was to descend the slope, form a line of battle at the base, and, at the sound of White's guns, sweep across the meadow. Quickly Hayes made his dispositions. Turning to Comly, who, dressed in a battle jacket buttoned to the throat, was nervously striding up and down, he directed that the Twenty-third lead the column, followed by the Thirty-fourth and the Thirty-sixth.

Slowly the brigade wound its way down. The descent was so precipitous and the woods so dense that Hayes and his staff had to dismount and leave their horses with aides. But at last they reached the bottom, and as the men emerged into the open Hayes formed them in a battle line. They were in plain sight of the enemy now and within close range, and both artillery and rifle fire began to strike them. Anxiously Hayes listened for the sound of White's guns, for he knew that no troops would stand too long under this kind of pounding. To his relief he heard almost immediately heavy firing on his left, indicating that White was engaged. He shouted an order to advance, and the brigade moved forward over the meadow at the set pace of a charging Civil War regiment, a "slow double-quick" that gradually picked up as the men neared their objective.

Because the meadow presented a relatively unbroken surface, the brigade was able to maintain an alignment unusual for Civil War units during the whole course of its advance. But its progress was the opposite of smooth. At this close range the enemy fire was deadly and tore great gaps in the line. Hayes had to be everywhere to inspire the men to keep going, exposing himself and shouting encouragement. One soldier recalled later that the colonel seemed "heated clear through." Still the attackers ground forward. Now they were at the base of the ridge where the Confederates stood—and here they came upon a creek that nobody had known was there. Across its waist-deep current they floundered and flung themselves on the bank. At this point Hayes called a halt so that he could reform the line. The men, knowing that from here on they would be going uphill, discarded their knapsacks. While they were resting, they were astonished to discover that they had an important guest. General Crook had accompanied the charge! But his riding boots had become filled with water, and he had had difficulty in getting over the creek. A lieutenant in the Twenty-third said impudently that his only objection to a general's leading a charge was that the commander had to be helped over water.

After a few minutes Hayes ordered "charge" sounded on the bugles, and the men rushed up the hill. They ran into an immediate hot volley, but they were not going to be stopped now. Right into the line of Rebel fortifications they smashed and kept on going. As they passed by an abandoned battery a young recruit in the Twenty-third emitted a whoop and placed his cap over the muzzle of one of the guns. The Confederates fell back to a second ridge and attempted to make a new stand. But suddenly their resistance dissolved as they saw the hopelessness of the situation. The First Brigade, followed by the Third, was on their front, and the Second was coming up on their flank. The gray line wavered and then broke in a rout toward Dublin. Hundreds of Confederates surrendered on the field. Among the captured was wounded General Jenkins.[7]

The abrupt and apparent ending of the battle left the Federals in a state of joyful shock. The men were "running wild in every direction," one participant would recall later, and some of them bayoneted Rebel prisoners before their officers could stop them. For a period nobody tried to get the troops in hand or to exercise any central control. Crook, who

---

[7] Hastings, MS. Autobiography, May 9, 1864; Hayes, MS. Diary, May 9; Arthur, "Dublin Raid," *Ohio Soldier*, January 19, 1889, 338; Journal of Twenty-third Regiment, Ohio Volunteer Infantry, MS. in Hayes Library, author unknown, probably Russell Hastings; Otis "Personal Recollections,"

had been all over the field during the fighting, was overcome by exhaustion and excitement and fell on the ground in a faint. His staff devoted their attention to reviving him. The only officer who kept his head and attempted to exploit the victory was Hayes. Collecting 500 men of his brigade and two artillery pieces, he ordered his horse brought to him and pressed toward Dublin, five miles way. Suddenly, near the town, he ran into stubborn resistance that indicated the presence of fresh enemy troops. These were, although Hayes did not then know it, cavalry from the command of his old antagonist of Buffington's Island, John Morgan. Two days before, Morgan had helped to drive off Averell when the latter appeared at Saltville, and then he had started to transfer his force by rail to Dublin to aid Jenkins. The first contingents to arrive seemed to have come just too late.

But possibly they had not. It was a critical moment in the battle, one of those times in war when the outcome sways in the balance and will swing to the side which is the bolder. The instinct of most brigade commanders in Hayes's situation would have been to halt, report the presence of the enemy in exaggerated terms, and wait for reinforcements. If Hayes had acted thus, Crook would probably have been impressed and would have paused to regroup, giving the Confederates time to bring up more men. They might not have been able to muster enough strength to smash Crook, but if they could have advanced while his army was still in a state of confusion, they could have administered him a sharp

---

Santa Barbara *Daily Press,* October 31, 1876; Hayes, "Cloyd Mountain," four-page manuscript account in Hayes Library; Clugston, MS. Diary, May 9, 1864; C. A. Sperry to Hayes, November 20, 1889; and J. L. Botsford to Hayes, November 27, Selected Soldiers' Letters. The reports on the battle are in *Official Records,* XXXVII, pt. 1, 10–16. Hayes handed in a brief document in which he stated that it was unnecessary for him to say anything because Crook had been present with the brigade during the battle. This was strange conduct for an officer in his position. An ambitious brigade commander would have handed in a report detailing his own actions and praising those of his subordinates, whose support for his promotion he would thus have gained.

check. At this dangerous juncture Hayes showed real quality. Although innocent of a military education, he nevertheless appreciated one of the most vital principles in war—keep the momentum of victory going. He resolved to attack. The enemy force immediately before him, Morgan's men and the fugitives from Cloyd's Mountain who had rallied on them, was no larger than his. But for all he knew, he was outnumbered. So he resorted to his stratagem of deception. His order was to "yell like devils" and charge. Screaming as if they were 5,000, one of his officers recalled, they swept forward. At the same time Crook, now himself again, had the rest of his force collected and was moving forward in support. The combined effect of Hayes's noisy attack and Crook's approach was too much for the Confederates, who broke almost instantly. Crook's whole command surged forward and with the First Brigade in the van entered Dublin at twilight, triumphant but weary. "We had marched eleven miles and fought a fiercely contested battle," wrote adjutant Hastings of Hayes's staff.[8]

Hayes was pleased and proud at everything about Cloyd's Mountain. He knew that he had played his own part well and that he had won Crook's commendation. But above any feeling of self-satisfaction, he rejoiced in the performance of his brigade and especially in the feats of the Twenty-third. His favorite unit had been in the forefront of the fighting and had in his opinion carried the battle for the whole brigade. "Don't repeat my talk," he warned Lucy. "But the 23d was *the* regiment." That his praise was not exaggerated was attested by the regiment's casualties, an aggregate of 123, including 21 killed, by far the heaviest in the brigade's total of 172. Only one other regiment in Crook's force, the Ninth West Virginia of the Second Brigade, suffered more, 186.

[8] C. A. Sperry to Hayes, November 20, 1889, Selected Soldiers' Letters; Hastings, MS. Autobiography, May 9, 1864; Arthur, "Dublin Raid," *Ohio Soldier,* January 19, 1889, 339, February 2, 355.

Hayes could write his summation of the battle in good faith: "This is our best fight."[9]

The capture of Dublin was only the first of Crook's objectives, and not the most important one. His main mission was to wreck the Virginia & Tennessee Railroad and burn its most vital span, the New River Bridge, eight miles to the east of Dublin. He moved promptly to accomplish it the very next day. Before leaving Dublin, he fired the railroad station, the telegraph office, the water tank, and a large accumulation of military stores left behind by the Confederates. He set a part of his infantry to destroying the track between Dublin and the bridge, the men pushing the rolling stock down the steep embankment and burning and twisting the rails. With the rest of his force and his artillery and wagons, he marched to the New River Bridge, where his rail wreckers joined him at noon.

The Confederates knew that the 400-foot-long wooden bridge was Crook's next objective. But they were too weakened by their defeat at Cloyd's Mountain to contest his approach. Retiring to the east bank, they brought up artillery and attempted to shield the bridge with fire. Crook retaliated by unlimbering his own guns, and a noisy duel ensued for two hours. Noting that the enemy fire was not too effective, Crook directed that the bridge be burned. A company of specially designated men from Sickel's brigade, bearing torches and combustible materials, dashed out on the span and soon had the timbers ablaze. As the flames licked up the

[9] *Official Records* XXXVII, pt. 1, 12, 13; Hayes to Mrs. Hayes, May 13, 19, 1864, Hayes MS. Letters. The total casualties in the army were 688. White's Second Brigade incurred 391 and Sickel's Third 117. Although White was as hotly engaged as Hayes, his heavier losses are to be explained in part by those in one regiment, the Ninth West Virginia. The total Confederate casualties were 538. One participant, Egan, *Flying Yank*, 162, thought that the battle was one of the most destructive of the war, considering the time occupied and the numbers engaged. But he put the actual fighting time at only forty minutes, whereas Hayes, more correctly, estimated it at an hour and a half.

edifice, both sides paused as if by mutual consent to contemplate the awesome spectacle. Crook's infantry lined the bluffs on the west bank, and his bands broke into martial airs. Within two hours the great bridge had fallen into the river and was floating off on its current. "A fine scene it was," Hayes recorded with grim relish in his diary.[1]

Despite its long-range nature, the encounter at the bridge was not entirely bloodless. The Confederate missiles occasionally found a target, and one of them caused Hayes to witness the strangest death he saw in the war. When the party from Sickel's brigade ran out to fire the bridge, Hayes collected some troops from his brigade and moved down to the river's bank to cover the burners. He ordered his men to lie down in a depression. All obeyed except a saucy character who demanded: "Why don't you get off your horse and hide too?" Hayes repeated the order, but the trooper came back: "I'll get down when you do." Just as Hayes was about to insist that he be obeyed, a shell burst near them, wounding the recalcitrant "fatally and shockingly," as Hayes put it. The wound was evidently so shocking as to cause an examination of the person of the soldier—who was discovered to be a woman![2]

On the afternoon of that May 10 Crook seemed to be on the verge of accomplishing one of the most successful minor campaigns of the war. He had done everything that had been expected of him—he had severed the Virginia & Tennessee Railroad, he had destroyed the New River Bridge, and in the process he had pretty thoroughly smashed the Confederate forces opposing him. Now presumably he would advance eastward toward Salem, tearing up more of the railroad as he

---

[1] Arthur, "Dublin Raid," *Ohio Soldier*, March 2, 1889, 386; MS. Journal of Twenty-third Ohio, May 10, 1864; Clugston, MS. Diary, May 10; Hayes, MS. Diary, May 10.

[2] Hayes to E. C. Arthur, June 10, 1889, MS. in Hayes Library. Hayes did not identify the "soldier" other than to say she was a dismounted cavalryman,

went, and, as Grant's instructions had provided, link up with Sigel for a drive on Lynchburg. But Crook did nothing of the kind. Instead he retreated north to Meadow Bluff. He said later that he decided to retire when he saw an intercepted telegraphic dispatch announcing that Lee had defeated Grant in northern Virginia. Not having heard from Sigel or Averell and not knowing their whereabouts, he feared that he was isolated, that Lee would send forces west by rail to cut him off. The route to Meadow Bluff was not the one he had advanced on, but it was shorter, and at Meadow Bluff he could be supplied from Gauley Bridge and he would be in position to make contact with Sigel. Crook's explanation is not entirely convincing. It was strange that a soldier of his experience and reputed cunning did not think to check the accuracy of an enemy dispatch, which, it turned out, was untrue. If he acted on the basis of the dispatch alone, then he lost his head and possibly his nerve as well. A more likely interpretation is that Crook became suddenly oppressed with his logistics problem. He was 140 miles or so from his base and connected with it only by bad roads, he was running short of ammunition and rations and could not forage in this desolate country, and he was carrying with him his own wounded and 300 prisoners. Under the circumstances, he could not be censured too severely for wanting to get away.[3]

He moved out immediately. Hardly had the bridge toppled into the river when the artillery and wagon trains began to cross the New at an upstream ford. The infantry marched three miles downstream and crossed at Pepper's Ferry, using the one scow usually present at Virginia ferries. It was far

which would indicate she belonged to one of the West Virginia units. J. T. Webb in a letter to his mother, June 9, 1864, Webb Family Correspondence, gave a somewhat different version of this incident. He described the killing of the soldier but did not mention Hayes as being present. He added that the woman was a member of the Fifth West Virginia.

[3] Schmitt (ed.), *George Crook*, 115–16. Sigel had advanced up the Valley; at New Market on May 15 he would meet a reverse and would have to retire. His defeat occurred after Crook began his retreat, and Crook did not learn

into the night before the last trip was completed, and the men had to light huge fires on both banks to illuminate the ferry. On the east side several hundred Negroes of both sexes and all ages appeared and announced they were going to accompany the army to freedom. To placate their astonished deliverers, the contrabands entertained for hours with music and dances. It was a weird scene, the fires lighting up the wild landscape, the dusky figures chanting and stamping, and the Northern soldiers watching intently and not quite understanding what emotions animated these people from another world. The Negroes, as was their wont everywhere when dealing with the warriors in blue, injected overtones of the ideological character of the war into their songs.

> *When evah you heah de fife and drum,*
> *You may be sho de wah's begun.*
> *My old massa ust to live mighty high,*
> *Ust to drink coffee, but now he drinks rye.*[4]

Crook permitted the Negroes to join the column. His decision pleased the antislavery sentiment of the soldiers, but it added one more supply burden to the already strained facilities of the quartermaster service. Some of the fugitives brought their own wagons with them, which would clog the mountain roads and hold up the march. The majority walked, carrying in their arms their children and few belongings.

On the next day the army marched nine miles to Blacksburg. The reasons for the short progress were several. Rumors, exaggerated ones, of a Confederate force hovering nearby dictated caution. North of Blacksburg lay Salt Pond Moun-

---

of it until reaching Meadow Bluff. Averell, after failing to strike Saltville, rode to Wytheville, where he was also repelled. He then went to Dublin and tore up trackage east of the town for eighteen miles. On May 14 he started north to join Crook and overtook the retreating column the next day.

[4] Arthur, "Dublin Raid," *Ohio Soldier*, March 2, 1889, 387.

tain and Peter's Mountain, and Crook wanted the men rested before attempting these formidable barriers. A fierce rainstorm came on in the afternoon, forcing an early resort to camp.[5] But short marches would be the rule during the whole of the retreat. Fifteen miles a day would be the maximum, and on some days as little as six or less would be considered good. It was not the rains, which fell every day, or the execrable mountain roads that held up the schedule, although both of these helped mightily. Rather, both the men and the horses were too exhausted to move very fast, and a serious shortage of food and forage soon developed to render these conditions truly pitiable. There was never much doubt that the expedition would make its way to Meadow Bluff, and the retreat never degenerated into a debacle. But the little force stumbling ahead over the mountain ridges did not look like a conquering army returning in triumph.

The stress factor began to take its toll on the first day out of Blacksburg, May 12. The column managed to cover fifteen miles, but it had to ascend rugged Salt Pond Mountain in a steady rain. As the narrow road could accommodate only the wagons, the men had to pick their way along its edges. In the clinging mud the progress of the whole column was painful. Hayes had charge of the wagon train, and a trying job he found it. "Rode all day in mud & rain back and forth," he summarized disgustedly in his diary. Many of the horses, weakened by insufficient forage, dropped dead in the harness. Loads then had to be shifted and wagons abandoned. The marchers toiled on until after midnight and went into camp on the mountain. Officers and men fell down on the wet ground to sleep, many of them, like Hayes, without blankets.

---

[5] Ibid., March 16, 1889, 402; Hayes, MS. Diary, May 11, 1864. A small Confederate force under General William L. ("Mudwall") Jackson was observing the column, but it made no serious attempt to interfere. For an account by a soldier under W. L. Jackson, see David Poe, *Personal Reminiscences of the Civil War* (Buckhannon, 1911), 38–9.

"A terribly severe day's work," Hayes recorded, "one of the worst in all my experience."[6]

At five in the morning on the thirteenth Hayes was sitting on a stump before the fire near which he and his staff had slept. The rain fell on his slouch hat and dripped onto a rubber blanket which he had flung around his shoulders. Some of his men sensed that he had had no breakfast. One stepped forward and offered him some coffee in a tin cup. Another handed him a few slivers of cracker. Hayes dispatched both items with relish and then talked briefly with the men, telling them that Crook was a good general and that the expedition had been a success. That day the army marched fifteen miles over Peter's Mountain and camped on the northeastern side.[7] They had passed the worst terrain. Salt Sulphur and Little Flat Top mountains lay ahead, but they were less forbidding, and then would come the descent to the Greenbrier Valley. But now the specter of hunger rose up in more menacing form. The incident of the soldiers giving food to Hayes had been grimly symbolic. Regular rations were no longer being issued, and officers and enlisted men were subsisting on what they could scrounge. What they got was mostly corn, which they ate parched, boiled, or raw on the cob.

The struggling column was able to cover only six miles on the fourteenth, and on the fifteenth, when it reached Union near the Greenbrier Valley, but four. Something of the desperation beginning to grip all of them was reflected in entries in Hayes's diary. "Out of grub. Live off of the country. . . . Starvation only to be kept off by energetic and systematic foraging. General Crook anxious. . . ." Crook was indeed anxious and was showing signs of strain. When the Thirty-sixth Ohio captured a bushwacker, the general snappishly

---

[6] Hayes, MS. Diary, May 12, 1864; Comly, MS. Diary, May 12; Arthur, "Dublin Raid," *Ohio Soldier*, March 30, 1889, 418; Egan, *Flying Yank*, 176–7.

[7] Arthur, "Dublin Raid," *Ohio Soldier*, March 30, 1889, 418; Hayes, MS. Diary, May 13, 1864.

ordered that the man be shot. The Ohioans performed the execution with gusto and left the body lying on the road with a paper pinned to the breast reading: "This is the fate of all bushwackers."[8]

Crook must have known that the men were approaching the breaking point. But he knew too that unless he drove them on they would perish on the road or be killed by guerrillas. His goal was Alderson's Ferry on the Greenbrier River. Once across the river, the column would be only a day's march from Meadow Bluff—and food. Crook caused word to be sent down the ranks that he had ordered a wagon train of supplies to be waiting at Meadow Bluff. The men responded with a last effort and lurched into Alderson's late on the sixteenth. In this valley area food was relatively plentiful, and foraging parties soon brought in a rich variety, including chickens, bacon, flour, and beef. On this fare the men, with the resiliency common to American soldiers in all wars, revived instantly in body and spirit. But they still had their work cut out. Because of the constant rains, the Greenbrier was high, and only one old flatboat was available to transport the whole force and its wagons across. But everybody, officers and men, turned to the job. Even Crook and his staff pitched in, the general personally clubbing some stubborn mules that objected to swimming the stream. It took the better part of two days to effect the crossing, but on the afternoon of the eighteenth the little army camped safely on the north bank. Hayes fell into a philosophical mood as he watched the frenzied activity at the ferry. These men had been without news of the outside world for three weeks and even now they cared nothing about what was happening in the larger war, he reflected. They were satisfied to have saved their own lives.[9]

On May 19 the column trudged an easy ten miles into

---

[8] Hayes, MS. Diary, May 14, 15, 1864; Comly, MS. Diary, May 14, 15; Arthur, "Dublin Raid," *Ohio Soldier*, March 30, 1889, 419.

Meadow Bluff. The rain that had followed it for nine days and nights suddenly ceased, and the sun broke forth with welcome warmth. As if they considered the change in the weather a good omen, the men marched in jauntily and with an air of pride. They had been out 21 days, they had marched 270 miles through 11 counties, they had crossed 17 mountain ridges, they had forded and ferried more streams than they cared to remember, they had experienced 16 days of storm and rain, and they had gone without regular rations for 10 days. It was a rare record, and they felt good about it. Hayes hit on a felicitous phrase to describe their feelings. They were, he said, "a happy little company." They were also a hungry company. The promised wagon train had not arrived from Gauley Bridge, and there were no rations at Meadow Bluff. "Began to feel like a man that is hungry," one doleful soldier recorded in his journal. The train came up the next day, however, to furnish a fortunate ending to the campaign.[1]

Hayes now contemplated the great raid with proud satisfaction. He described its results in letters to Lucy and Uncle Sardis—the cutting of the Virginia & Tennessee Railroad, the destruction of the New River Bridge, the victory at Cloyd's Mountain, and the prisoners and artillery pieces brought off. He did not forget to cite his own exploits, and he bragged mightily about the Twenty-third. But his highest praise was reserved for Crook. "This campaign in plan and execution has been perfect," he declared. "Altogether this is our finest experience in the War & Gen Crook is the best General we have ever served under not excepting Rosecrans." Under Crook he was ready for whatever came next.[2]

[9] Hayes, MS. Diary, May 16, 17, 1864; Comly, MS. Diary, May 17; Clugston, MS. Diary, May 17; Egan, *Flying Yank*, 180; Arthur, "Dublin Raid," *Ohio Soldier*, April 13, 1889, 434.

[1] Hayes, MS. Diary, May 19, 1864; Clugston, MS. Diary, May 22; Arthur, "Dublin Raid," *Ohio Soldier*, April 13, 1889, 435; Baggs, MS. Journal, May 20, 1864.

[2] Hayes to Mrs. Hayes, May 19, 1864, and to Sardis Birchard, May 19, Hayes MS. Letters.

Chapter 10

To Lynchburg—and Back

T HE MEN OF Crook's division had hardly settled down
to the enjoyment of camp life when the rumors sprang up—
a new commander had taken over the department from Sigel,
an important movement was in the offing, and they were
going to have to make another long march. Colonel Hayes
was in a better position than the rank and file to pick up news,
but if he knew more than they he did not put it in his diary
or his letters home. Perhaps a growing realization of the
necessity for reticence about military matters in personal
communications held back his hand, for in a number of
guarded allusions he indicated that he was pretty much aware
of what had happened and what was about to happen. A new
commander was indeed in charge. Generalissimo Grant, disgusted with Sigel for failing to advance in the Valley, had
named David Hunter to direct operations in the Department
of West Virginia. Hunter had proceeded to Cedar Creek in
the Shenandoah Valley, where Sigel's field army of 8,500 men
rested, and from here on May 21 he had ordered Crook's
force of 6,000 infantry and Averell's cavalry, now raised to
4,000 riders, to join him at Staunton.[1]

---

[1] *Official Records*, XXXVII, pt. 1, 492, 508.

Hayes knew that the division was going to move to Staunton and the exact route on which it would march. He had also a general idea of the nature of Grant's orders to Hunter. A general notion of these orders was all that Hunter had, for as transmitted in several documents Grant's directives were not completely clear and not always consistent. The mission envisioned for Hunter was sound enough. While the Army of the Potomac was engaging the Confederate army north of Richmond, Hunter was to advance south to Staunton and then turn east to Charlottesville and Gordonsville, breaking up enemy communications on the Virginia Central Railroad and compelling the Confederates to detach strength from the Richmond theater to meet him. Around Gordonsville he would meet a raiding cavalry column under Philip Sheridan which would conduct him to the Army of the Potomac. It was essentially the same move Grant had projected earlier for Sigel and Crook. But Grant, as he had done with these two generals, suggested an additional objective: that Hunter might go on to capture the industrial and agricultural center of Lynchburg, considerably to the south of the Staunton-Charlottesville line. Grant meant that Hunter should move to Lynchburg via Charlottesville, thus blocking the only railroad line on which the Confederates could reinforce against him, but the supreme commander did not make his purpose clear to Hunter. The confusion would have a fatal effect on the actions of Hunter, who independently had concluded that Lynchburg should be his main objective.[2]

While his superiors were perfecting their plans, Hayes was preparing his troops for action. Whatever might eventuate, he was proudly certain that his brigade would have a large role in it. The unit as now constituted consisted of the Twenty-

---

[2] Pond, *Shenandoah Valley*, 23–4, 34–5. That Hayes knew the general feature of the plan is evident from a reference in a letter to the probability that Crook's division would join the Army of the Potomac.

third and Thirty-sixth Ohio and the Fifth and Thirteenth West Virginia and boasted of 2,400 men. "I have seen them all in line today," Hayes wrote with quiet confidence. "They form a fine body of troops." The First Brigade was one of three in Crook's Second Division, the other two being still commanded by Colonels White and Sickel. The division could do anything led by a general like Crook, Hayes believed. Impatiently the colonel waited for the movement to begin. But Crook had to hold up, waiting for the delivery of shoes, of which the command was short, and other supplies. But finally, on May 31, the column wound out of Meadow Bluff and headed for Staunton, 125 miles away over the Appalachian ranges.[3]

Five days before, Hunter had started for the same destination. From Cedar Creek, he had only seventy miles to go, and he did not face any serious opposition until he reached Piedmont. Here a hastily gathered Confederate force, mostly cavalry, tried to block him, but Hunter easily smashed through it, inflicting heavy losses. On June 6 the Federals entered Staunton, while the Confederate forces left in the area retired to Waynesborough and Rockfish Gap on the railroad to the east. Hunter, who had to pause while awaiting Crook's arrival, employed his time in destroying military stores, factories and workshops, and railroad bridges and stations in the town and its vicinity.[4]

---

[3] *Official Records*, XXXVII, pt. 1, 571–2; Hayes to Mrs. Hayes, May 25, 26, 1864, and to Sardis Birchard, May 26, 29, Hayes MS. Letters. As indicative of the strengths of regiments at this stage of the war, the Twenty-third numbered 534 men, the Thirty-sixth, 533, the Fifth, 572, and the Thirteenth, 774; *Official Records*, XXXVII, pt. 1, 122, Hayes's report. Estimates of the size of Crook's force vary. Hunter stated that the combined troops of Crook and Averell totaled 10,000, ibid., 96. Pond, *Shenandoah Valley*, 28, puts Averell's strength at 4,400, which would leave Crook with only 5,600. But unless Hayes's brigade was oversized, it would seem that the three-brigade division must have been at its normal strength of around 6,000.

[4] Johnson and Buel (eds.), *Battles and Leaders*, IV, 485–6; *Official Records*, XXXVII, pt. 1, 95; Cecil D. Eby, Jr. (ed.), *A Virginia Yankee in the Civil War: The Diaries of David Hunter Strother* (Chapel Hill, 1961), 251.

Crook, meanwhile, was toiling ahead on his much longer march, with Averell's cavalry following in his wake. The route led east to White Sulphur Springs and Callaghan, north to Warm Springs, and then east again through Millborough, Goshen, and Middlebrook. The march rate varied from ten to nineteen miles a day, with the average being somewhere in between. This was fair speed but not the best the division was capable of. It was not enemy opposition which slowed the advance, for nothing more than small parties of gray cavalry were met during the whole trek, or the mountain terrain, which the division well knew how to surmount. Crook had to devote considerable time to foraging for food. He had started out with insufficient supplies and had warned Hunter he would have to "drain" the country as he passed through. But as willing as Crook was to drain, he would not permit individual pillaging or wanton oppression of civilians. Only authorized details were permitted to forage, and these operated under strict rules of discipline. This careful procedure was new to Hayes, who heretofore had been inclined to harsh views of the rights of Rebels, and it made a deep impression on him. The volunteer officer who had quarreled with Reno on a similar issue was ready to take guidance from a professional whom he admired.[5]

Crook was further delayed by his orders to destroy the Virginia Central Railroad, which he struck at Goshen. "Still halted, destroying Central R. R.," Hayes noted. "A big squad of men turn it over, rails and ties, and tumble it down the embankment; burn culverts and ties as far as possible. The R. R. can be destroyed by troops marching parallel to it very fast." The wrecking job did not go as fast as Hayes thought it would, but the work was thorough almost all the way to Staunton. The division crossed North Mountain into the Shenandoah Valley on June 7 and marched into Staunton the

---

[5] *Official Records,* XXXVII, pt. 1, 561, 607.

next day. "We seem to be clear of West Virginia for good," Hayes exclaimed gratefully in a letter to Lucy. He added that, although they were now in Hunter's army, Crook was considered the best general on the scene, "the man of all others."[6]

Although Hayes had never met Hunter, he had for some reason formed an unfavorable opinion of the general, and closer acquaintance would only strengthen his original evaluation. Hunter was an easy man to dislike. In his appearance and manner, he was one of the most unattractive officers in the army. Almost sixty-two years old, he was of middle height and broad build. His complexion was swarthy, his features were prominent and somewhat grim, and his thin hair was so black that observers were certain it was dyed. He customarily wore a straw hat, swayed his head from side to side when speaking, peering around with, as one critic put it, "an elevated squint," and only his Hungarian-style mustache suggested a touch of the warrior. Unlike most West Pointers and regulars, he had a violent, almost a crusading desire to eradicate slavery, and his convictions had earlier involved him in a controversy with Lincoln. While commanding on the Southern coast, Hunter had assumed he could free the slaves in his department by military edict, and Lincoln had had to overrule him. Hunter was frequently embroiled in controversy. He was prejudiced and intolerant and likely to fly off in sudden fits of anger and denunciation. Once he decided that a particular military situation called for a certain move, he could not be dissuaded from his plan.[7]

So now at Staunton he convinced himself that his proper objective was Lynchburg. Although his orders certainly al-

---

[6] Hayes, MS. Diary, June 1–8, 1864; Hayes to Mrs. Hayes, June 8, Hayes MS. Letters. Although Hunter's command was styled the Department of West Virginia, he and also the War Department usually referred to his force as the Army of the Shenandoah.

[7] Richardson, *Secret Service*, 196; *Sketches of War History, Ohio Commandery,* IV, 141–2; H. A. Du Pont, *The Campaign of 1864 in the Valley of Virginia and the Expedition to Lynchburg* (New York, 1925), 37–8.

lowed him the option of advancing on that city, he should
have reflected on Grant's language. The supreme commander
had made it plain that he desired Hunter to grasp the Char-
lottesville-Gordonsville line before proceeding farther south,
and he had at least indicated that he did not think Hunter
should stay at Lynchburg very long, not longer than was necessary to wreck the town's industrial resources. That Hunter
had a fair comprehension of what he was supposed to do was
demonstrated on June 9 when he advanced eastward on the
Virginia Central Railroad. But on running into Confederate
opposition he pulled back. His push was probably intended
as a token to show he had attempted to follow orders, for he
promptly announced that he was proceeding to Lynchburg
via Lexington. The move would have been a good one if the
purpose of his mission had been to raid Lynchburg and get
out right away. But Hunter was leading an army of 18,000
men of all arms, which was burdened with a large baggage
train. He was leading it to almost certain disaster. If he had
gone first to Charlottesville before advancing on Lynchburg,
he would have controlled the railroad line which linked the
Valley to Richmond. As it was, he was marching off and leaving this avenue open to the enemy. He was also putting himself in a position where he could hardly make contact with
Sheridan. Worst of all, if he had to retreat, he could not fall
back down the Valley but would have to take a roundabout
route to West Virginia. He seems to have deluded himself
that Grant would prevent Lee from dispatching reinforcements and that even if the reinforcements came Sheridan
would cut them off around Gordonsville. Crook, much more
realistic, predicted that Lee would react vigorously to a move
on Lynchburg and that even if the Federals captured the town
they would not be able to hold it long.[8]

The army left Staunton on June 10, moving in four col-

---

[8] Eby (ed.), *A Virginia Yankee*, 250–1.

umns on nearly parallel roads, one infantry division and a
cavalry division to the right and one of each to the left. Only
parties of gray cavalry appeared sporadically to contest the
way, and by the afternoon of the next day the invaders were
before Lexington. The weak Confederate forces retired without putting up much of a fight. Called the battle of Lexington
in the record books, the affair was nothing more than, in
Hayes's phrase, "an artillery and sharpshooter's duel."[9] The
town was something of a Confederate center, the home of
Stonewall Jackson and John Letcher, lately governor of Virginia, and the site of the Virginia Military Institute, whose
cadets had turned out to help repel Sigel at New Market. Its
associations aroused all of Hunter's crusading zeal. Although
the general claimed that shots had been fired at his men from
the Institute, it is evident that he wanted to punish the town
as a matter of principle. He let the troops loot the school and
then burned the building. He also fired the home of Governor Letcher and some other private dwellings and crated up
a statue of George Washington and sent it to Wheeling, on
the ground that Virginians should not be allowed to possess a
relic of the first President. Hayes, the new and more humane
Hayes, was horrified at the destruction. "This does not suit
many of us," he wrote. "Gen. C, I know, disapproves. It is
surely bad." It was also stupid, he decided. Many of the
townspeople had Union sympathies, but Hunter had alienated
them beyond recall.[1]

At Lexington, Hunter picked up all kinds of interesting
news. John C. Breckinridge, who commanded the gray forces
that had repelled Sigel and who had then gone to join Lee,

---

[9] *Official Records,* XXXVII, pt. 1, 96, 120, 122–3; Hayes, MS. Diary, June 10,
11, 1864; Hastings, MS. Autobiography June 10; Schmitt (ed.), *George Crook,*
116–17.
[1] Eby (ed.), *A Virginia Yankee,* 253; Ward, *Twelfth Ohio,* 77–8; Hayes, MS.
Diary, June 12, 1864; Hayes to Mrs. Hayes, June 12, Hayes MS. Letters.
Hunter also wished to burn the town's Washington College but was dissuaded by his officers.

was reported to have come back to Rockfish Gap. Another Confederate force was said to be moving west from Richmond and obviously headed for the Valley. Sheridan's cavalry column was rumored to have met a reverse and to have fallen back. All the stories turned out to be true. Lee, when he realized the danger developing in the Valley, had ordered Breckinridge and his approximately 2,000 men to return. Breckinridge had gone first to Rockfish Gap, but when he saw that Hunter had headed south had rushed to Lynchburg. To make doubly certain that Lynchburg would be held, Lee had ordered Jubal Early and 8,000 troops of the Second Corps to move to the Valley, and this force was rolling west on the Virginia Central Railroad. And finally, Sheridan had run into tough opposition at Louisa Court House and had had to retreat. Hunter could not at the moment accurately assess the varied reports, but he should have gathered one vital message from them. If he was going to continue to Lynchburg, he would have to get there fast. But he lingered at Lexington, waiting for a portion of his raiding cavalry to return and for a wagon train with much needed supplies to arrive. He was giving the Confederates precious time in which to concentrate against him.

Not until June 14 did Hunter leave Lexington. Then he marched south twenty-four miles to Buchanan. From there he turned east and crossed the Blue Ridge at the picturesque Peaks of Otter. As the troops came over the summit, they gasped at the sight of the entire southern side of the mountain covered with rhododendrons in full bloom. Hayes's adjutant reached the base and looked back at the column winding down through the mass of color. He noted that as the soldiers filed past him each man had a rhododendron bouquet in the muzzle of his gun, making the drab marchers seem like "a moving bank of flowers." At Liberty (now Bedford), Crook's men came upon a section of their old railroad target, the Virginia &

Tennessee, and paused to wreck it. The work did not seriously delay Crook's division, but Hunter was having trouble with his other units, which he could not keep closed up. He did not get his whole army before Lynchburg until late on the afternoon of the seventeenth. It had taken him four days to cover a little more than fifty miles.[2]

Only Confederate cavalry and artillery units appeared to contest Hunter's approach. Crook, who was in the advance, ordered White's Second Brigade to attack, and the defenders, after a short resistance, retired into the city's fortifications. Crook said later that he had to do all the work, with no assistance from anyone. Hunter was not on the field, although he came up later. An enterprising commander might have exploited the success by going right into Lynchburg, even in a night assault, which was what some of the regimental officers thought Hunter might do. The general elected, however, to call off the battle and go into camp.

All during the night disquieting reports kept coming in to headquarters. Observers could hear trains moving into Lynchburg and drums beating and men cheering. Some skirmishers of Hayes's brigade out on the picket line noticed another force camped alongside of them in the darkness. "What Brigade is that?" one of their officers called out. "Gordon's Brigade of Early's Division. Who do you uns belong to?" came the reply. "The same," the Federal answered before ordering his men to get out. Hunter was ready to believe that the Confederates were reinforcing, but he refused to concede that the additions represented a corps. He resolved to attack on the morrow. His analysis of the situation was almost right. What had happened was that Early, with the van of his troops, had arrived in Lynchburg the day before and had taken over the command. More of Early's corps came in during the night, but all of it would not reach the scene until the next day. If Hunter had

---

[2] Hastings, MS. Autobiography, June 15, 1864; Hayes, MS. Diary, June 14–16; *Official Records*, XXXVII, pt. 1, 98–9.

attacked on the morning of the eighteenth, he would not have encountered a full corps.[3]

But the Federal commander spent the morning demonstrating against the enemy works and did not open his attack until the afternoon. Then he arranged his battle line thus: Crook's division on the right, the artillery brigade in the center, and Jeremiah Sullivan's division on the left. Still farther to the left were the two cavalry divisions. Hunter intended to make his main move with Crook's force, which would attempt to flank the enemy left, whereupon the whole line would advance. Quickly Crook's men disappeared in the woods. They had not been gone for more than twenty minutes when the Confederates rushed out of their defenses and attacked the Federal center and left. So heavy did the assault become that Hunter ordered Crook to return to support Sullivan. Crook got back fast, and the two divisions stemmed the graycoats and eventually drove them back to their works. But the display of Rebel aggressiveness shook Hunter badly. Although the force opposed to him was no larger than his and probably not as big, he was convinced, as were his officers, that he faced Early's entire corps and was outnumbered. He reflected too that he was far from his base and was running short of ammunition and rations. In the situation, he saw no recourse but to retreat. That night, while Early prepared an attack for the next day, the Federals fell back on the road to Liberty. Hayes put it aptly when he said they backed out on the Liberty road.[4]

---

[3] *Official Records*, XXXVII, pt. 1, 99; *Sketches of War History, Ohio Commandery*, IV, 141–2; Schmitt (ed.), *George Crook*, 117; Comly, MS. Diary, June 17, 1864.

[4] Du Pont, *Campaign of 1864*, 76–8; *Official Records*, XXXVII, pt. 1, 100, 123; Comly, MS. Diary, June 18, 1864; Eby (ed.), *A Virginia Yankee*, 265–6; Hayes, MS. Diary, June 18. Most accounts of Lynchburg put the Confederate strength at 12,000. This estimate seems too low. An official Confederate analysis stated that Breckinridge had 9,000 under him before Early's 8,000 arrived. It is true, however, that a large proportion of Breckinridge's troops, perhaps 5,000, were not considered reliable for field duty. See *Official Records*, XXXVII, pt. 1, 758.

It was one thing to withdraw from the fighting front, but it was quite another to conduct an endangered army, and especially one on short rations, out of the fighting theater. Now Hunter's error in leaving the railroads in the region in possession of the enemy rose up to haunt him. He could not retire down the Shenandoah Valley through Lexington and Staunton, his natural line of retreat, for Early, moving faster by rail, could attack him in flank and cut off his escape. Yet somehow the Federal army had to get to a base of supplies. Hunter took the only possible route—through Buford's Gap in the Blue Ridge to Salem and from there north to White Sulphur Springs and Meadow Bluff, or, in other words, all the way back to the Kanawha Valley and West Virginia. Hunter's decision was correct enough, in the circumstances, but when he made it he was in a state of apparent shock resulting from the collapse of his campaign. He remained dazed in the initial stages of the movement and relied heavily on Crook for advice. Indeed, Crook, who had left a field depot at Meadow Bluff, probably made the actual decision to return to the Kanawha.[5]

The army retreated with all the speed it could manage. On the day after the battle, the nineteenth, it passed through Liberty and on the following day it reached Buford's Gap. Here Crook posted Hayes's brigade to hold the rear until the rest of the command got beyond Salem. Early followed the retreat until the twenty-second, punching at the blue column with cavalry attacks. Hayes noted in a contemptuous diary entry that the Rebel jabs did no hurt to Crook's division but invariably captured some equipment from Hunter's units.[6] When the Confederate commander saw that Hunter was heading for the far Kanawha, he sensibly called off the chase and returned to Lynchburg.

But still the Federals continued their precipitate with-

[5] Du Pont, *Campaign of 1864*, 84–5; Schmitt (ed.), *George Crook*, 117–18.
[6] Hayes, MS. Diary, June 19–22, 1864.

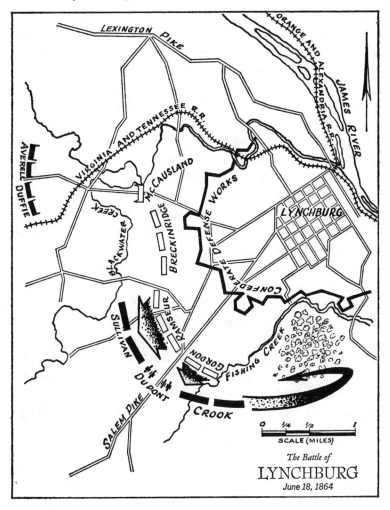

The Battle of
LYNCHBURG
June 18, 1864

drawal, marching well over twenty miles each day. It was now the need of supplies that drove them on. Later men who had been on this march would remember that some soldiers slashed young trees with their knives to get the inner bark to chew on and that others scoured the ground behind the cavalry to pick up kernels of corn left by the horses.[7] There may have been individual cases of such suffering. But the evidence indicates that Hunter's troops were relatively well fed, better than were Crook's in the retreat from Dublin. Several herds of cattle were driven along with the army, and fresh beef was issued every night. Yet the men grew steadily weaker. Many fell down asleep on the road or fell out of the line of march, and officers had to be constantly alert to pick up these unfortunates. Frequently, when a unit halted every man in it would drop on the ground, and to get it started again the officers would have to arouse each man and stand him on his feet. Something of the nightmarish quality the march finally assumed was reflected in a terse line in Colonel Comly's diary: "Every body crazy."[8]

What was causing all the trouble was not so much the lack of rations as it was the kind of rations. It was frequently noted during the war that when soldiers were denied for any period their customary diet—hard bread or hardtack, flour, salt meat or bacon, coffee—they suffered in health and morale. Hunter's troops had none or little of these staples for a week, and the cumulative effects on men already in poor physical condition were devastating. This was an exhausted army. Crook's men, when they were hardly recovered from their trek to New River, had marched 123 miles to Staunton. Then they and Hunter's contingent had trudged 100 miles to Lynchburg. Now the whole force was being asked to traverse another 150 miles to Meadow Bluff. There was also a psychological factor that added to the stress of the situation. Everybody felt it, officers and men. They were boxed off in a trap in the mountain wilderness, away from other Federal forces, away from

---

[7] Du Pont, *Campaign of 1864,* 91; Otis, "Personal Recollections," Santa Barbara *Daily Press,* November 1, 1876; Schmitt (ed.), *George Crook,* 118–21.

[8] Comly, MS. Diary, June 18–21, 27, 1864; Eby (ed.), *A Virginia Yankee,* 269; Charles M. Keyes, *The Military History of the 123rd Regiment of Ohio Volunteer Infantry* (Sandusky, 1874), 70–4; Baggs, MS. Journal, June 28.

the outside world, away from supplies, and unless they kept on marching and marching they would die right there. Hayes later admitted to the strength of this emotion: "We had to go night and day for about a week to get out."

So they marched, and at last, on June 25, they stumbled into Meadow Bluff at midnight. "Starved and sleepy," Hayes wrote in his diary, and added a phrase whose vague construction revealed his and the men's condition: "The hardest of the war." But here the marchers met a bitter disappointment. The officer in charge of the stores had become alarmed at rumors of Confederate guerrillas in the area and had retired to Gauley Bridge. At sunrise, with little sleep, the weary soldiers took the road again. On the twenty-seventh, when they were within a day's march of Gauley Bridge, they saw a wagon train coming to meet them. They knew now that they were safe, but the bonds of comradeship that had united them in danger disappeared in an instant when they went for the food. "All the hardships of the march had been borne with little complaints," Comly noted sadly, "but there were three fights among the men in five minutes after we met the supply train, and everybody quarreling like wolves." The march did not stop because the army was again on a supply line. Hunter had to get to a base from whence he could transport his force back to the Virginia theater, and the only possible destination was Charleston. So the column continued on to the camps near that city and settled down for a brief period of rest. If any unit needed rest more than others, it was Crook's division, which since the beginning of the campaign had marched 440 miles.[9]

"Back home again in the Kanawha Valley," Hayes began a casting up of the results of the Lynchburg campaign. It had

---

[9] Hayes to Sardis Birchard, June 20, 1864, Hayes MS. Letters; Hayes, MS. Diary, June 25, 30; Comly, MS. Diary, June 27; Hastings, MS. Autobiography, July 1.

been in many ways a successful operation, he concluded. Hunter's army had destroyed some vital links in the Confederacy's rail system and had forced Lee to detach men from the defense of Richmond. But more could have been accomplished by an enterprising commander. Hayes was sure that Crook would have taken Lynchburg. He hoped that he and his brigade would be placed under Crook as part of an independent command. Hayes was becoming increasingly proud of his brigade. "It is now to me like my own Regiment," he confessed. The statement marked another progression in his education. The colonel who had once thought that the regiment was the ultimate unit and that he would want to command no other could now identify himself with a larger organization. He would never lose his affection for the regiment he had led or depart completely from his role as the colonel of the Twenty-third Ohio, but his vision of command was definitely enlarged.[1]

He revealed another changing side of his character in a lecture he felt constrained to write Lucy on the nature of war and of his war particularly. She had written him criticizing President Lincoln for refusing to employ retaliation to protect Union prisoners in the South from "brutal rebels." "All a mistake, darling," he chided. "All such things should be avoided as much as possible. We have done too much rather than too little." He then described how Hunter had turned Mrs. Letcher and her two daughters out of their home in Lexington and on ten minutes' notice had burned the place. Crook's officers and men had been "disgusted," he told her. He cautioned Lucy not to be misled by catchphrases like "brutal rebels." "There are enough 'brutal rebels' no doubt, but we have brutal officers and men too," he emphasized. "I have had men brutally treated by our own officers on this raid. And

---

[1] Hayes to Sardis Birchard, June 20, 1864, and to Mrs. Hayes, June 30, Hayes MS. Letters.

there are plenty of human rebels. I have seen a good deal of it on this trip. War is a cruel business and there is brutality in it on all sides, but it is very idle to get up anxiety on account of any supposed peculiar cruelty on the part of rebels. Keepers of prisons in Cincinnati, as well as in Danville, are hardhearted and cruel."[2]

Colonel Hayes was growing as a man as well as a soldier. He was still for a hard, driving war, and he would accept no result but victory and a restored Union. But he had learned that one could be unrelenting and efficient without hating individuals. His new attitude sprang in part from his association with and his admiration for Crook. But it went deeper than that. Crook's meticulous procedures in enemy country were purely military—done for military reasons for military ends. Hayes looked beyond these narrow limits to a concept of war as a political instrument. He seemed to have caught a part of Lincoln's vision—that the defeated must be lived with after the victory.

---

[2] Hayes to Mrs. Hayes, July 2, 1864, ibid.

Chapter 11

Return to the Valley

O N July 12 Colonel Hayes was at the Swan House in Parkersburg, West Virginia. It was a bad hotel, he noted in his diary: "Landlord not sound in politics or diet!" He found time to write to his mother explaining why he was at this Ohio River town instead of back in camp at Charleston. "We are here on our way East," he confided. Hunter had suddenly embarked his army on steamers and moved down the Kanawha to Point Pleasant and up the Ohio to Parkersburg, the western terminal of the Baltimore & Ohio Railroad. Crook's part of the army had a new and impressive title. The general had been designated as commander of all troops in West Virginia south of the Baltimore & Ohio line, and perhaps out of a desire to assert a measure of independence from Hunter he had styled his force the Army of Kanawha. Hayes went on to relate that he had taken advantage of the movement to meet Lucy and the boys briefly at Chillicothe. He added that he was not sure why they were being hurried forward so fast, but it had something to do with "the trouble in Maryland."[1]

There was indeed trouble in Maryland. Jubal Early, after herding Hunter out of the Valley, had a clear field before him, and, with Lee's enthusiastic concurrence, he proceeded to take advantage of it. Resting his men but briefly, he moved north

---

[1] Hayes, MS. Diary, July 7–12, 1864; Hayes to Mrs. Sophia Hayes, July 12, Hayes MS. Letters; *Official Records*, XXXVII, pt. 2, 9, 18–19.

to Staunton and Winchester, and on July 6 he crossed the Potomac at Shepherdstown and marched to Frederick, Maryland. He was obviously heading for Washington itself, and his presence created panic in the whole area. It also threw into cruel focus the confused command system controlling the capital's defenses which made any effective resistance to Early impossible. There were thousands of troops in the Washington region, but they were scattered from the city's defenses to points all over Maryland. Worse, there was no single commander over these forces, no one man who could direct and coordinate their efforts. The closest approach to a central authority was represented by General Henry W. Halleck, Chief of Staff to Lincoln and Grant, whose impressive title could not conceal that he was little more than a military secretary and adviser. Both Lincoln and Grant, who was stalled before Richmond, would have been glad to have Halleck issue orders in this emergency, but "Old Brains" had never liked responsibility even when his command position had been more sharply defined. He liked it less now and refused to do more than offer scholarly suggestions. Hunter, the general who ordinarily would have commanded the defense of the theater and who had the only field army available, was far away in West Virginia.

In the circumstances, it was small wonder that Early brushed aside a Federal force that attempted to delay him at Monocacy Junction and pushed toward the Washington defenses. On July 11 and 12, the latter being the day when Hayes at Parkersburg was writing about some vague trouble in Maryland, the bold raider probed at the fortifications around the city. It has been a matter of argument ever since whether Early could have forced his way in with a little more aggressiveness. The consensus is that even if he had entered he could not have stayed very long. As it was, Early had to retire after making no more than a demonstration. The threat his movement posed had caused the government to call on Grant for help, and Grant had responded quickly. He dispatched the Sixth Corps, some 12,000 strong, under Horatio G. Wright by water to Washington and also ordered two divisions of the Nineteenth Corps, just arriving in the East from Louisiana, to proceed to the capital. The van of Wright's corps was coming in one end of the city while Early was knocking at the other. At the appearance of this formidable reinforcement Early withdrew. But he did not flee in fright or retire very far. Crossing the Potomac at Edwards' Ferry, he camped at Leesburg, where he was still uncomfortably close to Washington.

His proximity forced the Union high command to take a hard strategic look at the whole Washington theater. If Early was permitted to remain in the area, he would be a constant threat to the capital. Grant either would have to detach the Sixth Corps for permanent defense or, if he recalled it, would always have to send it or some other unit back when Early made a move. The problem of Early had to be dealt with. At the very least, the raider had to be pushed far enough up the Valley so that he would no longer be a menace. Another and brighter possibility presented itself. If enough Union forces could be brought together quickly in the Washington region, they might be able to trap the Confederate army and thus eliminate it completely as a strategic factor in the Valley theater. Early at Leesburg was apparently in a position that invited entrapment. All that was necessary, it seemed, was for Wright's corps to move west and for Hunter's army to advance east, and the converging columns could crush Early between them. The problem would be to bring the two Union forces together at exactly the right moment, the kind of movement that is never easy in war. It was aggravated by the great distance separating Hunter from the area of proposed operations. Both that general and Grant, however, had foreseen something of the difficulty and had acted to meet it even before Early's threat had become acute.

Hunter knew that in retreating to the Kanawha Valley he had removed himself from the seat of war. He knew too that he could not get back to it by marching east—the compounded problem of distance, terrain, and supplies was insuperable. The shortest route, in time, was to use water transportation to Parkersburg and from there advance east on the Baltimore & Ohio to wherever he was needed. Grant initially would have been satisfied to see Hunter merely reach a position where he could protect the railroad. But when Early approached the Potomac, it was evident that Hunter would have to come farther east. He was ordered to take the direction of all forces operating against Early and to proceed by rail to Cumberland, Maryland, and from there by train or march, depending on the conditions of the railroad, to Martinsburg, West Virginia.[2]

Hunter had started to accumulate water transport right after reaching Charleston, and he pushed his efforts with additional vigor when informed of the critical situation developing in Maryland. But low water on the rivers impeded his passage to Parkersburg—the troops often had to land and march around shoals—and the necessity of making repairs on sections of the railroad hindered him in getting to Cumberland. Hunter himself reached that city on July 8, but his advance division under Sullivan did not arrive until two days later. (On the eighth Early was already at Frederick, and on the tenth he was approaching Washington.) Hunter could not justly be censured, but his apparently sluggish progress caused sharp criticism in Washington. Already suspected of misman-

---

[2] *Official Records,* XXXVII, pt. 1, 689, pt. 2, 59, 63. The reader is reminded that in the theater of operations the states of Maryland, West Virginia, and Virginia come together in puzzling proximity. The armies moved in and over parts of all three states, often in a short period of time.

agement in the Lynchburg campaign, he seemed about to give a repeat performance. Although part of the trouble stemmed from nothing more than Hunter's neglect to report consistently on his whereabouts, both General Halleck and Secretary of War Stanton were convinced that he was too slow and indecisive to deal with the audacious Early. They were certain of this before Early approached Washington and more certain after he withdrew toward the Potomac and the possibility of trapping him arose. Hunter was hardly the man to lead a quick, converging column, the critics pointed out to Grant. The supreme commander was sufficiently impressed to direct that Wright should exercise the command of the troops moving out against Early and that any part of Hunter's force joining Wright should be under the latter's authority.[3]

While this scheme was unfolding at the highest command level, Hunter was moving closer to a position where he could join with Wright. He advanced Sullivan's division of 7,000 and a cavalry force of 2,000 to Martinsburg and then to Harper's Ferry and ordered Crook's division to come on from Parkersburg as fast as possible. On the evening of July 14 Hunter himself arrived at Harper's Ferry. Here he received a directive from Halleck to unite with Wright at Edwards' Ferry on the Potomac, where Early was expected to cross on his return to Virginia. (Early was already over and on the way to Leesburg.) Halleck's dispatch contained some unexpected news and a humiliating suggestion. Wright, who was junior in grade to Hunter, was to have command of the combined expedition, the Chief of Staff announced. He went on to recommend that the "immediate command" of Hunter's troops be turned over to Crook. Hunter had been in the army game long enough to recognize a slap in the face. In aggrieved letters to Stanton and Lincoln he complained that he had been given the choice of relinquishing the field command to one of his

---

[3] Ibid., pt. 2, 123, 210, 222–3, 261.

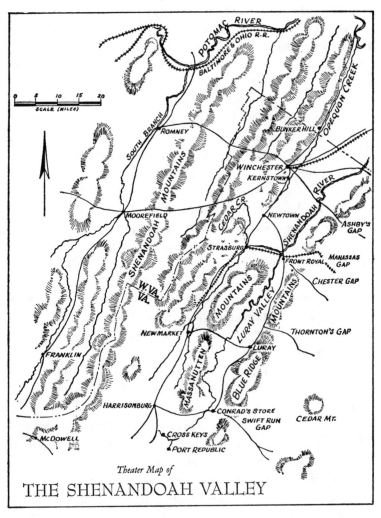

Theater Map of

THE SHENANDOAH VALLEY

subordinates or volunteering to serve under a junior officer.
Thus affronted, he saw no recourse but to ask to be relieved.
It took a letter from Lincoln to soothe him even in part. No
reprimand or censure was intended, the President assured

him. Wright had most of the troops in the area of operations and was the logical person to command the pursuit of Early. The assignment of Crook had been proposed only to free Hunter from the necessity of serving under a general he ranked.[4]

Hunter was not completely mollified, but he was enough of a soldier to accept the situation. He had already ordered the troops with him under Sullivan to cross the Blue Ridge and move south via Hillsborough to Leesburg. Sullivan had marched, but on reaching Hillsborough had paused and gone into camp. Now Hunter dispatched Crook, who with the rest of the army had arrived at Martinsburg, to hurry on to Harper's Ferry in advance of his troops. In an order that concealed his bitterness from the troops, Hunter announced that Crook, superseding Sullivan, was to take command of the forces proceeding to join Wright. Not troubling to hide his feelings from anybody else, Hunter informed his superiors that Crook had gone to Hillsborough, but that as Crook was no longer under his command he did not consider himself responsible for what might happen. At the same time Wright, hearing that a detachment of Hunter's was at Hillsborough and fearing that it might be attacked by Early, put his own corps in motion toward Leesburg.

Only the most optimistic observer in the Federal command system could have thought that these separate commanders directing these uncoordinated movements would catch a wily operator like Early. The most realistic one, Grant, indicated that he expected a very modest result. Through Halleck he issued instructions to Wright to pursue Early only far enough to ascertain that the Confederate was retreating to Richmond and then to return to Washington. He directed Hunter to advance cautiously to Gordonsville and if he had to fall back to retire in such a way that he could cover Washington. In the

---

[4] Ibid., pt. 2, 123, 210, 222–3, 261.

vivid language he was capable of using on occasion Grant told Hunter not to let himself get "squeezed out to one side" so that he would have to withdraw to West Virginia again. He also authorized Hunter, in words the latter must have liked, to employ economic warfare, to "eat out Virginia clear and clean," so that crows flying over it would have to carry their provender with them.[5]

Colonel Hayes made his entrance into this tangled situation with Crook. He and the general and the rest of Hunter's command arrived at Martinsburg on the night of July 15. While Crook pushed on to Harper's Ferry to find Hunter, Hayes and his staff wandered around the town looking for a place to sleep. Hayes spied a veranda on a building near the street and said: "This will do for me." The group settled down and were soon deep in slumber. In the morning they discovered that they had reposed on the veranda of a German beer saloon. Hayes was troubled with a bad boil on his hip and decided to make his quarters temporarily in the building. With obvious relish, he informed his strait-laced wife that he was sleeping on the floor in the barroom. He added that half his brigade had gone to join Crook thirty miles east and that he and the rest expected to follow shortly. He analyzed the strategic situation without much optimism: "The combinations to catch the Rebs seem to me pretty good, but I expect them to escape. Raiding parties always do escape."[6]

The combinations were not quite as good as Hayes thought, although his prediction as to their effect would turn out to be correct. On July 16 three Union forces were in potential

---

[5] Ibid., 341, 342, 343, 351–2, 354, 365–6, 368. Although Hunter resented his inactive role, he showed no anger toward Crook. Indeed, he asked the War Department to make the latter a major general, and the promotion was promptly granted by brevet grade.
[6] Hastings, MS. Autobiography, July 16, 1864; Hayes, MS. Diary, July 14–16; Hayes to Mrs. Hayes, July 17, Hayes MS. Letters.

position to envelop Early. Wright had crossed the Potomac and was moving on Leesburg. Crook on that day had assumed command of the division at Hillsborough and after sending his cavalry out to try to learn something about the enemy's whereabouts had marched south a short distance to Purcellville. Hunter was at Harper's Ferry, with units of his command scattered between there and Martinsburg. The difficulties in the way of combining these separate columns were enormous. Each one was operating in effect as an independent force. Although Wright could give directions to Crook, the Sixth Corps commander was not likely to try to control an officer who was not with him and of whose location at the moment he was uncertain. Hunter had yielded all authority over Crook and was restricting his activities to his immediate area. Even if Hunter had been disposed to exercise command, he could not have done so effectively. He was on one side of the Blue Ridge, and Crook was on the other. They would be doing well if they did no more than achieve a loose coordination.[7]

In the circumstances, it was a relatively easy matter for Early to slip between the forces of Wright and Crook. He left Leesburg on the sixteenth and with his trains and plunder crossed the Blue Ridge at Snicker's Gap and encamped at Berryville on the west side of the Shenandoah River. Wright at Leesburg and Crook at Purcellville, only six miles apart, although they could not justly be blamed, nevertheless looked slightly foolish. As if realizing the embarrassment of the situation, Wright moved quickly to recover the initiative. He ordered Crook to push through Snicker's Gap and prepared to follow with the Sixth Corps. Crook forced the gap easily, but when he tried to cross the Shenandoah, called by the soldiers the Shining Door, he found Early aggressively ready to contest the passage. The Confederate, flinging forward his

---

[7] Pond, *Shenandoah Valley*, 81; *Official Records*, XXXVII, pt. 2, 354.

whole force on the eighteenth, drove Crook back with severe losses. The Eastern troops in Wright's force, coming up after the engagement had ended, noted with patronizing amusement that Crook's mountain men spoke of the meeting as "a right smart little fight." Wright's soldiers might be entertained by the dialect, but their commander had not supported Crook and he did not show much disposition to get into a smart little fight himself. On the next day he cast about for a crossing above or below his present position and on finding none concluded he might have to attempt it where he was. But that night Early mysteriously vanished, and on the next day was reported to be on the Valley pike heading south for Strasburg. What the soldiers named the "Snicker's Gap war" was over.[8]

The reason for Early's disappearance was soon disclosed. It was the result of a sudden move by Hunter, the general who hitherto had cast himself in the role of an onlooker of events. Hunter might have his faults, but he had the knowledge and instincts of a soldier and he knew an opportunity when he saw it. Early had presented him with an inviting one by retiring behind the Shenandoah River line. Hunter, to the north, could move down the west side of the river and plant himself in Early's rear while the Confederate had his attention focused on Wright in his front. Hunter moved quickly to exploit the opening, using as his instruments Hayes, who led the best fighting brigade in the command, and Averell, whose cavalry force was at Martinsburg. Hayes's brigade had left Martinsburg on the seventeenth and moved in two columns to the area below Harper's Ferry. On the next day Hunter heard that Crook was about to attack at Snicker's Gap. He immediately ordered Hayes to unite the

---

[8] *Official Records*, XXXVII, pt. 1, 287, pt. 2, 368–9; Pond, *Shenandoah Valley*, 81–4; Aldace F. Walker, *The Vermont Brigade in the Shenandoah Valley* (Burlington, 1869), 41–2; Richard B. Irwin, *History of the Nineteenth Army Corps* (New York, 1892), 359–60.

brigade at Key's Ferry and march to Snicker's Ferry and strike
Early on the flank. Hunter's directive was deceptive in that
its wording did not indicate any great sense of urgency or
reveal to Hayes that he might expect much opposition. Hayes
was to attack in conjunction with a cavalry force on the other
side of the river and after driving the Rebels off, presumably
an easy matter, was to report to Crook, who Hunter mistakenly thought was still at Purcellville. For all Hayes knew,
he was going to participate in nothing more than a probing
movement at the river fords. Hunter should have made it
clear that Crook was preparing to deliver a full-scale assault.[9]

When Hayes advanced and ran into determined opposition
and at the same time heard heavy cannonading from Snicker's
Gap (this was Crook's "right smart little fight"), he not un-
naturally concluded that something was wrong. He moved
forward cautiously, skirmishing the whole of the afternoon,
and stopped for the night near Kabletown, about ten miles
from Harper's Ferry and the same distance from Snicker's
Gap. He reported the situation to Hunter and drew a sharp
reprimand. "General Crook notified me yesterday morning
that he intended to move forward and attack the rebels at
Snicker's Ferry," said the general, imparting information he
should have confided earlier, "and the firing you heard was
no doubt General Crook's attack upon the enemy . . . and
I am very sorry you did not move forward and assist in
the attack as you were ordered as you would have taken the
enemy in flank, and in all probability have terminated the
fight in our favor." Hayes must press on and make contact
with Crook, the general insisted.[1]

Hayes tried it again on the nineteenth but found the going
even rougher. On that day Wright's force on the other side

[9] Hayes, MS. Diary, July 17, 1864; *Official Records*, XXXVII, pt. 2, 377.
[1] Hayes, MS. Diary, July18, 1864; Comly, MS. Diary, July 18; *Official Records*,
XXXVII, pt. 2, 392.

of the river remained quiet, and Early, even though he was contemplating retreat, had ample strength at hand to deal with Hayes. When Hayes, after hours of heavy skirmishing, approached Snicker's Ferry, Early threw a whole division at the Federals. Hayes had to retire fighting to prevent being enveloped. He withdrew his regiments one by one, keeping a unit on the line while passing others to the rear, moving them, as the appreciative Comly wrote, "hand over hand." By nightfall the brigade was back at Kabletown and thankful to be there. "We lost nothing," recorded Comly, "though it was a close shave."[2] On the following day Hayes, taking no chances, moved to Key's Ferry.

While Hayes was making his futile push, Hunter was directing still another offensive, and this one achieved more success. The general sent Averell's cavalry, supported by an infantry brigade, a force of 2,300, dashing at Winchester, the capital of the Valley. At the same time he ordered Hayes at Key's Ferry to march eastward to Charles Town, fortify himself, and try to open communication with Averell. In a strange plea that he should not have made, Hayes asked for time. He had no entrenching tools, he said, and asked if he could not fall back closer to Harper's Ferry and try to get some news of Crook before moving. Hunter's snappish reply was to proceed to Charles Town at once. That Hayes was still uninformed of Hunter's strategic purpose and un-

---

[2] Hayes, MS. Diary, July 19, 1864; Comly, MS. Diary, July 19; Hastings, MS. Autobiography, July 19. Pond, *Shenandoah Valley*, 85–6, gives a hostile and misleading account of Hayes's actions. This valuable pioneer work, ordinarily of judicious tone, does not indicate that Hayes faced any opposition in his attempted advance. Hayes's adjutant, Russell Hastings, claimed that Hayes would have gone on to attack Early if he had not been burdened with a large wagon train. Hayes revealed no such purpose in his brief diary entries. It would seem that Hayes, operating with uncertain information and under a commander whom he distrusted, was more cautious than he should have been. His method of retreat to Kabletown, the passing of regiments successively to the rear while one always held the front line, was commonly used by unit commanders who had to retire their men fighting.

aware of the seriousness of the situation was evident in a letter he wrote Lucy. The whole thing was very funny, he said. He was looking for Crook and Crook was looking for Rebels, and neither knew where the other was. It was also evident that he desperately wanted to get back under Crook's command. His desire was immediately gratified. Hardly had he reached Charles Town when he received an order from Crook to join him at Berryville. Tactfully Hayes informed Hunter that as he supposed this was the commanding general's wish he would obey the order. Hayes might be relieved to leave Hunter, but that general's strategy, even though clumsily implemented, was bearing fruit. Averell smashed up a division of Early's before Winchester, and it was his presence above the town, coupled with the movements back and forth of Hayes's brigade, whose import Early could not accurately determine, that decided the Confederate commander to retire toward Strasburg. Averell and Hayes had opened the gate to the Valley for Crook.[3]

As soon as it was ascertained that Early had withdrawn, Averell moved forward to Kernstown, about three miles south of Winchester, and Crook joined him there on July 22. The long chase of Early had apparently ended and in apparent failure. The raider had been pushed back, but he had not been caught. But to General Wright, it seemed that the object of the campaign had been accomplished and Grant's instructions carried out—Early had retired and would probably now rejoin Lee at Richmond. Wright therefore put the Sixth Corps on the road to Washington. His action would pose a problem for Grant. The supreme commander also thought that Lee would call Early back to Richmond, and in that case he would want the counter reinforcement of Wright. But if Wright and Hunter together could break

[3] *Official Records*, XXXVII, pt. 2, 392–3, 401–3, 418; Hayes, MS. Diary, July 20, 21, 1864; Hayes to Mrs. Hayes, July 20, Hayes MS. Letters.

up the Confederate railroad complex around Gordonsville, Grant preferred that Wright stay where he was. The news that Wright was in Washington tipped Grant's mind to a decision. There was no point in sending the Sixth Corps back to the Valley. Let it come to the lines before Richmond, Grant instructed Halleck on July 23, but let the almost 5,000 men of the Nineteenth Corps he had also sent north remain in Washington as a defensive force. As for Hunter's troops, they must be very tired, Grant thought, and that general should take up a position to protect the Potomac line.[4]

At the moment Hunter himself was on the Potomac line, still at Harper's Ferry, but his principal field force under Crook was at Kernstown. Immediately upon arriving there, Crook had issued an order for the organization of what he still insisted on calling the Army of Kanawha. It was made up of the First Division under Colonel Joseph Thoburn; the Second Division under Colonel Isaac H. Duval, which included Hayes's brigade; and the Third Division under Colonel James A. Mulligan, a colorful Irish-American officer. Ordinarily Crook's command was a two-division outfit, but the presence within it of troops formerly of Sigel's army necessitated the creation of a third division for Mulligan, who had come along with Sigel's troops. On paper Crook had 14,000 infantry troops plus two cavalry divisions, but his actual infantry strength was probably not greater than 12,000. It was too small a force to be facing Early's somewhat superior army in such an exposed position, and it should have been drawn back to a line below Harper's Ferry. It was kept where it was because its generals, with unwarranted optimism, misread completely Early's capacity and purpose. Hunter informed Lincoln that he was not strong enough to hold the Valley if the Confederates returned. But they were not going to return, he predicted; Early would undoubtedly pro-

---

[4] *Official Records* XXXVII, pt. 2, 411–14, 422.

ceed to Richmond. Crook nourished the same delusion. He told Hunter he would stay at Kernstown a day or two, just long enough to induce the Confederates to think he would not follow them and thus persuade them to send a part of their force to Richmond, which was the very thing Grant did not want them to do.[5]

Seldom has a military prognosis been so wrong. Early had no intention of going to Richmond and every intention of renewing the offensive. He was waiting only to determine the strength of the force opposed to him, and when he learned that the Sixth Corps had left for Washington and Crook's command was alone at Kernstown he struck immediately. On July 23 his cavalry and patrols appeared before the Union lines and skirmished heavily. Even when they returned the next morning, Crook and his officers had no apprehension of danger. Crook apparently thought that the Confederates were making a reconnaissance in numbers, and at about noon he decided to attack them. He formed his division on both sides of the Valley pike with Duval on the right, Thoburn in the center and somewhat to the rear, and Mulligan on the left. Mulligan was ordered to advance, and to support him Crook detached Hayes's brigade and placed it on the Irishman's left. Hayes had never met Mulligan, but he recognized the division commander by a green scarf he wore. Hayes introduced himself, and the two men compared orders. "My orders are to fight with you and keep my line with yours," Hayes volunteered. Mulligan answered that his instructions were to attack whatever was in his front. Hayes said that he would move when Mulligan did. "Very well,"

---

[5] Ibid., 417, 423–4. Duval might be described as a soldier of fortune. Born in Virginia (West Virginia), he had left home when young for the Far West. He had acted as an agent for the national government in dealing with the Indians, had participated in the California gold rush, and had joined an insurrection in Cuba. Returning to the United States, he volunteered his services in 1861, became colonel of a West Virginia regiment, and achieved rapid promotion; Lang, *Loyal West Virginia*, 351.

said Mulligan, "I shall be ready to move in five minutes."[6]

As Hayes placed his brigade in line, he received another order, presumably from Crook, to advance with Mulligan and gradually wheel to the right to take in flank a Rebel force supposed to be passing around the Federal right. Just then Hayes noticed gray troops on a ridge of hills perpendicular to his own left, and Dr. Joe Webb, who had a good eye for taking in a situation, rode up and said that the hills were covered with enemy soldiers. Hayes sent an aide to inform Crook of this development and reported it personally to Mulligan. The Irishman said he had the same information. He and Hayes agreed that they were in a tough spot—the Confederates could fire down the length of the Union line or attack it in flank—but that they might as well advance as stand still. The blue line started forward. Immediately a sheet of flame burst forth from the hills and enveloped the whole column. Mulligan fell, mortally wounded, with five balls through his body. His troops wavered and stopped.

Hayes continued on and found himself somewhat in advance of the main line. Struck by the full force of the enemy fire, he tried to change his front to face it, but in the din he had difficulty in making his commands heard and the men were becoming too confused to obey orders even if they heard them. Seeing that his left was being doubled back, he ordered a withdrawal. As the movement began Hayes's picture album, almanac, and map fell out of his pocket. He and some of the men charged back twenty yards and recovered the items. At some stage in the fighting, probably in this retirement, Hayes's horse was struck down by a bullet, and he was hit in the shoulder by a spent ball. Within a few minutes he was able to form a new line behind a stone fence. Here he could

---

[6] Ibid., pt. 1, 309, 311; Hayes, two-page manuscript titled "Winchester" in Hayes Library; hereinafter cited as Hayes, "Winchester." The Federals referred to this battle as both Kernstown and Winchester.

check temporarily the Rebel onrush, and here he learned for the first time of the sad course of the day's battle.[7]

It was no reconnoitering party that had approached Crook's lines that morning, but Early's whole field army of approximately 17,000 men, and Early had not come to scout but to attack. His original plan was to demonstrate all along his front to mask his main movement, a flank attack on the Federal right. But after the battle began, he was informed that the enemy left was exposed, that by placing a force on the ridge of hills east of the Valley pike he could overlap the blue flank. Quickly he swung a division over to the indicated sector. This was the force that appeared to dismay Hayes and Mulligan. Thus the battle opened with everything favoring the Confederates—Early operating with a definite plan and with his army well in hand; Crook moving under a misapprehension of the situation and preparing to attack a superior enemy with a fraction of his army. The outcome was almost inevitable. When the gray flanking column crumpled the Federal left, the whole Federal line fell into confusion, and at the same time Early attacked in the front and on his left. The Federals broke in retreat after only a short resistance and streamed back on both sides of the pike toward Winchester.[8]

Only by the most determined efforts was Crook able to prevent the withdrawal from turning into a rout. He had a number of units that were relatively fresh—Duval's other brigade and Thoburn's division had escaped the brunt of the attack—but his problem was to find officers on the field

---

[7] Hayes, "Winchester"; Hayes, MS. Diary, July 24, 1864; Hayes to Mrs. Hayes, July 26, Hayes MS. Letters; Comly, MS. Diary, July 24; J. T. Webb to mother, July 28, Webb Family Correspondence; *Official Records*, XXXVII, pt. 1, 311–12, Hayes's report.

[8] The reports on the battle are in *Official Records*, XXXVII, pt. 1, 286–329. Colonel Duval's, which tells of Hayes's detachment to Mulligan, is on pp. 309–10. Crook's report appears on p. 286.

who could keep their heads level and their troops in hand. He rode up to Hayes at the stone fence and ordered the colonel to hold the position until a battery of artillery was brought off and then to protect the line of retreat on the right of the road to Martinsburg. Officers like Hayes were in constant demand during those hectic moments. Even General Averell of the cavalry had to ask Hayes at one stage to form his brigade in support of the horsemen. Hayes's brigade fell back in line of battle to Winchester, but on reaching the town marched through in column. The inhabitants were out on the street, the faces of most of them plainly showing the jubilation they felt at the Federal defeat. But an old Quaker woman, known to be a Union sympathizer, stood with tears running down her cheeks. Lieutenant William McKinley reined his horse to the curb and said in a low voice: "Don't worry, my dear Madam, we are not hurt as much as it seems, and we shall be back here in a few days." Early struck at the bluecoats for eight miles before calling off the chase. At nine that night the bulk of the army stopped at Bunker Hill, twelve miles north of Winchester, although some units continued on almost to Martinsburg.[9]

On the next day the retreat was resumed in a drizzling rain. Hayes's brigade again covered the rear. Rebel cavalry caught up to the column just south of Martinsburg, and Crook ordered Hayes to form a line of battle until military stores could be removed from the town. Sharp skirmishing ensued, and at one point a Confederate cavalryman rode out between the lines and challenged any Yankee to come out and fight him. A Federal cavalryman went forth to meet him, and suddenly both forces stopped their fire to watch the spectacle.

---

[9] Ibid., 310, 311–12, 436; Hastings, MS. Autobiography, July 24, 1864; Comly, MS. Diary, July 24. Duval in his report gave Hayes special mention for his conduct during the retreat, calling the colonel of the First Brigade "brave and gallant." For accounts of the retreat dealing with other units, see *Official Records*, XXXVII, pt. 1, 293–4, 297, 304.

If the audience hoped for a saber fight, it was disappointed. The Rebel opened with his pistol, and the bluecoat, in Comly's words, "replied with observations in kind," finally bringing down his foe's horse. The Confederate thereupon ran back to his lines, and both sides resumed the battle with renewed vigor. When the stores were removed, the Federals evacuated the town. The Rebel cavalry piled in right after them, and Crook sent Hayes and some of his own cavalry to clear them out.[1]

Crook had to decide at Martinsburg on which route he would continue his retreat. His shortest avenue was to move straight east eighteen miles to Harper's Ferry. But here he would have to march with his wagon trains parallel to the Confederates and with his whole column vulnerable to a flank attack. It seemed too risky, and he informed Hunter that he would cross the Potomac far up at Williamsport and come down to Harper's Ferry on the north side. Making the passage in safety, the army reached Sharpsburg on July 26. Hunter at first contemplated holding Crook at this point to guard the South Mountain passes, but concluded he had better concentrate his forces. So Crook proceeded immediately to Sandy Hook, recrossed the river to Harper's Ferry, and moved south a few miles to fortified lines at Halltown. Hunter, Crook, Hayes, and the whole army were back where they all had started from half a month before.[2]

It was a time to take stock, and Hayes had started casting up accounts as he moved down to Halltown. Looking back at what had happened at Kernstown, he regretted most the casualties in his brigade. The losses had indeed been heavy, 396, greater than the totals in Mulligan's and Thoburn's divisions, which were 317 and 155 respectively. His beloved

---

[1] *Official Records*, XXXVII, pt. 1, 311–12, Comly, MS. Diary, July 25, 1864; Hayes, MS. Diary, July 25.
[2] *Official Records* XXXVII, pt. 2, 437, 451; Hayes, MS. Diary, July 26–29, 1864.

Twenty-third had incurred 136 casualties, which with the same number for another of his regiments, the Thirty-sixth Ohio, were by far the highest figures for any of the regiments engaged.[3] Hayes could not see that either he or his brigade was in any way responsible for the disaster. They had simply met defeat at the hands of a superior force. Still, he mused to Lucy, "this is all a new experience, a decided defeat in battle." If any blame was to be assessed, Hayes, like Crook and most of the infantry officers, thought it should go to the cavalry, which had failed to warn of the strength of the enemy. This was pure special pleading. Although Crook's cavalry was not of the best, it could hardly be censured for the surprise at Kernstown. It was Crook himself who had decided that Early would return to Richmond.[4]

Hayes's unreasoning worship of Crook blinded him to some real shortcomings that his superior had displayed in the campaign. Crook did not possess enough strength to deal with Early in such an advanced position as Kernstown. But he was almost equal to the Confederate, and with a little more daring he might have turned and struck a damaging blow. Like Hunter at Lynchburg, he let his opponent obtain a psychological ascendancy over him, and his retreat had been almost as precipitate and circuitous as Hunter's to West Virginia. Crook was a competent soldier, but he lacked the spark that raises generals above the average. He was not the man to drive Early anywhere or to clear the Valley.

At Halltown Crook's weary soldiers prepared to rest and recover their morale. The more knowing among them could deduce that the rest period would not last long when on July 29, the day after their arrival, they saw Wright and the Sixth Corps and a division of the Nineteenth Corps march

---

[3] *Official Records*, XXXVII, pt. 1, 288. The total losses in Duval's division were 513. Duval's other brigade and Thoburn's division did not see heavy fighting.

[4] Hayes to Mrs. Hayes, July 26, 1864, Hayes MS. Letters.

into the Halltown camp. The news of Kernstown had constrained Grant to reconsider bringing Wright back to him.
It was evident that Early was not going to return to Richmond
but would remain in the Valley. The threat had to be met,
and Grant acceded to Halleck's urgent pleas that Wright
be sent to Hunter. Hopefully the high command thought
that the combined force, under Hunter's command, could
hold Early off if he attempted another raid and perhaps even
defeat him. Equally hopeful at a lower level was Hayes, who
mistakenly believed that Wright was to command the army.
"It looks as if we would move up the Valley of Virginia again,"
Hayes confided to Lucy.[5] Usually accurate in his predictions,
he was wrong this time. Early had yet another raid to make
and Hayes some more hard marching to do before the army
would see the Valley again. When Hayes returned to that
lovely spot, he would serve under a new commander, the
most dramatic general he would meet during the war.

---

[5] Hayes to Mrs. Hayes, July 29, ibid.

Chapter 12

Sheridan Comes

O N JULY 29, the day that Wright joined Hunter at Halltown, Early at Martinsburg started two brigades of cavalry under John McCausland across the Potomac above Williamsport. McCausland appeared at Chambersburg, Pennsylvania the next day and demanded that the town put up a large ransom—$500,000 in currency or $100,000 in gold—or suffer burning. When the money was not forthcoming, the raiders applied the torch and departed. They had acted under Early's orders. The Confederate commander, incensed by reports of Hunter's earlier depredations, had decided it was time to give Northern civilians a dose of the same medicine. Although the destruction of the town had little justification or reason—Chambersburg was in no sense a military or industrial center—the mere presence of the gray column in southern Pennsylvania had enormous repercussions. In fact, seldom in the history of war has so small a force had so much impact on the course of larger operations. It was immediately assumed in Washington that a large Confederate force was loose above the Potomac and that other towns would meet the fate of Chambersburg. Even when McCausland fled west at the approach of Federal cavalry under Averell, who would shortly strike the raiders a damaging blow, the scare did not subside. Early's whole army must be somewhere in Pennsylvania, the nervous reasoning ran, poised to move on defenseless Harrisburg or Baltimore and possibly again on Washington itself.

One of the persons most excited at the possiblity was General Halleck, who was bearing reluctantly the burden of command. After the debacle at Kernstown, Grant had insisted to the War Department that somebody closer to the Washington scene than he must give coordinating orders in an emergency. Secretary Stanton had responded by pushing off the function on the Chief of Staff. Now there was an obvious emergency, and Halleck, as much as he might dislike it, had to act. He acted with bustling energy but without much direction. First, he ordered Hunter to move Wright's and Crook's units back to Maryland, specifically to Emmitsburg, almost on the Pennsylvania line. At the same time he apprised Grant of the crisis and begged for more help. Grant was impressed enough to send a division of cavalry north and with it the remainder of the Nineteenth Corps. The situation of the latter unit was peculiar. One division of it, approximately 6,000 men, was with Hunter. But its commander, General William H. Emory, was in Washington with 4,600 men, and 2,000 or so more were steaming up the Virginia coast. Halleck directed Emory to move with the detachment in Washington west to Frederick and unite with Hunter's column advancing to Emmitsburg. Exactly what Halleck hoped to accomplish with all this frenetic ordering about of separate units he never paused to explain. At no time did he have any notion as to the location of the enemy force he was forging combinations to trap. Early's main body remained south of the Potomac, and the only Rebels north of it were riding west while Halleck was calling troops east. The men who were recalled would have to perform some of the most useless marching and countermarching done in the war.[1]

---

[1] *Official Records,* XXXVII, pt. 2, 510–19; Irwin, *Nineteenth Army Corps,* 363–4. As an example of the confusion the student will encounter in trying to understand this hardly studied campaign, Irwin, adjutant general of the corps and a careful writer, states that Emory and his whole force were at Halltown and moved east with Hunter.

When Hunter received Halleck's orders to proceed to Emmitsburg, he protested that he could not move immediately—the weather was intensely warm and Wright's and Crook's troops were exhausted from their long marches. Back came a peevish reply that the men would have to start even if a night march was necessary. So at four in the afternoon on July 30 the army moved out from Halltown, crossed the Potomac, and covered fourteen miles into Maryland. Night marching was an ordeal that good infantry officers resented as being hard on the soldiers and accomplishing but small results. Hayes had never liked it, and he liked it even less now when his men were in poor condition. The effects were "disastrous" on the marchers, he exploded in his diary, noting that when his brigade made camp north of Middletown on the thirty-first only fifty to a hundred men in a regiment came in in a body. As he passed through Middletown, he took the opportunity to look up the Rudys, with whom he had stayed while recuperating from his wound suffered at South Mountain. The reunion was joyful, and Rudy told the colonel he would come a hundred miles to get him if he was wounded again.[2]

Hayes found all the people in the area as friendly and relaxed as the Rudys, and he soon concluded that the army was looking for a danger that did not exist. The Rebel force supposed to be north of the Potomac was a "myth" he opined in his diary. Hayes's private analysis was so obviously based on fact that it soon became official doctrine. Everyone, even General Halleck, conceded that the threat, if there had been one, had passed, and the Chief of Staff consented to let Hunter rest his worn troops around Frederick and Monocacy Junc-

[2] Hayes, MS. Diary, July 30, 31, 1864; John M. Gould, *History of the First-Tenth-Twenty-ninth Maine Regiment* (Portland, 1871), 422–3, hereinafter cited as Gould, *First Maine;* Hayes to Mrs. Hayes, August 2, Hayes MS. Letters.

tion. An observer from the Nineteenth Corps who saw Hunter's men in their camps noted sympathetically that they were "ragged, famished, discouraged, and half of them in ambulances." He also reported that they made no secret of their contempt for their commanding general.[3]

Soon Hunter's troops were to have renewed reason to criticize their general. The flat ending to the great scare pointed up again the weaknesses in the theater command structure—the divided responsibility, the separated forces, and the consequent inability to achieve a common purpose. It was a situation that supreme commander Grant could not continue to ignore, and that busy officer, prodded by Lincoln and nagged by Halleck, was at last on the point of acting. He realized that he would have to put all the Valley and Washington forces under a single head, and while he was casting about for a selection he ordered Hunter to return the army to the Halltown lines. The move was an obvious one— Halltown was a secure defensive base and a logical offensive base—but the men who had to make it saw only that they were going to have to trudge back to where they had started from. They blamed Hunter for another foolish decision, and on the march they made a point of doing the blaming so loudly that their officers heard them. If Hayes caught the comments of his men, he took no notice. He evidently thought that the recent fiasco would bring a change in commanders, and he was content to wait for that development. Back in camp at Halltown he was soon able to announce the welcome news to Lucy. His brigade was now a part of an assembling "tolerably large army," he revealed, and the aggregation was under a new commander, Philip Sheridan. Although Hayes had no

[3] Hayes, MS. Diary, August 1, 3, 4, 1864; *Official Records*, XXXVII, pt. 2, 531–2, 565, 576; John William De Forest, *A Volunteer's Adventures*, edited by James H. Croushore (New Haven, 1946), 163–4.

direct knowledge of Sheridan, he was pleased with the choice
and hopeful that it portended a more active role for the
army. "We are likely to be engaged in some of the great operations of the autumn," he predicted.[4]

Even after the recent sad record of events Grant had been
reluctant to place all the Valley forces under one general.
The hesitancy of the supreme commander to take this obvious
and logical action is one of the unexplained mysteries of the
war. For some reason, he shied away from the responsibility
of naming a commander for this theater, although it was
close to his own headquarters and easy to supervise. Possibly
he delayed because the Valley army was a part of the Washington defenses and therefore related to the capital's political
scene, the one thing Grant wanted to stay clear of. As much
as anything, Grant may have been governed by the strong
streak of personal tenderness in his nature. He had a real
regard for Hunter and from the start of the campaign had
defended him against all criticism. Even when he realized
he would have to make some kind of change in the Valley
command, Grant shrank from hurting Hunter. After considering two other possible choices, he settled on Sheridan,
then leading the cavalry of the Army of the Potomac. He
toyed with the idea of making Sheridan commander of the
troops in the field and leaving Hunter in administrative
control of the department, and he did not formally decide to
appoint "Little Phil" as the independent commander until
he visted Hunter's camp on the Monocacy and found that
Hunter had no objection to being relieved. But after this
period of fumbling, events moved fast. The order assigning
Sheridan was issued on August 7, and on that same day the

---

[4] *Official Records*, XXXVII, pt. 1, 697–8; Irwin, *Nineteenth Army Corps*,
365; Comly, MS. Diary, August 6, 1864; Hayes, MS. Diary, August 6, 7;
Hayes to Mrs. Hayes, August 8, Hayes MS. Letters.

new commander arrived at Harper's Ferry and assumed the direction of the department.[5]

Most people were disappointed when they first saw Phil Sheridan. He did not look, especially on foot, like much of a general. Only thirty-three years of age in 1864, he had a young, almost boyish face. The impression of immaturity was intensified by his slight stature. He was barely five feet five inches high, and although his shoulders were broad and his chest deep he seemed to be an inconsequential little man. That was the first impression, but it disappeared immediately when he mounted his huge black horse, Rienzi. In the saddle, with his powerful upper body he loomed like a giant. His men saw him always riding, accompanying the infantry column and inhaling the dust just as they did. They appreciated his attention to the details of the march, his supervision of the trains, and his evident intelligent grasp of the military art.

They would appreciate him even more when they followed him in battle. Sheridan had that charismatic quality of leadership that could lift masses of men to seemingly impossible endeavors. The possessor of an awesome stock of profanity, he loosed it on anyone who pleaded that he could not make the last desperate effort that would bring victory. One admiring but shocked observer heard him shout at a cavalry staff officer who reported that his superior's horses were too tired to execute a charge: "—— —— tell him to *charge*! —— tell him I say *charge*!! We've got the rebels on the hip —— we've whipped them on the left and front, and he must charge the right, and do it —— quick. I don't give a —— for horse flesh today."[6] No Union general had a more driv-

---

[5] *Official Records*, XXXVII, pt. 2, 558, 573; Pond, *Shenandoah Valley*, 111–21; Philip H. Sheridan, *Personal Memoirs of P. H. Sheridan* (New York, 1888), I, 461–6; Ulysses S. Grant, *Personal Memoirs of Ulysses S. Grant* (New York, 1885–6), II, 317–31.

[6] Sheridan, *Memoirs*, I, 346–7; George T. Stevens, *Three Years in the Sixth Corps* (New York, 1870), 391; Gould, *First Maine*, 499, 507.

ing desire for victory, and none was more ruthless in employing officers and men in any way necessary to attain it. And Sheridan would be remarkably successful in the Valley. Although he had commanded an infantry division in the West, his only experience in independent command had been with the cavalry; yet he would demonstrate real talent for handling an army of combined arms. The only possible reasons to deny him a ranking with the great captains of the war are that he exercised command for but a short period and that he enjoyed a definite numerical superiority over his antagonist.

Sheridan's command was officially styled the Middle Military Division, but he himself called the force under him the Army of the Shenandoah. Just how big it was is the usual matter of dispute where Civil War armies are concerned. On paper there were well over 40,000 men in the department. Many of these, however, were in garrison at various points in the Valley or guarding railroads, supply depots, and river crossings. It is probable that for field service Sheridan had available 31,000 infantry and 6,000 cavalry. The size of Early's army is open to the same kind of conjecture. The Confederate general had had under him at one time close to 20,000 men. But the strength of his force had always been subject to fluctuation because of its relation to Lee's army—in periods of crisis at Richmond, Lee would withdraw units from Early and return them when the threat had passed. Moreover, Early had suffered substantial losses in the summer campaign and would incur greater ones in the autumn, and his replacement system produced highly sporadic results. Early estimated that he could not bring more than 12,000 troops to battle, a figure that is probably somewhat too low, 15,000 or 16,000 being a more likely total. However the contrasting figures are reckoned, Sheridan had a substantial numerical advantage, at least two to one and possibly more. But a two-to-one edge was not decisive in the Civil War. Armies with as much leverage had failed to win and had even endured bad defeats. To carry out the offensive mission assigned to him Sheridan would need a large force and one that could undergo tough fighting.[7]

Sheridan's objective, as outlined by Grant, was much the same as the one the supreme commander had previously hoped Hunter could accomplish. Sheridan was to advance up the Valley and try to bring the gray army to battle and destroy it. As a subordinate but important part of his assignment, he was to devastate the economic resources of the region he traversed. But although the Federal strategy was boldly offensive in concept, Sheridan was under injunction to be properly cautious in executing it. Northern estimates inflated the size of Early's army to well over 30,000, and the Union commander understood that he was not supposed to attack unless he felt he had a fair chance of success. Accepting the official evaluations, Sheridan was resigned to proceeding warily against a foe fully as strong as he. Also restraining him was his lack of knowledge about the composition and quality of his own hastily scraped together army.[8]

The infantry of the Army of the Shenandoah comprised three corps. In Sheridan's first opinion the elite unit was the Sixth Corps of the Army of the Potomac. Its general, Horatio G. Wright, was a solid if unimaginative soldier, and its division and brigade leaders were men of experience. The corps itself had one of the best fighting records in the Eastern theater. Actually, it was not nearly as good a unit as it seemed. The Sixth had been in the Army of the Potomac too long. It had known too many defeats, and its officers and men were afflicted with the Potomac psychosis that Robert E. Lee and

---

[7] Johnson and Buel (eds.), *Battles and Leaders,* IV, 531–2; *Official Records, XLIII,* pt. 1, 975–82.

[8] *Official Records,* XLIII, pt. 1, 54.

his lieutenants were invincible. It would always perform creditably, but it would require a large infusion of Sheridan's hot passion for victory to make it forget the past. By contrast, the Nineteenth Corps had known nothing but victory, but its experience had not given it the qualities of a battle-hardened outfit. The corps's service had been in Louisiana, and its successes had been scored over weak opposition. How it would stand up to a first-rate foe remained to be seen. Its commander, ponderous William H. Emory, was capable but no more, and the level of his subordinate officers left something to be desired. Observers noted that the corps's loose conduct indicated a lack of discipline at the top.

The Sixth and Nineteenth were regulation-sized corps, about 12,000 men each. The third infantry unit, the Eighth Corps, however, could count only a little over 7,000 troops. The Eighth was Crook's force, at first called the Army of West Virginia, but later given a number to bring it in line with its modest size and to achieve a consistent terminology. The smallest of the three corps, it had the simplest organization, only two divisions, the First under Thoburn and the Second, Hayes's outfit, under Duval. It enjoyed a peculiarly personal reputation with the rest of the army. Whereas the accounts of participants nearly always refer to the two larger units by number, they invariably speak of "Crook's corps" or "Crook's command." The Eighth was easily the most distinctive of the corps. A ragged and somewhat run-down aggregation when Sheridan took it over, it was still obviously a rough-and-tough outfit. Most of its experience had been with raiding, and Hayes and other officers thought of it as being more than anything a large raiding party. Sheridan might have had some doubts as to how it would perform in a set battle, but he must have known that if the mountain troops could do anything they could march. And good marchers would have a vital role in the general's first strategic plans.

When Sheridan assumed the command, Early was at Bunker Hill, about twelve miles north of Winchester. From here the Confederate leader could easily move to menace the Baltimore & Ohio or the Potomac crossings. Sheridan judged that his initial move should be to force Early back from his forward position, and the Union commander devised an artful and attack-proof scheme to accomplish his objective. On August 10 he moved out from the Halltown lines on a broad front, the Sixth Corps on the right, the Nineteenth in the center, and the Eighth on the left, with strong cavalary forces screening both flanks. Fearing that he might be attacked while marching, Sheridan resorted to an unusual tactical formation. As much as possible, he kept the men to the fields. The regiments of each corps advanced in line of battle, one unit behind another. Thus a corps occupied a front as wide as a regimental line as it moved. When the first regiment reached its destination, it halted in battle array; the second regiment to arrive filed to the right of the first, and so on until the whole brigade was in line. It was a device that preserved a battle formation while moving and yet did not lose much time, the army covering seventeen and eighteen miles a day, a good record by any standard. Rolling forward in this manner, Sheridan occupied a line running in a north-south direction from Clifton to Berryville, with Wright at Clifton, Emory on Wright's left, and Crook at Berryville. This position, to be used again by Sheridan, became known as the Clifton-Berryville line. It was an offensive natural for the Federals. Holding it, Sheridan was parallel to Early at Bunker Hill and so situated as to be able to attack the Confederates in flank. Early responded by yielding Bunker Hill and falling back to cover Winchester.[9]

Sheridan had not made his move merely to draw Early back

---

[9] Hayes, MS. Diary, August 10, 1864; Gould, *First Maine*, 476–7; Frank M. Flinn, *Campaigning with Banks in Louisiana . . . and with Sheridan in the Shenandoah Valley* (Boston, 1887), 163–4, hereinafter cited as Flinn, *Cam-*

to Winchester. The Union commander had expected his foe to react in the way he did, and he hoped now to bring on a battle under conditions favorable to himself. On the eleventh Sheridan sent his army in a general westerly direction toward Winchester. His immediate objective was to seize the crossings of Opequon Creek, a stream that took its rise a little south of Winchester, ran past the town on the east, and, continuing down the Valley, emptied into the Potomac. If he could accomplish it, he would cut off Early's line of withdrawal and force the Confederate to fight whether he wanted to or not. The three corps advanced in the same broad-front formation as on the previous day and seized the fords with no opposition. Early made no effort to defend Winchester. Realizing that he was outnumbered, the gray leader had no mind to be trapped into a premature battle. He retreated rapidly up the Valley pike toward a more defensible position at Strasburg, where he could wait for promised reinforcements from Lee. Sheridan, seeing the enemy slipping away from him, pushed vigorously on; if he could not bring the Confederates to bay he would at the least shove them farther south. By nightfall the Federal army held a line from Millwood, a little southeast of Winchester, to Stony Point on the left, where Crook's command, which had been in the forefront of the chase, rested.[1]

On the next day Sheridan moved on to Cedar Creek, a tributary of the Shenandoah, with Crook's corps leading the advance. Expecting to meet opposition at the crossings, Sheridan formed his army in line of battle on the north bank, with the Sixth Corps on the right, the Nineteenth in the center,

---

paigning with Sheridan. The march formation employed by Sheridan was obviously known to other generals. How frequently it was used during the war cannot be determined. Usually the sources do not describe such commonplace matters, commonplace, that is, to the soldier-writers, as the way an army marched. It is probable that this particular formation was resorted to only on rare occasions and in relatively open country, like the Valley.

[1] Hayes, MS. Diary, August 11, 1864; Irwin, *Nineteenth Army Corps,* 372; Flinn, *Campaigning with Sheridan,* 164-5.

and the Eighth on the left. Reconnaissances sent out that night and the following morning developed that the Confederates were strongly posted south of the stream, with their main force holding Fisher's Hill. It was also evident that Early was not going to attack but would try to make the Federals come to him.[2] For three days the armies sparred cautiously, each one trying to divine the other's intention and hoping to entice the other into a rash move. It was exciting work, but for Crook's men the same kind of small fighting they had always done. Colonel Hayes, who admitted in his diary that he had "some narrow escapes" in one of the skirmishes, soon saw that Sheridan was not yet ready to risk a showdown battle. In letters home Hayes correctly surmised that the general was feeling out the enemy and testing his own army for future action.[3]

Although Hayes would have welcomed larger actions, he voiced no criticism of Sheridan's strategy, which he recognized as necessary. More and more, the once hasty volunteer officer was becoming resigned to realities and also the absurdities of the military machine. One day while Hayes and his staff were resting on the ground under a clump of trees a spruce little staff officer rode up to the group. The visitor was obviously fresh out of West Point and anxious to demonstrate it. Not bothering to determine the identity of any of the reclining figures, he looked at a puddle of water nearby and snapped out: "You men, there! Is that water clean?" Hayes rolled over lazily, disclosing the eagles of his rank, and said softly: "Yes, I guess it's clean." The staffer gave one startled look and left. Hayes, who once would have fumed at such an encounter, dismissed this one with an amused laugh.[4]

Nor did Hayes think any less of Sheridan when the com-

[2] Flinn, *Campaigning with Sheridan*, 165–7; Walker, *Vermont Brigade*, 57.

[3] Hayes, MS. Diary, August 12–15, 1864; Hayes to Sardis Birchard, August 14, and to Mrs. Hayes, August 16, Hayes MS. Letters.

[4] Comly, MS. Diary, August 12, 1864.

HAYES AND HIS STAFF IN 1864

This picture was taken at Cumberland, Maryland, in the spring of 1864.
Hayes is in the center of the front row; at his left is Dr. Joseph Webb,
the brigade surgeon and his brother-in-law.

GENERAL HAYES

*This photograph, probably made late in 1864 or early in 1865 and obviously
touched up somewhat, shows Hayes as a brigadier general.*

THE TWENTY-THIRD GOES HOME

Hayes's regiment was mustered out of service in Cleveland, Ohio, in July, 1865.

THE TWENTY-THIRD REGIMENT, O.V.I., BAND, CHARLESTON, W. VA., 1863

Left to right, front row: William Arthur, Edwin Arthur, John Arthur, John Cramer, George Smith, Theodore Belding, Alfred Arthur, William Arthur, Jim Huffman; top row: Thad Coffin, Jim String, John Oswald, Ed Spring, Eugene Coffin, Chris Miller, Arnold Issler.

manding general decided he would have to retire his army
back down the Valley. On August 14 Sheridan received word
from Grant's headquarters that a corps from Lee's army had
joined Early. Although the information was exaggerated—it
was a division instead of a corps—Sheridan believed that
he now confronted an enemy army of over 40,000. Reasoning
that against such a force he could not hope to hold his extended position at Cedar Creek, he resolved to withdraw to a
more defensible line. He began the movement with great
secrecy on the night of the fifteenth, pulling the Nineteenth
Corps back fifteen miles to Winchester. On the following
night the Sixth and Eighth corps followed. So quietly was
the transfer accomplished that Early did not learn of it until
it was completed. Then the Confederate general put his
own army in motion, but he was too late to catch the Federals
on the march. From Winchester, Sheridan retired to the
Clifton-Berryville line, where he waited a day for a division of
the Nineteenth Corps coming from Washington to pass
through Snicker's Gap, and then he moved to Charles Town.
Here on the twenty-first, Early, who had advanced to Bunker
Hill, essayed an attack, but he did not press it when he saw
the Union army standing in battle array, from right to left,
the Sixth, Nineteenth, and Eighth corps, behind hastily constructed field entrenchments. But Sheridan, even though he
held a strong position, wanted a stronger one, and at midnight
withdrew to the Halltown line.[5]

There followed a period of probing by both armies, Early
stabbing at the Federal lines, chiefly those of Wright and
Crook, and Sheridan stabbing back, seeking to ascertain
Early's strength and purpose. Hayes played a leading role in
one of the most successful of the Federal efforts. On the

---

[5] Hayes, MS. Diary, August 16–21, 1864; Irwin, *Nineteenth Army Corps*,
374–5; Walker, *Vermont Brigade*, 57–9; Stevens, *Three Years in the Sixth
Corps*, 396.

afternoon of August 26, after the army had waited all day for an expected Confederate attack, an order from headquarters came down to Colonel Duval to make a reconnaissance on the Confederate right in strength, with a whole brigade. Duval chose to execute the movement with Hayes's First Brigade. Although the division commander accompanied the troops, he left the tactical direction to Hayes. Moving out at dusk, the brigade formed in line of battle in a woods and suddenly burst forward on the enemy picket line. The surprise was complete. The attackers inflicted twenty casualties and picked up twenty prisoners whose unit identities would furnish clues to Early's strength and who could be interrogated as to the numbers in their units. As the astonished graycoats were being carried back to the Union lines, they asked their captors: "Who the Hell *are* you uns?" It was a competently carried out little affair, and Hayes received high commendation from his superiors. He passed on their praise to Lucy and added of the episode: "We enjoyed it much."[6]

Heartened by this success, Crook four days later threw Duval's whole Second Division forward in a heavier effort. This push achieved unexpected results. The attackers not only broke the enemy picket line but drove two Rebel brigades from their first line of works before retiring with a bag of almost a hundred prisoners. But the Federals incurred some losses of their own. Whereas Hayes had suffered only three wounded in the earlier reconnaissance, he had three killed and twenty-one wounded in this affair, and for Crook's corps the casualties totaled 142. But although Hayes grieved for his men, he liked this kind of fighting. It was the sort the West Virginia troops were used to—the rush in and hit them and then rush out style of raiders. In fact, Hayes confided to Uncle Sardis, the men were having "the best times we have had

[6] *Official Records*, XLIII, pt. 1, 360, Crook's report, 400, Duval's report, 405, Hayes's report; Hayes, MS. Diary, August 22, 23, 1864; Comly, MS. Diary, August 22; Hayes to Mrs. Hayes, August 23, Hayes MS. Letters.

since our first raid under Crook." And though the constant skirmishing was having a costly effect on his numbers, the size of his favorite unit, the Twenty-third, as the result of good recruiting, stood at 600, a remarkable regimental strength at this late date in the war.[7]

Early's probings, and the vigorous Federal reaction to them, had the effect of convincing the Confederate commander that he could not smash into Sheridan's Halltown fortress. He turned therefore to the project which had always intrigued him the most, the breaking of the Baltimore & Ohio rail line. Retiring from Sheridan's front, he returned to his favorite striking point at Bunker Hill. But Sheridan, whose main objective from the beginning was Early's army, had no intention of letting his antagonist work his will on this important artery of communication unhindered. And Sheridan had at his disposal a move that was certain to force Early to yield his position at Bunker Hill. All that Sheridan had to do was to step forward to the Clifton-Berryville line, whereupon Early would have to swing back to cover Winchester and the Valley pike. Sheridan made the move now, first advancing his army by cautious stages to Charles Town. No opposition was met, as Early had his eyes fixed on the railroad to the north and was unaware of what was happening on his strategic flank. To subordinate officers like Hayes it appeared that the Confederates had left the immediate scene and that active operations were ended for the moment. This modest result of the campaign was satisfactory to Hayes. He had developed a great faith in Sheridan, and he was convinced that the general knew exactly what he was doing. It had been "a happy month in the main," he mused in his diary, and to Uncle Sardis he wrote: "We are a happy army."[8]

---

[7] Hayes, MS. Diary, August 26, 27, 1864; Comly, MS. Diary, August 26; *Official Records*, XLIII, pt. 1, 360, 405, 408–9; Hayes to Sardis Birchard, August 27, Hayes MS. Letters.

[8] Hayes, MS. Diary, August 28–31, 1864; Hayes to Sardis Birchard, August 30, and to Mrs. Hayes, September 1, Hayes MS. Letters.

If Hayes expected September to be another relatively quiet month, he immediately received a jolting notification that things were going to be different, as well as a reminder of the fallibility of military predictions. On September 3 the happy army was completing its movement to the Clifton-Berryville line, the Sixth Corps stopping at Clifton, the Nineteenth forming on the Sixth's left, and the Eighth heading for Berryville. Late in the afternoon Crook's troops made camp and prepared to settle down for the night. Suddenly, about an hour before sunset, a hail of shots rang out, and Confederate attackers materialized out of nowhere to drive in the blue picket line. It was immediately evident that the Rebels were present in strength. Crook was completely mystified by their appearance. What had happened was that he had run onto a division of Early's army moving back to Richmond. This was the unit that Lee had sent to Early at Cedar Creek. Now finding a need for it, Lee had asked for its return, and the division had started to move east by the shortest route over the Blue Ridge, unaware that a part of Sheridan's army stood squarely in its way. The Confederate commander, R. H. Anderson, was as surprised as Crook at the encounter, but he realized that he had the element of surprise on his side and ordered his men to attack.

Crook hurriedly posted Thoburn's First Division, the unit nearest at hand, to cover the Winchester pike, placing most of the troops to the right of the highway. At the same time he ordered Duval's Second Division, which was somewhat to the rear, to double-quick it up to the front and form on Thoburn's left. Before Duval could get all his regiments into line, the Confederates attacked again and drove several of Thoburn's regiments back in disorder on Duval. Crook, who had intended to use Duval to hit the enemy flank, now had to change his plan. Duval's was the only force that could stem the gray onrush. There was not much doubt that Duval could do it. The Federals were at least equal in numbers to the Rebels and strongly positioned behind stone-wall fences, and they met the attackers with a murderous fire when the latter came within range. But in the heat of the moment the outcome seemed a matter of touch and go to the unit commanders. Hayes was disturbed because all of his regiments had not arrived, and he breathed easier as he saw the last ones come up. When his favorite Twenty-third approached, he went out to meet it and personally conducted it to the battle line. The fresh troops reached the scene just as the Rebels recoiled under the fire from the stone walls, and the Federal officers, reacting with the instincts of battle veterans, immediately sent their men forward in a counterattack. The bluecoats pushed the Confederates back, beyond the ground that had been lost, maintaining the chase until eight o'clock and then returning to their camp in the darkness.[9]

The impromptu little battle had been a real slugging match, fought by both sides with lethal tenacity, much of it in darkness with friend indistinguishable from foe. Crook's losses were 166, and of these Hayes's brigade suffered 63. Colonel Comly, who confessed that the battle was the first up to that time in which he felt certain of being killed, recorded an example of the spirit of the Union soldiery. Near dusk he saw two men helping a third one to the rear. Thinking they were skulkers, Comly rode up and recognized the man being aided, a big Irishman who had recently come into the Twenty-third as a substitute. Angrily Comly ordered him and the others to return to the front. The Irishman protested that he was wounded, but Comly would have none of it. Finally the man asked for the colonel's hand, and Comly let

[9] *Official Records,* XLIII, pt. 1, 360–1, 400–1, 405; Hayes, MS. Diary, September 3, 1864; Hastings, MS. Autobiography, September 3; Hayes, two-page manuscript on Berryville, in Hayes Library; Keyes, *123rd Regiment,* 87–8; William T. Patterson, MS. Diary, June 23–November 6, 1864, in Ohio Historical Society Library, Columbus, entries of September 3, 4.

him take it. "Feel," said the soldier. He stuck the hand all the way into a hole in his shoulder. When Comly withdrew it, blood from the wound spurted up Comly's arm to his own shoulder. Horrified, Comly spoke: "Forgive me! Go back to the Doctor, quick." The man started off but after a few steps fell dead.[1]

Even Hayes was impressed by the savagery of the encounter. He told Lucy that he had never been in as much danger before, but, he added characteristically, "I enjoyed the excitement more than ever before." It was his brigade, he said with pride, that by its steadiness had turned the battle from defeat to victory. He was proud of the brigade—it had marched and fought more than any unit in the army, he boasted to Uncle Sardis—but saddened by its losses. He had started the campaign with 2,400 men, but now he could count no more than 1,200—and almost none of the fifty per cent absent were stragglers.[2]

When Early received word of the collision at Berryville, he hastened there with most of his army. If he had any idea that he might attack the Federals, he abandoned it when he saw their strongly entrenched lines stretching northward to Clifton and beyond to Summit Point. Instead, recognizing the threat that Sheridan's unsuspected movement posed for Winchester, the Confederate commander retired behind the line of Opequon Creek and dispatched Anderson's division to Lee by a more southerly route. Sheridan, for his part, was satisfied to hold the ground he occupied. The only change he made in his dispositions was to shift Crook's corps from the left of the line at Berryville to the right of it at Summit Point, posting the tough mountain troops where he did to cover his flank and communications to Harper's Ferry. The two armies probed at each other with the customary skirmishes, but on

---

[1] Comly, MS. Diary, September 3, 1864.
[2] Hayes to Mrs. Hayes, September 4, 1864, and to Sardis Birchard, September 6, Hayes MS. Letters.

the tenth heavy rains set in and continued for three days to halt all operations.[3]

In the brief respite from campaigning Hayes had time to contemplate the current political situation. No matter how immersed he might become in the fascinating game of war, he could never shed completely his civilian interests, and one of these interests, destined to grow increasingly important with him, was politics. Because of his background and because he had a sharper than average mind, he understood better than most soldiers the relationship between politics and war. That relationship was at the moment acutely personal. In late August some of his friends had persuaded the Republican-Union convention of the Cincinnati district to nominate him for a seat in the House of Representatives. He accepted the nomination with no outward show of enthusiasm but with obvious satisfaction and pride. He made only one stipulation —he would not campaign for the office. If the voters wanted to elect a soldier, well and good, but he was not going to leave the army. When a friend suggested that he get a furlough and come home to stump, Hayes administered a stern rebuke: "An officer fit for duty who at this crisis would abandon his post to electioneer for a seat in Congress ought to be scalped. You may feel perfectly sure I shall do no such thing—."[4]

Hayes was also studying the presidential election. His old commander from the early West Virginia days, General McClellan, was the Democratic candidate against Lincoln. Hayes had a strong regard for McClellan as a man and as a friend of the common soldier. "No man ever treated the private soldiers better," he wrote Lucy. "No Commander was ever more loved by his men." But McClellan was running on a "peace" platform that proposed an armistice in military operations, but with no requirement that the South return to the Union

---

[3] Hayes, MS. Diary, September 4–15, 1864; Irwin, *Nineteenth Army Corps*, 376–7; Pond, *Shenandoah Valley*, 145–6.
[4] Hayes to William Henry Smith, August 24, 1864, typed copy in Hayes Library.

as a condition of the cessation in war. Although Hayes did
not believe that McClellan, if elected, would execute the
platform, he could not support a candidate who would let
himself be associated with it. Therefore he was for Lincoln,
but, curiously, he wanted his men to "think and talk well"
of McClellan. He assured Lucy that Lincoln was certain of
election if the military situation improved.[5]

Hayes could not see that it was going to change very much
in the Shenandoah Valley. He looked for no important operations to occur there in the immediate future. "Our policy
seems to be not to attack unless the chances are greatly in our
favor," he wrote Uncle Sardis. If Hayes was making some fuzzy
predictions at this time, it was not because his military perceptions were becoming dulled. Accustomed to serving under
sluggish and slow commanders, he did not yet quite appreciate
the temper of the new breed he had met. On September 17
he noted in his diary that Grant had arrived in Sheridan's
camp and was conferring with the general of the Army of the
Valley. But Hayes attached no significance to the visit. A
sergeant in the Nineteenth Corps who saw Grant come in
knew better. This veteran stared at Grant and said pensively,
"I hate to see that old cuss around. When that old cuss is
around there's sure to be a big fight on hand."[6]

On the day after Grant's arrival an order from Sheridan's
headquarters directed all his units to be prepared to move.
Hayes did not think much would come of the directive. "As
usual the order to move comes on Sunday," he complained
to Lucy. "We go on what direction or why I don't know."[7] He
was never more wrong. The movement would proceed under
the surest direction, and as a part of it Hayes would experience his greatest military adventure.

[5] Hayes to Mrs. Hayes, September 9, 1864, Hayes MS. Letters.
[6] Hayes to Sardis Birchard, September 12, 1864, ibid.; Hayes, MS. Diary,
September 17; De Forest, *A Volunteer's Adventures*, 172.
[7] Hayes to Mrs. Hayes, September 18, 1864, Hayes MS. Letters.

Chapter 13

Encounter on the Opequon

G RANT HAD COME TO Sheridan's headquarters to urge the Valley commander to seek a showdown with Early. Although Sheridan had been conforming his movements to the letter of Grant's instructions, which were not to attack without a reasonable chance of success, the supreme commander felt that the time had now come when Little Phil could strike with just such a chance. Numerous, though unverified, reports received at Grant's headquarters stated that part of Early's army had been drawn away to Richmond, and influential individuals and groups in the North were bringing pressure on the government to do something to break Early's grip on the Baltimore & Ohio. By a dramatic coincidence, on the day before Grant arrived Sheridan had secured convincing information that the Confederate division encountered at Berryville had gone to join Lee, leaving Early that much weaker. The notification had come from a loyalist Quaker girl in Winchester, Miss Rebecca Wright, whose name had been given to Sheridan by Crook. Sheridan sent a Negro to her house with a note asking what she knew about the composition of the Rebel forces. Hastily she wrote down the essence of a recent conversation with a Confederate officer. The colored man put the message in his mouth and succeeded in delivering it to Sheridan.[1]

---

[1] Sheridan, *Memoirs*, II, 2–9; Joel and Stegman, *Rifle Shots*, 558; *The Loyal Girl of Winchester* (Philadelphia, 1888), no pagination. The last item is a

Buoyed by the information, Sheridan had resolved to attack before Grant arrived. Instead of having to urge his subordinate to move, the supreme commander found himself listening with deep satisfaction to Sheridan's depiction of how he intended to hit Early. Grant, who had brought a plan of his own along, never took it out of his pocket. He approved Sheridan's plan, and before departing for the lines before Richmond he uttered one of the shortest directives in the history of war. "Go in," he said to Sheridan.[2]

The plan that Sheridan outlined to Grant was simple and sound. He would swing his army west to the fords over the steep-banked Opequon and make for Newtown, about six miles south of Winchester. At Newtown he would stand athwart Early's lines of communication to the south and could make the Confederates fight on ground of his choosing. Sheridan had made the plan on the assumption that Early would remain behind the Opequon crossings to cover Winchester. Such a position would have been an obvious one for the Confederate leader to take. Indeed, having lost a division from his army and believing that he faced a much larger foe, Early would have been well advised to seek an even more defensible line than the Opequon, to retire at least as far as Cedar Creek. He did neither of the sensible things open to him. Instead, obsessed as always with the prospect of laying hold of the Baltimore & Ohio, he moved part of his army forward to Bunker Hill and Martinsburg. On September 18, the day after Grant's departure, one of Sheridan's cavalry officers reported the presence of Confederate troops above

pamphlet detailing Miss Wright's war activities. A copy in the Hayes Library inlaid in a bound volume of Hayes's documents contains additional information. After the war she was given a job in the Treasury Department in recognition of her services. Hayes, as commander of the Military Order of the Loyal Legion of the United States, was instrumental in having the pamphlet reprinted.

[2] *Official Records*, XXXIV, pt. 1, 27.

Winchester. Instantly Sheridan, who had issued orders for the move to Newton, decided to revise his plan.

The news that Early's army was strung out all the way from Winchester to Martinsburg presented Sheridan with several choices of action. He could continue his move to the Confederate rear at Newtown. Or he could advance on Stephenson's Depot, a few miles north of Winchester, striking the center of the Confederate line and interposing between its flanks. He rejected both of these possibilities and determined instead to move directly on Winchester, snapping up the two divisions that Early had left there and then defeating the other gray units in detail as they returned to the scene. Sheridan's revised plan has drawn much criticism from military writers, including some who were with his army. These commentators contend that he should have adhered to his original design of going to Newtown. If he had, they argue, he would have forced Early's whole army to surrender or temporarily disperse or return to Confederate territory by a circuitous and tiring route. The critics have some logic on their side. But it must be noted that only one of the results they hold out would have been a decisive one —that Early would surrender his army, which was highly unlikely. The other two outcomes would not have taken the Confederate army out of the war permanently. A permanent disposal was what Sheridan was aiming at. His battle plan may have had technical defects, but Sheridan was a Grant man and he had the killer instinct of his commander. He did not want to win a mere chessboard triumph of maneuver but to destroy the enemy army. He would go for Winchester and by the most direct route.[3]

[3] Pond, *Shenandoah Valley*, 149–55; Du Pont, *Campaign of 1864*, 107–8; Edward J. Stackpole, *Sheridan in the Shenandoah* (Harrisburg, 1961), 180–9; L. W. V. Kennon, "The Valley Campaign of 1864, A Military Study," in *Papers of the Military Historical Society of Massachusetts* (Boston, 1907), VI, 44–5; Frederic Morton, *The Story of Winchester in Virginia* (Strasburg,

His insistence on bursting forward straight at Winchester was the most questionable feature in Sheridan's plan as finally worked out. He proposed to send one third of his cavalry and all of his infantry and artillery over a single avenue of approach, and that a difficult one to traverse. His battle orders stated that the army would move out at two o'clock in the morning on the nineteenth. First, a division of cavalry would dash across the Opequon at the Berryville ford and secure the Berryville pike. Immediately west of the stream the road ran for two miles between bluffs so abrupt that the passage was known locally as the Berryville canyon or gorge. The mission of the cavalry, and it was a vital one, was to clear any Confederate opposition out of the gorge and open the way for Sheridan's infantry. Then the Sixth Corps would cross the Opequon, followed by the Nineteenth, and when both units reached the open country beyond the canyon they would form in line of battle under Wright's command. When the Sixth and Nineteenth attacked, two more cavalry divisions were to sweep down from Stephenson's and engage the Confederate left. Sheridan expected that the combined assault would cause Early's army to break and flee southward. Now would come the entrance into the battle of Crook's corps, and the crowning movement of Sheridan's strategy. Assigned to take position at the Opequon crossing, the Eighth was to act as a reserve under Sheridan's direction. As the gray army broke, Crook's unit would fling itself over the Valley pike south of Winchester, and the retreating Confederates would find themselves caught between Crook and the cavalry which opened the Berryville pike and in the meantime shifted to the Federal left.[4]

1925), 167–8. Pond and Stackpole laud Sheridan's planning, the others criticize it.

[4] *Official Records*, XLIII, pt. 1, 46–7; Stackpole, *Sheridan in the Shenandoah*, 189–93; Pond, *Shenandoah Valley*, 155–6.

It was a bold plan, a variation of the classic double envelopment so prized by commanders since the beginning of war. It was also a good plan, worked out to the finest detail and with every eventuality presumably covered, and on paper it seemed easy to execute. But there were four elements in the situation that prevented the operation from developing exactly as Sheridan envisioned. Three were inherent in the plan itself, and one was beyond Sheridan's control. For all his careful attention to contingencies, the Union general overlooked some serious disranging possibilities. First, he staked too much on the time element. The success of his scheme would depend on the various parts of his army moving at a set time, attacking at a set time, and converging at a set time. He should have remembered that such clocklike precision was almost impossible to accomplish in battle. Second, he failed to realize the risk he incurred in sending virtually his whole army through the Berryville gorge. If for any reason the Sixth and Nineteenth corps got stalled in the passage, his entire schedule would be disrupted. Third, he erred in placing Crook's corps too far behind his main body. The reserve unit, when it was needed, would have to advance over two miles and through the same difficult gorge.

The factor that Sheridan could not have foreseen was the changed disposition of the Confederate army. Early heard on the eighteenth that Grant had visited Sheridan, and immediately the gray general realized that some important Federal move was afoot. In hot haste he ordered his detached units to pull back to Winchester. He did not have them there by nightfall, but they were within supporting distance. Whether or not Early would be able to concentrate his army before the Union blow fell would depend on how soon Sheridan delivered his attack on the morrow.

On the morning of the nineteenth the Union camps were astir with movement at two o'clock. In the chill darkness the troops formed in the column or marching formation and awaited orders to move off. While the infantry stood at ease, the cavalry division splashed over the Opequon and headed up the narrow pike between the frowning hills that might hide enemies in gray. No opposition appeared, however, until the riders reached the end of the gorge. Here a small Confederate force behind earthworks attempted to bar the way but was easily dispersed. Back went the word to Sheridan— the road was open, and the Sixth Corps trudged across the ford and entered the gorge.

So far everything was going according to Sheridan's schedule. Highly elated, the general rode with his staff to the head of the canyon to supervise the movement of his units as they emerged. The advance troops of the Sixth saw him sitting there as they marched out, and entering on their first battle under his command they were pleased that he had chosen to place himself at the very front of the battle and within range of enemy fire. Just at that moment the sun broke through the morning clouds, its rays touching and making even brighter the brilliant autumnal foliage of the Valley and heralding a lovely day.[5] The sight was splendid, but Sheridan was blind to its beauties. He was beginning to feel some gnawing misgivings. The Sixth Corps was taking longer to get through the gorge than he had expected, and beyond the rolling meadows over which he would have to advance the woods were obviously full of Confederates. It was nine o'clock before the Sixth reached the open country and formed in line of battle. But its wagon trains were still behind it in the gorge, blocking the advance of the Nineteenth Corps. In a cursing fury, Sheridan rode back and ordered officers and teamsters to clear the road. He finally got the snarl untangled, but it was around noon when the Nineteenth finally

[5] Stevens, *Three Years in the Sixth Corps*, 399–400; Walker, *Vermont Brigade*, 91–2.

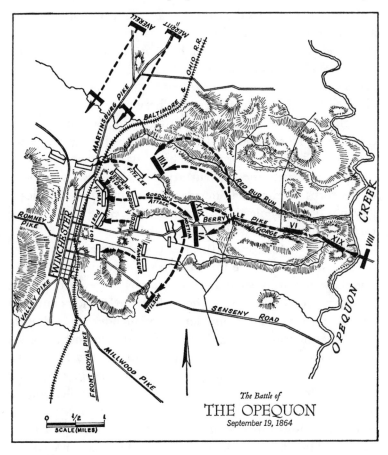

The Battle of
THE OPEQUON
September 19, 1864

arrived on the scene and formed on the right of the Sixth. Any chance of destroying the Confederates in detail had slipped away. Early had brought up the last of his divisions. If Sheridan wanted his battle, he would have to fight the whole gray army.

Sheridan realized that the situation for which he had devised his battle plan no longer existed. It was for him that moment of truth which comes to all generals soon or late and which determines the stuff they are made of. For Sheridan it came soon, at the beginning of his first big battle as an independent commander, and he met it with iron resolution. He might have disengaged and left the field to the Confederates or he might have tried, as Joseph Hooker had done with tragic consequences the previous year at Chancellorsville, to entice the Rebels to attack him. Scorning either easy choice, he responded with the instinct of the great battle captain. The Sixth Corps had been stabbing at the Confederate position since it had arrived, and now with both of his corps on the field Sheridan determined on a full-scale advance of his whole line, throwing the weight of the attack on the Confederate right to turn that flank.

At a little before or a little after noon—the accounts differ —the Union line drove forward into the woods where Early had kept his army sheltered. The attackers seemed at first to carry everything before them. But Early had a surprise in store for them. The Confederate commander realized quite well what Sheridan was trying to do, and, demonstrating his own brand of audacity, he resolved to counterattack. To lead his assault column, he designated one of his best division generals, John B. Gordon. As Gordon moved up, he noticed a slight gap between the lines of the Sixth and Nineteenth corps, and into this opening he poured his men in a fierce charge. The effect was more than he could have hoped for. Two Federal divisions, one from the Sixth and one from the Nineteenth, broke and fled to the rear. Their stampede infected the whole center of the Union line, which wavered and then fell back as the Confederates continued their pressure. Bluecoated fugitives jammed the Berryville pike all the way back to where Sheridan had set up his field headquarters at the western end of the gorge. The battle that had opened with such bright auguries for the Federals seemed about to turn into a crushing defeat.

Actually the signs were not nearly as bad as they looked. The Federals, after retreating almost to the point where they had begun their advance, managed to stabilize their line, and the Confederates, shrinking from the fire they there encountered, retired to their own line of defense. Early had committed his last reserve in the counterattack, but Sheridan had yet to throw in Crook's corps. The outcome of the engagement that the Federals called the battle of the Opequon and the Confederates the battle of Winchester still hung in the balance, and which way it would turn was now squarely in the hands of the West Virginia troops. Sheridan listened impassively as members of his staff urged him to call up the Eighth Corps and, in a reversal of the original plan, send it against the Confederate left instead of the right flank.[6]

The Eighth Corps had spent the morning hours at the Opequon ford. From the bluffs of the stream its officers and men could hear the sounds of the battle raging some three miles away and even see snatches of the action. Crook himself, soon after the firing opened, announced his intention of riding to the front, and, accompanied by his staff, he cantered through the gorge and at the western end found Sheridan watching the fight from a small hill. Crook apparently remained with his commander for the rest of the morning and

---

[6] The literature on the battle is voluminous. The reports are in *Official Records*, XLIII, pt. 1, 24–5, 46–7, 144–52, 162–3, 279–81, 361–3, 368–9. Accounts by participants are Sheridan, *Memoirs*, II, 11–24; Walker, *Vermont Brigade*, 93–9; Du Pont, *Campaign of 1864*, 110–11; Stevens, *Three Years in the Sixth Corps*, 401–2; De Forest, *A Volunteer's Adventures*, 172–90; J. Warren Kiefer to Mrs. Kiefer, September 20, 1864, Kiefer Papers; Kiefer, *Slavery and Four Years of War* (New York, 1900), II, 110–17; George N. Carpenter, *History of the Eighth Regiment, Vermont Volunteers, 1861–1865* (Boston, 1886), 177; *A Memorial of the Great Rebellion: Being a History of the Fourteenth Regiment New-Hampshire Volunteers* (Boston, 1882), 215, hereinafter cited as *Fourteenth New-Hampshire*. The best secondary descriptions are Stackpole, *Sheridan in the Shenandoah*, 194–231, and Pond, *Shenandoah Valley*, 157–67. In specific Confederate parlance, the meeting was known as the third battle of Winchester. Smaller engagements were fought in the vicinity in 1862 and 1863.

was with him when the center of the Union line reeled back in a seeming rout. The qualification is necessary because the accounts of participants differ as to the sequence of events after Sheridan decided that he would have to use Crook to save the day. At twelve-twenty, according to Crook's artillery chief, a careful reporter, Sheridan turned to the Eighth Corps leader and personally directed him to move his force to the front as quickly as possible. Crook, in his autobiography, said the same thing in more general language. He sent his whole staff flying back to hasten the advance, and Sheridan, to make sure that the job would be rushed, dispatched some of his own staff on the same errand.[7]

But Hayes, in a letter written a week after the battle, and his adjutant general, Russell Hastings, in a reminiscent work, said that Crook was at the Opequon ford when a staff officer from Sheridan came spurring down the road, presented Sheridan's compliments, and said that the commander wished Crook to move forward. Hastings supplied a colorful detail. He stated that Crook and Hayes and their staffs were lying in a clover field and when not observing the battle were engaged in a jesting conversation. But when the group saw Sheridan's messenger approaching every man sprang to his feet and each officer tightened his sword belt in anticipation of instant action.[8]

The discrepancies, like those in much of the war's literature, are impossible to reconcile. It is highly probable that Crook, a corps commander of combative instinct, rode to the front

---

[7] Du Pont, *Campaign of 1864*, 109–12; Schmitt (ed.), *George Crook*, 126.

[8] Hayes to Sardis Birchard, September 28, 1864, Hayes MS. Letters; Hastings, MS. Autobiography, "Battle of Opequon." A letter from J. T. Webb to his uncle, September 28, 1864, in Webb Family Correspondence, also states that the staff officer met Crook at the Opequon. The language of the letter is, however, similar to that of Hayes in his communication to Sardis Birchard, which suggests that this member of Lucy Hayes's family may have seen Hayes's letter before he wrote his own.

to be with his commander, and it is extremely improbable that he returned to the Opequon ford when by staying where he was he could receive directly any order Sheridan chose to give. Possibly Hayes and Hastings saw the staff officer deliver the march order to Duval and confused the division commander with Crook. Or perhaps the scene they thought they witnessed, or one something like it, occurred at some time after the Eighth Corps reached the field and somewhere along the battle line, maybe when Sheridan transmitted a specific instruction to Crook. The order the general sent to the ford merely directed the corps to move to the front. Sheridan could not be more particular until the Eighth was actually on the scene and ready to be disposed. As it happened, even the hard marchers of the mountains took a long time to traverse the Berryville gorge.

Although the corps started to march at a little past twelve-thirty, it did not emerge from the canyon until around two. Progress was maddeningly slow. The whole length of the passage was clogged with wounded, ambulances, and a large number of stragglers. Some of the wounded were walking to the rear and some were seeking care at a hastily set up field hospital, where the surgeons were beginning their grisly work of sawing off limbs, and many of both groups called to the men of the Eighth to hurry—that the Union line was at the point of breaking. If the division commanders, Thoburn and Duval, did not believe these warnings, they at least knew that they were not moving fast enough, and they finally ordered their units to get off the crowded road and march on either side of it. The troops picked up their march rate then, and they were not as likely to listen to the rumors of disaster at the front. They issued from the gorge in good spirits and to their delight saw Sheridan ride up to them. "Go for 'em, boys," the general shouted. The corps, which

had covered three miles in moving to the front, filed to the
right another three miles and took position on the right of
the Nineteenth Corps. It was now close to two-thirty.[9]

Sheridan directed the move to the right. What else he
ordered Crook to do became a matter of dispute between
the two generals. Crook himself claimed that Sheridan told
him only to take position next to Emory. Crook's artillery
chief said that he heard Sheridan say: "Crook, put in your
corps to support Emory and look well for the right flank."
But Sheridan wrote in his report that he instructed Crook
to use his force as a turning column, to find the enemy left
and break it, whereupon the commander would order a left
half-wheel of his own line to support the attack of the Eighth.
And Russell Hastings, who may have dramatized the story
of the delivery of the original march order to Crook but who
reliably described other aspects of the battle, related that
Sheridan, after directing Crook to find the enemy left, exclaimed: "Then strike and carry it at all hazards." Hastings
added that Sheridan further said that the two cavalry divisions
from Stephenson's Depot would soon arrive and would cooperate with Crook.[1]

The controversy hinges on a flank movement that Crook
executed at a crucial moment, and, according to the Eighth
Corps commander, on his own initiative. He had no express
direction to try a turning movement, Crook said, but in

---

[9] Hastings, MS. Autobiography; Patterson, MS. Diary, September 19, 1864;
Hayes to Mrs. Hayes, September 21, Hayes MS. Letters; *Official Records*,
XLIII, pt. 1, 401, Hayes's report. Hayes, in both his letter and his report,
fell into a bad error as to the time of the battle. He stated that the Eighth
Corps emerged from the gorge a little after noon and took position next
to the Nineteenth at one o'clock, placing the actions at about an hour and
a half before they occurred. His confusion on this point and the previous
one on the delivery of Sheridan's order to Crook illustrate that even a careful
observer writing soon after the event may incorporate inaccuracies in the
record.
[1] Schmitt (ed.), *George Crook*, 126–7; Du Pont, *Campaign of 1864*, 119–20;
Official Records, XLIII, pt. 1, 47; Hastings, MS. Autobiography.

obeying Sheridan's order to look well to his own right he
reconnoitered the Rebel left, found it vulnerable, and decided to attack. As related by Crook and his supporters, the
general placed Thoburn's First Division to the right and
rear of the Nineteenth Corps, from whence it shortly moved
forward at General Emory's request to occupy the right of
his line. Crook then moved with Duval's Second Division
far to the right and discovered that he lapped the Rebel left
flank. Immediately he sent Captain William McKinley of
his staff to Thoburn with special orders—Duval was going
to attack and Thoburn was to join him. McKinley, following
Crook's direction, next sought out Sheridan and informed
the commanding general that Crook was about to advance
and asked that he be supported by the whole Union line.[2]

It is a pretty story, plausible in parts, but it does not stand
up under examination. Interpreted literally, it would mean
that Sheridan brought the Eighth Corps up to the front
merely to strengthen his line for defensive purposes. He was
impelled into offensive action solely by Crook's bold seizure
of the initiative. But even if there were no counter evidence
this analysis is demonstrably wrong. Sheridan had come to
the field to fight, and he had not abandoned his plan just
because he had suffered a partial reverse. That he had lost
none of his aggressive spirit was evident by his actions after
Crook's force reached the field. He rode down the length of
the battle line shouting the good news. One auditor heard
him say: "Crook and Averell are on their left and rear—
we've got em bagged, by ——!"[3] The battle was, in fact, fought
exactly as Sheridan had originally planned to fight it, except

[2] Schmitt (ed.), *George Crook*, 127; Du Pont, *Campaign of 1864*, 119–21;
Official Records, XLII, pt. 1, 361, Crook's report. In his report Crook did not
go nearly as far as he did in later writings. From his language in this document, it would be impossible to tell who was directing operations.
[3] J. Warren Kiefer to Mrs. Kiefer, Kiefer Papers; Walker, *Vermont Brigade*,
101–2.

that the Eighth Corps was thrown to the enemy's left instead of to his right. Whatever Sheridan's exact language, it is obvious that he meant for Crook to strike the Rebel left and that the Eighth Corps leader so understood the order and that he proceeded to execute it with great competence.

Leaving Thoburn in his assigned position and under orders to attack at the sound of Duval's guns, Crook personally conducted the Second Division on its trek to the far right. The line of march led to the north and then to the west and finally turned south. Across fields and valleys and over wooded hills the men toiled, every one of them conscious that the outcome of the battle might depend on the time they made. Many remembered that in this immediate area, at Kernstown, the corps had suffered its worst defeat in the previous July, and they looked forward to wiping out that humiliation. Shortly after the turn to the south was made the sounds of firing on the main battle line became more audible, and Crook halted the division in a dense forest and formed it in line of battle. Hayes's First Brigade was to lead the way, with Johnson's Second following in support. The orders were to advance at a fast walk, to remain silent until within a hundred yards of the Confederate guns, and then to charge with a yell at full speed.[4]

As the division emerged from the cedar shelter, a line of skirmishers spread out to the front. Soon Rebel cavalry appeared to engage the skirmishers, and then enemy artillery shells began to drop in the ranks. But the blue ranks continued to move forward at the same steady and inexorable walking gait. In the military sense the Federals were proceeding blind. Nobody, not even Crook, knew the exact location of the Confederate left, and the ranking officers had

---

[4] Hastings, MS. Autobiography; Hayes to Mrs. Hayes, September 21, 1864, Hayes MS. Letters; *Official Records*, XLIII, pt. 1, 400.

only the most general notion of the terrain ahead. The attackers were following one of the simplest maxims of war—move
to the sound of the firing. But now this firing was swelling
in fury, a clear indication that the point of decisive contact
was near at hand. Somewhere off in those dark thickets
was the Rebel main line and the Rebel artillery. Hayes, riding
at the head of the lead brigade, judged that it was time to
begin the rush. He gave the order and the troops uttered a
great shout and swung forward at the double-quick step of
charging infantry.[5]

Bursting across a field under heavy fire, the First Brigade
struck a fringe of underbrush and went on. Now was the
moment for the final dash that would overrun the Rebel line
and bring victory. Suddenly, to their surprise and horror,
officers and men saw a creek before them and directly in their
front a slough, "a deep, miry pool" in Hayes's words, twenty
to thirty yards wide, slow-running and muddy and even to the
most unpracticed eye difficult to cross. The stream was Red
Bud Run, an affluent of the Opequon. The Federal officers
knew of its existence—Thoburn's division was posted south
of it—but even though Duval's division had crossed it in the
move to the right apparently neither Crook nor his subordinates had thought they would encounter its course again.
Least of all, nobody had known about the forbidding slough.[6]

On its bank the attackers now milled about in growing confusion, while from the other side the Confederates redoubled
their musket and artillery fire at the stationary blue target. It
was a critical moment in the battle, and it posed a difficult

---

[5] Comly, MS. Diary, September 21, 1864; Hastings, MS. Autobiography; Hayes
to Mrs. Hayes, September 21, Hayes MS. Letters.
[6] *Official Records*, XLIII, pt. 1, 400–1; Hayes to Mrs. Hayes, September 21,
1864, Hayes MS. Letters; Comly, MS. Diary, September 21. As is usually the
case with descriptions of Civil War terrain, statements on the width of the
slough differ, the highest estimate being forty to fifty yards.

decision for Hayes, the ranking officer on the scene. Hayes, a colonel and a brigade leader, would have to determine what to do, and what he did would control the course of Crook's flanking movement and ultimately the movements of the whole army. Down through the chain of command all day the orders had run, from army to corps and division headquarters, the orders that embodied the way generals thought battles should be fought, the orders that were supposed to move units according to a preconceived plan and to set places at set times; and at last, as was often the case in a Civil War battle, because of an accident, a stream that was not on somebody's map, the outcome had come to rest with a minor officer, a man who commanded no more than 1,200 men.

Hayes hardly hesitated. To hold the brigade on the creek was to court destruction; the Confederate guns would soon pound it to pieces. To retreat would be to violate orders and was unthinkable. There was only one possible course, and in the minute that he had for contemplation Hayes must have taken it by instinct. Somehow he had to get his men over the slough. Again by instinct, the reaction of the good infantry officer, he realized that if he sat his horse and ordered them to cross they would not do it, or would attempt it so feebly as to fail. They would have to be led. He spurred his mount into the morass and shouted: "Come on, boys." Some of the men plunged in after him, but others hung back. The regimental officers had caught the cue, however, and ran about crying that Hayes was nearly over and that the brigade must follow him. In the troops piled, struggling forward in the waist-deep water and through the clinging mud of the bottom. It was later reported that a number had drowned or suffocated, but those that died here were probably victims of the enemy fire that swept the surface. Midway across Hayes's horse became hopelessly mired, and the colonel abandoned him and proceeded, as he admitted to Lucy, "on all fours."

Hayes was the first man to reach the other side. But others were close behind him, his brigade and Johnson's Second, and soon appeared General Crook, who helped the unit officers rally the troops for the final charge.[7]

Little prodding was needed. Both officers and men, as if some spark of common knowledge had passed between them, realized that the battle was theirs. The whole of Duval's division arose, and without specific orders from their officers and with units from its two brigades intermixed, drove for the Rebel line. As Duval went in, Thoburn had heard the shout from the Second Division as its line neared the Red Bud and had sent his own division forward. Curiously, in this exultant moment Thoburn's men reacted in exactly the same way as Duval's—they anticipated orders. At one stage Thoburn directed a change of front, but before the order could be conveyed every man had faced and marched to the enemy's fire. His line advanced with Duval's, the two divisions eventually becoming as commingled as the units of Duval's division. Hayes aptly characterized the long and loose formation as a "crowd."[8]

In a headlong rush the charging Federal line bore down on the Confederates, who waited behind stone fences. The defenders put up a stiff resistance, and the Union losses were heavy. Among the first casualties was Colonel Duval, who fell badly wounded. Immediately Crook placed Hayes in command of the Second Division. Two men had brought Hayes his horse, and the new commander rode proudly ahead

---

[7] Hastings, MS. Autobiography; Comly, MS. Diary, September 21, 1864; Hayes to Mrs. Hayes, September 21, Hayes MS. Letters; F. M. Kelley to Hayes, December 22, 1886, Selected Soldiers' Letters; Du Pont, *Campaign of 1864*, 123. The slough, as Hayes found after the battle, was about a hundred yards long, and his line above and below it crossed without too much difficulty. He passed this information on to Lucy with an admonition never to show his letters outside the family: "No one knows a battle except the little part he sees."

[8] *Official Records*, XLIII, pt. 1, 368–9; Comly, MS. Diary, September 21, 1864; Hayes to Mrs. Hayes, September 21, Hayes MS. Letters.

of his troops as they neared the enemy works.[9] The attackers
went over the stone fences "pell mell," as Hayes put it. Back
about 500 yards the Rebels retired and took a position behind
another line of stone walls. But now there was no stopping
Crook's men. They outnumbered the Confederates, and their
right lapped the left and rear of the gray line. And a new
element had entered the battle on the Union side. Sheridan's
two cavalry divisions from Stephenson's, "that splendid
cavalry" Hayes called them, had suddenly appeared on the
weak Rebel left flank. Moving first at a trot and then at a
thunderous gallop, the horsemen smashed into the Confederate line just as the infantry attacked in front. The Rebels
broke, and the blue foot and horse soldiers piled after them in
frenzied excitement. A cavalry captain who knew Colonel
Comly paused to lean down from his steed's neck, embrace
and kiss the commander of the Twenty-third, and cry "Isn't
it glorious?" before riding on. The Confederates retreated
a mile before attempting another stand, but they had little
stomach to fight more and soon retired. In triumph the
Eighth Corps swarmed toward Winchester.[1]

When Crook's troops had marched off to the right earlier
in the afternoon, the rest of the army had stood at ease.
Sporadic fighting flared up now and then all along the line,
but Sheridan was holding back until he could hear from
Crook. The commanding general's exultant announcement of
Crook's movement had apprised the whole army of what was
coming, and officers and men waited impatiently for Crook's
attack to develop. Precisely at three o'clock the troops on the
main line heard the sound of heavy firing on the far right and

---

[9] Hayes in some notes written after the war, stated that the horse had been
wounded while mired in the slough, mortally it turned out, and he eventually had to abandon him; MS. in Hayes Library.
[1] Hayes to Mrs. Hayes, September 21, 1864, Hayes MS. Letters; *Official
Records*, XLIII, pt. 1, 401; Comly, MS. Diary, September 21; Keyes, *123rd
Regiment*, 91.

then a great shout. It was Crook's corps charging the first
enemy works. The noise of the battle rolled ever closer, and
finally some of the soldiers on the right of the line went out
to see if they could discover what was happening. They
never forgot the sight that greeted them—the Eighth Corps
emerging from the woods, its flags flying and its long line
tramping forward at the marching step, and, now with its
front cleared, in perfect alignment.[2]

The minute that Sheridan realized the success of Crook's
movement he rode down the front, his face aglow with the
flame of battle. Perspiration rolled from his forehead, and
his black charger was flecked with foam. Everywhere he
shouted the same order—go in. "Press them, General," he
cried to one officer, "they'll run." He need not have urged
anybody. The soldiers of the Army of the Shenandoah were
veterans, and they saw as clearly as Sheridan did that one
hard rush would dissolve the wavering enemy line. They had,
in fact, anticipated the order, as Crook's men had theirs
earlier, and the instant Sheridan gave the word they were off.
Like a huge crescent, as one participant put it, the Federal
line surged toward Winchester. It was not a battle any longer
but a chase. The Confederates, wearied and weakened by
hours of fighting and hemmed in in front and rear, offered
hardly any resistance. They surrendered or fled, the last of
them, a wild mass of fugitives, retreating through Winchester
and up the Valley pike. As the whooping blue hunters neared
the town, they noticed Sheridan riding with them. The general swung his hat above his head and shouted: "Boys, it's just
what I expected." The Sixth and Nineteenth corps made fast
time to Winchester, but the Eighth, which was closer when the
rush started, was there before them. It was fitting that the
corps which had done so much to make the victory complete

---

[2] Gould, *First Maine*, 496–8; De Forest, *A Volunteer's Adventures*, 186–7;
Carpenter, *Eighth Vermont*, 181; *Fourteenth New-Hampshire*, 22–3.

should be the first to enter the capital of the Valley. It was also fitting that the first unit of the Eighth to march in was the Second Division. Its new commander might have claimed with much justice that if any one man was responsible for the result he was that man. Colonel R. B. Hayes did nothing of the kind. When he came to think of it, modestly but foolishly he gave the credit to Crook.[3]

The sun was going down when the remnants of Early's army disappeared to the south. The exultant Federals stood on a victorious field. It was a moment of fierce and unrestrained joy. Later there would be a time to cast up the human costs of the victory, which were grievous, some 5,000 casualties, of whom nearly 700 were killed.[4] But now the soldiers wanted to do nothing but applaud their chiefs. They went wild with excitement when Sheridan rode down the line, accompanied by Wright, Emory, and Crook. Cheer after cheer rolled up to the darkening Valley sky, and after the generals had passed, the men threw their hats in the air and turned to hug one another in sheer elation.[5] If Colonel Hayes took any part in the ceremony, he did not record it. As soon as he could get his division in hand he marched it a few miles south of town and with quiet efficiency put it into camp.

---

[3] Stevens, *Three Years in the Sixth Corps*, 403–5; Walker, *Vermont Brigade*, 104; Carpenter, *Eighth Vermont*, 183–4; J. Warren Kiefer to Mrs. Kiefer, September 20, 1864, Kiefer Papers; Mason Tyler, *Recollections of the Civil War* (New York, 1912), 278; Hayes to Mrs. Hayes, September 21, Hayes MS. Letters.

[4] Irwin, *Nineteenth Army Corps*, 393; Pond, *Shenandoah Valley*, 168–9; *Official Records*, XLIII, pt. 1, 116, 123, 401. The losses by corps were as follows: Sixth, 1,699; Nineteenth, 2,074; Eighth, 794. The casualties in Hayes's division were 191, of whom 37 were killed. Early's losses are a matter of dispute. Usually estimated at 4,000, they may have been higher.

[5] Irwin, *Nineteenth Army Corps*, 392–3; Flinn, *Campaigning with Sheridan*, 195.

Chapter 14

Red September and Brown October

SHERIDAN'S HARVESTING" the poet called his effusion. A. J. H. Duganne, the author, had some reputation in his day. Boston-born, he lived and wrote in Philadelphia and New York before the war, and his verses and fiction won a wide audience. At the outbreak of hostilities he helped raise a New York regiment and as its lieutenant colonel went off to fight in Louisiana. His service began meritoriously enough but ended in capture and a Confederate prison, and upon his exchange he was so broken in health that he had to request a discharge. Returning to New York in 1864, he resumed his writing, and, exploiting the popular interest in the campaigns of that year, he concentrated on the production of war ballads. His tribute to Sheridan was composed in the turgid language he favored and was not particularly good verse. But in one very significant sense it caught the spirit of Sheridan's army—the bright exultation of the army in that autumn of victory and its terrible determination to bring stern retribution to the Shenandoah Valley. Duganne sang of that "Red September" and that "Brown October" when Sheridan "led out the war."

Sheridan did not seem to be leading out anything immediately after the encounter of September 19. Probably

[265]

wisely, he did not attempt a night pursuit of the Confederates. Early retreated rapidly up the Valley pike but, finding he was not being followed, slowed his march. But he kept going, allowing his weary troops only a short rest, and by early morning of the twentieth he had taken a strong position on Fisher's Hill, about twenty miles south of Winchester and two miles south of Strasburg. Sheridan, by contrast, did not put his army on the road until the morning, and then he marched in somewhat leisurely fashion fifteen miles to Cedar Creek. It was late in the afternoon before his lead units, the Sixth and Nineteenth corps, reached the crossings of the stream. They immediately moved to the other side, the Sixth forming to the right of the turnpike and the Nineteenth to the left. Sheridan posted his two larger corps knowing that the Confederates were watching his every move from a signal-and-observation station on the right of their line at Three Top Mountain. But when the Eighth Corps came up still later, he kept it concealed on the north bank. The Federal commander was resolved to give battle. He knew that at the Opequon he had struck the Confederates a damaging blow, and to keep the momentum of victory going he intended to strike them again. But until he had decided on a definite plan of operation he was not going to give away the location of every part of his army. His thinking was apparent to the subordinate officers. "We hide in woods after dark," Hayes noted in his diary.[1]

While his army was still moving up, Sheridan rode forward to examine the Confederate line. He saw a position of forbidding natural strength made even more formidable by fieldworks. At the point where Early had halted, the twenty-mile width of the Valley abruptly narrowed to limit the space

---

[1] Stackpole, *Sheridan in the Shenandoah,* 246–7; Pond, *Shenandoah Valley,* 173–5; Stevens, *Three Years in the Sixth Corps,* 409–10; Hayes, MS. Diary, September 20, 1864.

for maneuver of an army on the offensive. Here, at the edge of the north fork of the Shenandoah River, the Massanutten Mountains reared their lofty peaks and, stretching southward for thirty miles, divided the Valley into two parts. East of the range, and out of the area of operation, was the narrow Luray Valley. West of it was the wider but by military standards the still severely circumscribed Main Valley. From the Massanuttens on the east to Little North Mountain on the west the Main Valley was no more than five miles wide, and Early was entrenched across it. The Confederate right rested on the Massanuttens, which presented no passable gaps and which were in turn anchored to the Shenandoah River, and the left lay on Little North Mountain, less precipitous but still a rugged obstacle to an attacker. Between the mountain flanks on the ridge of Fisher's Hill was the main Confederate line, and a small stream called Tumbling Run ran past the foot of the ridge. Early considered his position virtually impregnable. His only fear was that his right might be turned through the Luray Valley, and to prevent such an eventuality he placed most of his cavalry to the east.[2]

What thoughts went through Sheridan's mind as he looked at the heights of Fisher's Hill are not known. He said later that he realized the position was too strong to attack frontally and he decided that night to take it in the left flank. But there is strong evidence that earlier in the afternoon, perhaps at the advice of General Wright, he toyed with the notion of a direct assault on the Confederate right. He discussed the movement with his three corps commanders. Wright and Emory approved it, but Crook warmly dissented and argued for a turning attack like the one that had brought victory on the Opequon. Sheridan, without making a decision, told the generals to meet him at his headquarters that evening.

---

[2] Walker, *Vermont Brigade*, 110–11; Irwin, *Nineteenth Army Corps*, 396–7; Du Pont, *Campaign of 1864*, 133–4.

To this second council Crook came accompanied by his division officers, Hayes and Thoburn. While the Eighth Corps commander welcomed all the support he could muster, he had brought Hayes along to perform a specific and important function. Taciturn by nature, Crook did not think he talked well or persuasively, and he felt handicapped in making a formal presentation of his views. Moreover, he had the West Pointer's inbred reluctance to speak out freely to a superior. He had developed a tendency, in situations like the present one, to call on Hayes to represent him, Hayes the civilian officer and lawyer who talked well and freely. So now Crook proposed that the Sixth and Nineteenth corps should occupy the enemy's attention in front while with his own corps he worked his way around the Rebel left on Little North Mountain, and then, turning to the commander of his Second Divison, he said: "Colonel Hayes, I want you to tell General Sheridan what you think of putting our men in on the enemy's front." Hayes began bluntly: "General, it would be simply murder." He went on to second Crook's plan, adding as a clinching point that the West Virginia troops had been climbing mountains for three years and could go over North Mountain with little difficulty.[3]

Sheridan was convinced. That night, as he said truthfully but not quite frankly in later statements, he decided to use Crook's corps to turn the Confederate left. The plan advanced by Crook and Hayes appealed to the army commander for another reason than that it would avoid a costly frontal assault. Sheridan had from the first set his sights on capturing or destroying Early's army, and Crook's scheme

[3] Sheridan, *Memoirs*, II, 35; Kennon, "Valley Campaign," *Papers of Military Historical Society of Massachusetts*, VI, 45–6; Du Pont, *Campaign of 1864*, 134; Schmitt (ed.), *George Cook*, 129–30; Hayes, two-page manuscript account of battle of Fisher's Hill, in Hayes Library, hereinafter cited as Hayes, "Fisher's Hill"; Williams, *Hayes*, I, 247–8; Lang, *Loyal West Virginia*, 334, note. In the quotation from Crook in Lang the military titles are abbreviated.

seemed to hold out the best prospect of accomplishing this end. If Crook could get in the Confederate left rear, then Wright and Emory could smash in from the front, and the Federals would have Early in a vise. To make the trap complete, to secure the double envelopment which was his dream, Sheridan sent most of his cavalry through the Luray Valley with orders to seize the roads that were Early's only escape route to the south. It was to be an exact repetition of the arrangement that had come so close to succeeding on the Opequon.

Having quickly settled on a plan, Sheridan characteristically proceeded to put it in motion with the greatest deliberation and the most careful attention to detail. He spent the whole day of the twenty-first in placing his army in position and instructing his officers as to the precise roles they were to play. This time, if preparation could prevent it, there would be no slip-up, no delaying change in plans that would give the enemy time to escape. As the success of Crook's movement, which in turn was the key to the success of the operation, would depend on secrecy and surprise, Sheridan decided not to advance the Eighth Corps until after darkness fell. Throughout the day Crook's troops remained concealed in the woods north of Cedar Creek. But the other two corps Sheridan shifted about with ostentatious display, moving them directly at Fisher's Hill. He had a twofold purpose. By seeming to menace the Confederate front he hoped to convince Early that the Federal attack would come at this point and that the whole blue army was before the ridge. At the same time, by pushing closer to the Confederate main line, he was getting the bulk of his force in a better position to cooperate with Crook when the moment arrived for the final rush. After hours of heavy skirmishing and by dusk the Sixth and Nineteenth corps had extended their line to within 700 yards of Fisher's Hill and to high ground that afforded a clear view of the Rebel works. The men of these corps had done their work. Now they could only wait for the morrow and for the appearance of Crook's troops far to the right on Little North Mountain.[4]

That night the Eighth Corps crossed Cedar Creek quietly and encamped in another wooded hiding place near Strasburg. Its men too looked forward to what the next day might bring, and with a particular tenseness, because they knew what their role was going to be. The Eighth was so small that news traveled fast through the ranks. And after the losses of the recent weeks the corps was below even its normal size— Hayes's division did not number much more than 3,000 and Thoburn's was only slightly larger.[5] The mountain troops were fully aware that because of their previous experience they had been selected to lead the movement on which the outcome of the battle would hang. With the hardened poise of veterans, they accepted the assignment without either recrimination or exultation. They were sure they would have to do some rough marching, and somewhere along the way they expected to encounter some hard fighting and suffer some losses. Before sunrise on the twenty-second they were up and moving toward North Mountain. Crook, fearful of prying Confederate eyes from the signal station on Three Top, marched the men in the cover of woods and ravines, even making the color bearers trail their flags to avoid detection. Progress through the dense cedar thickets was ex-

---

[4] Hayes, MS. Diary, September 21, 1864; Irwin, *Nineteenth Army Corps,* 397; Walker, *Vermont Brigade,* 113; Flinn, *Campaigning with Sheridan,* 199–200; Stevens, *Three Years in the Sixth Corps,* 410–11; Stackpole, *Sheridan in the Shenandoah,* 249–50.

[5] Hayes's estimate of the size of his division is in a letter to Mrs. Hayes, September 23, 1864, Hayes MS. Letters. With Hayes temporarily command-ing the Second Division, the direction of his First Brigade was now in the hands of Colonel Hiram F. Devol of the Thirty-sixth Ohio. Lieutenant Colonel Benjamin F. Coates led the Second Brigade; *Official Records,* XLIII, pt. 1, 129.

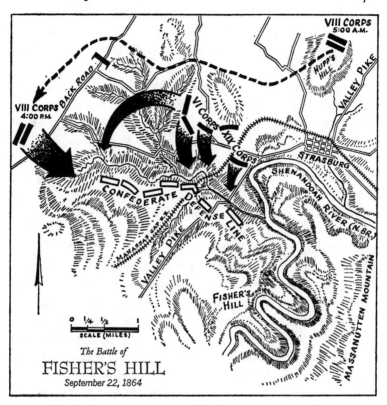

The Battle of
FISHER'S HILL
September 22, 1864

cruciatingly slow, and it became still slower as the troops
approached the timbered slope of the mountain.[6]

While the Eighth Corps was toiling forward, the camps of
the Sixth and the Nineteenth were astir with activity. Union
skirmishers moved down to the bank of Tumbling Run to
engage their gray counterparts, and Sheridan shifted a
division of the Sixth more to the right, partly to mislead
Early as to the point of attack and partly to place the division
so that it could act in conjunction with Crook. On Wright's

---

[6] Schmitt (ed.), *George Crook*, 130; Patterson, MS. Diary, September 22, 1864.

front a telescope had been mounted on a tripod, and at it Sheridan stayed for hours, sweeping the terrain from right to left and muttering frequently, as one soldier reported the words: "I'll get a twist on 'em, d—m 'em!" The general must have been surveying the Confederate line, for the march of Crook's column could be followed with the naked eye. Observers could plainly see the glint from the musket barrels of Crook's troops as they wound through the woods, and excitement mounted as it was realized that this was a version of the movement that had won at the Opequon. All along the front officers and men waited expectantly for the mountain corps to burst on the Confederate flank.[7]

They would have a long wait. Crook was going through a hard time on North Mountain. Until he reached the eastern face, he had marched his corps in column, with Hayes's division leading the way. Crook and Hayes rode in the advance, Hayes on a horse he had picked up from a teamster, an unprepossessing animal but one that could go anywhere a man could. But when he reached the slope of the mountain, Crook halted and brought up Thoburn's division alongside and to the left of Hayes's. He then marched both "by flank," so that when he faced them to the front he would have two lines of battle. It was a good formation to employ in advancing on an enemy known to be in close proximity, but it was not conducive to speed. Still the corps edged forward, over rocks and through underbrush, crossing the eastern side and then starting to descend. Crook and his officers found that their horses could not traverse the rugged path and had to dismount. But Hayes's team horse picked his way ahead with no trouble. At a point where Crook judged he had passed the enemy flank he swung his divisions to the left and front. Confederate pickets had spotted them now and were banging away, and batteries from the center of the Rebel line were

---

[7] Walker, *Vermont Brigade*, 116–18.

beginning to open fire. Crook gave the order to charge, and in a yelling line the whole corps sprang forward.[8]

In few battles of the war did the appearance of a flanking force have the immediate and total effect on an enemy army occasioned by the emergence of Crook's two divisions from the recesses of North Mountain. Early had considered his position impregnable, and while he had expected to be attacked he had not thought the blow would fall in this quarter. The Confederate leader had some of the qualities of a good general—energy and aggressiveness, notably—but he always tended to overlook an important detail. In this case he had neglected the vital factor of terrain. He had thought that the enemy would attack where he was strongest, on his right or front, whereas even a glance at the terrain should have told him that his left flank was the most vulnerable. Early had some 12,000 men on the field, none too many to hold a four-mile front, but if he had strengthened his force on the left a little more he would have prevented the debacle that now ensued.

Although the charge of the Eighth Corps packed plenty of punch, its impact was almost entirely psychological. Early's men, imbued with the confidence of their general, had felt wholly secure about their left, and when a horde of Yankees was reported on the rear of that flank it was too much to stand. This was the Opequon all over again. In an instant the dire news flashed down the length of the Confederate line, which began to fall off in pieces. The left flank broke immediately under the onslaught of the Federal attack. "They ran like sheep," said Hayes, uncharitably disregarding the confusion sweeping the gray ranks. As Crook's troops rushed down the mountain, their lines and units became merged and intermixed, as at the Opequon, and the soldiers, in effect, took over the direction of the battle. At one point Colonel

---

[8] Schmitt (ed.), *George Crook*, 130–2; Hayes, "Fisher's Hill."

Thoburn attempted to halt his division and align it in some order. His efforts were hopeless. "The bold, restive spirit" of the men could not be restrained, Thoburn wrote. While he was stopping some, others would break away and take after the enemy. "I had to abandon the idea of good order and lines," Thoburn admitted, "and let them go ahead." Colonel Hayes did not record that he tried to hold his men back. Knowing what the spirit of the volunteers could accomplish when aroused, he probably cheered them on.[9]

Crook's corps had reached the rear of the Rebel flank at about three-thirty, and it started its charge shortly before four. The anxious watchers on the Union line below heard the now familiar yell that the mountain troops emitted in battle and the rattle of musketry, and then they saw Crook's line emerge from the woods. Plainly visible was a color bearer waving a flag over a captured battery. Immediately staff officers from corps and division headquarters, shouting the news, galloped down the line with orders for a general advance. What followed was again reminiscent of the scene on the Opequon. The army moved forward, responding to the directions of its generals, it is true, but also moving because of its own grasp of the situation and on its own volition. The men understood perfectly what they had to do and probably would have done it without orders. In the apt words of one participant, each soldier became for a period his own commander. The whole line of the Sixth and Nineteenth corps suddenly surged forward and up the rough side of Fisher's Hill. Some artillery fire struck the attackers, but they met no real resistance and when they reached the crest of the ridge they saw the reason—the Rebel infantry was fleeing south as fast as it could travel.[1]

---

[9] Hayes to Mrs. Hayes, September 23, 26, 1864, Hayes MS. Letters; *Official Records*, XLIII, pt. 1, 369–71, Thoburn's report 402–3, Hayes's report. For other reports on this phase of the battle see ibid., 48, 363–4, 378–9.

[1] Walker, *Vermont Brigade*, 118–20; *Fourteenth New-Hampshire*, 249–50; Stevens, *Three Years in the Sixth Corps*, 411–13; Flinn, *Campaigning with*

Only momentarily did the Federals pause, and then all three corps, the men again animated by that common impulse to action which was becoming a characteristic of this army, leaped to the pursuit. A few units, seasoned outfits that knew what would be required of them, took some time to prepare. The men of the Twenty-third Ohio went back to the point where they had begun their original charge and where they had left their knapsacks, and there they divested themselves of every item that might impede their action, even their coats. "They stripped as if for the prize ring," Colonel Comly observed admiringly. But most of the troops simply went forward as they were and as best they could, moving, as one of them put it, in "a confused delirious mass." In the van rode Sheridan, burning with the excitement of battle and exhorting the men with mighty shouts. "Run, boys, run!" he cried. "Don't wait to form! Don't let 'em stop!" When some soldiers told him they were too tired to run, he answered: "If you can't run, then holler!" For eight miles, to Woodstock, and even after the sun sank the jubilant victors pushed the chase, the great "Fox Chase," as the men of the Twenty-third insisted on calling the battle. But Early managed to make his escape in the darkness. To Sheridan's intense chagrin, his cavalry, suffering under inept leadership, failed to plant itself across the Rebels' line of retreat, and for the second time the Union commander was denied the complete victory he so thirsted for. The Confederate army of the Valley was badly shaken, but it was still intact as a fighting force and still to be reckoned with.[2]

Sheridan, 200–1; J. Warren Kiefer to Mrs. Kiefer, September 23, 1864, Kiefer Papers; Kiefer, *Four Years of War*, 120–3; De Forest, *A Volunteer's Adventures*, 191–203; *Official Records*, XLIII, pt. 1, 26–7, 47–8, 152–4, 282–4.

[2] Walker, *Vermont Brigade*, 120; Comly, MS. Diary, September 22, 1864; Hayes, MS. Diary, September 23. The capacity of Sheridan's army to analyze situations and anticipate orders, as demonstrated at the Opequon and Fisher's Hill, was a rare phenomenon. Units in other armies did the same thing, but it was unusual for a whole army to possess the gift. The explanation lay partly in the smallness of the Valley army, which invested it

Sheridan's dissatisfaction with the result attested that he had that most vital ingredient of the great battle captain—the desire to finish an enemy off. Disappointed as he was that he had not accomplished his purpose, he still had ample reason to feel proud of what he had been able to do. It was a lustrous achievement. In two battles he had inflicted stunning defeats and heavy losses on the enemy. At Fisher's Hill the Union casualties were only 528, while Early's were at least 1,200.[3] Thus in the dual engagement of "Red September" each army had suffered losses of about 5,000 men, but Early had lost many more in proportion to his total and such attrition he could hardly stand. Sheridan had done more than deplete Confederate manpower. He could also show an impressive list of material captured—flags, military stores, and guns, sixteen of the latter falling to him at Fisher's Hill alone. Lastly, the Union commander had scored important territorial gains. At the opening of the campaign Early had been at Winchester. After Fisher's Hill the Confederate leader retreated to a point below Harrisonburg, where Sheridan would shortly follow him. The military front had been moved over seventy miles southward, and from the Potomac boundary a hundred miles. The whole North exulted at the news from the Valley, and Sheridan's victories would help return Lincoln to a second term in November.

These were the immediate results of the September campaign, and they were important. But there was something perhaps even more significant that came out of the late

---

with a remarkable cohesion and facility to communicate. Possibly because of its size, this was an army with a small-unit psychology—its regimental, brigade, and division commanders had the quick perceptions and the individual independence of company officers.

[3] Irwin, *Nineteenth Army Corps*, 400; Stackpole, *Sheridan in the Shenandoah*, 256. Early's losses were doubly serious because 1,100 of them were prisoners and hence would not return. Of the Union corps, the Sixth had casualties of 238, the Nineteenth of 114, and the Eighth of 162. Hayes's division lost 83 men, half of the total of Crook's corps.

battles, something of particular meaning for the future, for Sheridan the leader who still had to lead, and for his army, which still had to fight. Sheridan had demonstrated high qualities of generalship at both the Opequon and Fisher's Hill. He had made good plans and had executed them with a sure hand, and he had fought each battle almost as exactly as he had planned it. Although the Opequon was accounted the bigger victory, Fisher's Hill was a better-managed battle. In the latter encounter Sheridan had seized the initiative, and he held it throughout, shaping the battle completely as he desired it, and if his cavalry had not failed him he might well have destroyed the enemy army.

His soldiers knew now that Phil Sheridan was a general. They had viewed him when he first took the command with some skepticism. He was, after all, a cavalryman, and although undoubtedly a hard fighter, what did he know about handling infantry? Their original impression prevailed during the weeks of maneuvering around Halltown. They liked it that Sheridan always rode with them on the marches, and they responded to the dramatic leadership that he gave them. But they continued to think of him as no more than a dashing leader. Then came the Opequon and Fisher's Hill, and suddenly they saw Sheridan in a new light. He was still aggressive and dashing, but now he was more. He was a careful and deliberate planner and a master of strategy and tactics, a solider who knew his business. He would fight his men in battle, but he would never waste them. The Army of the Shenandoah had gained a respect for its commander that it would not lose. That feeling would a month later save the general and the army in the most dangerous crisis both ever faced.

One unit in the army dissented in part from the glow of admiration for Sheridan, and, curiously, it was the corps which had had the most to do with winning the victories that had made Sheridan's reputation. The Eighth Corps had some reservations, and none of its members expressed them with more vehemence than Colonel Hayes. That the men of Crook's command should react as they did was not surprising. The mountain troops had come into the Valley with something of a chip on their shoulders. Fresh from the small war of West Virginia, they expected that the Sixth and Nineteenth corps would patronize them. Nor were they disappointed. The men of the two larger corps boasted loudly of their larger experiences and sneered openly at the petty past of the Eighth. Crook's men, for their part, looked on the critics as dandies who would not fight when the going was rough. Bitterly the troops of the Eighth remembered Snicker's Ford and the failure of Wright's corps to support them. After the Opequon and Fisher's Hill the Sixth and the Nineteenth were disposed to forget and forgive. Being fighting men, they had to admire the bravery of Crook's corps, and at Fisher's Hill they expressed their feelings by emitting a mass cheer for the mountain men as they passed them in the final charge.

The Eighth, however, was not inclined to be so generous. Although its officers and men basked in the evident admiration felt for them, the corps was still a sensitive and edgy outfit, quick to take offense at slights real or imagined. Although it liked the admiration, it thought that it ought to have even more and suspected that the esteem would not last very long. In large part, its reactions were the product of its past experience and its size. Accustomed to operating as virtually an independent unit in West Virginia, the Eighth was not yet used to working with other units as a part of an army. It could have made the transition more easily had it not been so small. Numbering only a little over 7,000 at its maximum, the aggregation that previously had styled itself the Army of West Virginia or the Army of Kanawha and that was now called the Eighth Corps was in reality nothing more than a conventional division. Its anomalous status provoked a mood of jealous suspicion—people were laughing at the little Eighth or, worse, were ignoring it. The corps was convinced that consistently it was denied proper recognition in the official reports and in the press. About the press the corps was right, but its explanation was wrong. The Sixth and the Nineteenth did receive better publicity, for the simple reason that nearly all of their regiments were from the Northeast and that therefore the metropolitan journals of that section sent numerous correspondents to cover the action of the Valley army. Most of the regiments of the Eighth were from Ohio and West Virginia, and although the Cincinnati papers had some reporters in the field they were comparatively few, and in any case the corps did not get much attention in the New York press, where it counted most.

Hayes was extremely bitter about the reporters. All of them were with the two larger corps and the cavalry, he complained to Uncle Sardis. "Gen Crook has nobody to write him or his Command up. They are of course lost sight of." Oddly, Hayes, ordinarily a man of sharp perception and judicious temperament, did not think to analyze why the correspondents were so distributed. Like everybody else in the Eighth, he simply regarded it as the result of a conspiracy—a plot to discredit Crook. That an officer of Hayes's standing should let himself get involved in this kind of inter-corps bickering was not surprising. Sniping at other units and officers—the military version of the political game—was a favorite and familiar avocation at every headquarters in every army. Hayes came to the business late because never before had he been for any appreciable period in any army large enough to nourish such emotions. Now he was following a natural course, marking up another progression in his development as an officer. But it was not a progression that reflected much credit on his character or his judgment.

Hayes's reaction went beyond the normal bounds of personal or unit sensitivity. He was not disturbed at any neglect of his own deeds, and only in a secondary way was he concerned with the reputation of the corps. True, he wanted it known that the Eighth was responsible for the September victories and that *his* brigade had led the attack at the Opequon and that *his* division had led again at Fisher's Hill. But these matters were only incidental to the main point— the Eighth Corps had been able to do what it did because it was commanded by Crook. Crook had planned and executed the great flanking movements at both battles. He was "the brains of this army," but now people were trying to strip the laurels from him. As for Sheridan, he was all right, honest and brave, but: "Intellectually he is not Gen Crook's equal." Much of this was palpable and demonstrable nonsense, as Hayes must have known if he had taken time to reflect. Some of it he picked up from talk at Crook's headquarters, but essentially it was a product of his own making, an outgrowth of his inordinate worship of his superior which tended to blind him to reality. He manifested his feeling in another way two weeks later when he received news of the birth of a son. He insisted on calling the boy George Crook Hayes.[4]

Hayes composed his thoughts on Crook and Sheridan while the army was resting at Harrisonburg after its pursuit of Early from Fisher's Hill. He had little time to write anything during the three days that the army pushed up the fifty-mile stretch of the Valley pike to Harrisonburg. The Federals moved fast and kept on the heels of the retreating Confederates almost to New Market. Sheridan hoped he could bring Early to bay somewhere along the route, but the Confederate leader obviously had no intention of accepting battle. When Early veered off the pike below New Market and moved to the east,

---

[4] Hayes to Sardis Birchard, September 26, 28, 1864. This son, the second of Hayes's war-born children, survived the war by only a year.

Sheridan gave up the chase and marched to Harrisonburg, reaching there on the twenty-fifth. Early hurried through Keezletown to Port Republic, where he paused momentarily, and then continued on almost to Brown's Gap on the Blue Ridge. "Old Jube" was not trying to escape over the mountains, as some of the Federal observers concluded, but was placing himself in a position to receive reinforcements. Lee was returning the division he had taken away earlier in the month, and Early was merely moving to meet it. This unit, some 3,800 strong, arrived on the twenty-sixth, and it, together with additional cavalry forces that came in, about made up for the losses in the two recent battles. Aggressive Early began to think in offensive terms again.[5]

While Early was reorganizing his army after its long retreat, Sheridan at Harrisonburg was letting his rest from its long pursuit. The men needed a respite, and Sheridan let them lay up in camp for ten days. "A glorious rest" Colonel Comly called it, although both officers and men suffered from the lack of certain supplies. The water in the area was inadequate to support the needs of such a mass of men, barely enough being available for cooking purposes. Over the long line of communication back to the lower Valley the transport trains brought up plenty of food but little else. The men would have welcomed particularly a chance to get into fresh clothes. Still they were happy in this moment of peace stolen from the rush of war, and they manifested their feelings in pathetic attempts to recapture the ways of peace. They wanted something to love. Comly noticed that every man in the Twenty-third who could get one had a pet dog. Some had sheep or lambs which they led on a rope during a march, and one soldier carried a rooster around with him. They would

---

[5] Hayes, MS. Diary, September 23–25, 1864, brief entries of the marches; Irwin, *Nineteenth Army Corps*, 401–2; Flinn, *Campaigning with Sheridan*, 203.

try to run down even rabbits or raccoon. "They are all crazy after children," Comly observed, "petting them and 'hovering' them as tenderly as mothers."[6]

Colonel Hayes, when he was not agitating himself about Crook's reputation, was also happy during this interlude. He was satisfied with his part in the campaign, and he was more than flattered that he had Crook's trust. Crook demonstrated his regard in unmistakable fashion. Although Duval was expected to return to the army when he recovered from his wound, the command of his division was temporarily open. It was an assignment a brigadier general could claim, and a number of officers of this grade on inactive duty at Harper's Ferry promptly asked for the division. One of them even came to Harrisonburg with his staff to apply personally. Crook told him the division was satisfactorily officered and to get back to Harper's Ferry. Assured that he would retain the command until Duval could again take it, Hayes relaxed in his tent quarters. He read whatever novels and magazines he could lay hands on and in letters home speculated on the military situation. The present campaign was about ended, he concluded, and undoubtedly Sheridan would soon move his army back down the Valley to some defensible line.[7]

Hayes had correctly read the thoughts of the Union commander. There was little that Sheridan could hope to accomplish on the end of his extended line at Harrisonburg. He did send his cavalry south to Waynesborough to destroy the Virginia Central bridge at that point, a thrust which caused Early to move to Waynesborough and then to Mount Sidney, south of Harrisonburg on the Valley pike. Early's exact location and his purpose occasioned Sheridan some perplexity. The Union commander thought, as he wrote Grant, that

---

[6] Hayes, MS. Diary, September 26, 27, 1864; Comly, MS. Diary, September 26, 28.

[7] Hayes to Sardis Birchard, September 27, 1864, and to Mrs. Hayes, October 1, 2, Hayes MS. Letters.

Early had retired behind the Blue Ridge or, if he had not, that he would head for the mountain barrier if attacked. Grant hoped that Sheridan himself would see fit to cross the Blue Ridge to Charlottesville and Gordonsville and wreck the railroad complex in that region. But the Valley commander vetoed the idea, arguing that he could not supply his army on such an expedition. The Valley campaign was in effect ended, and the most effective way to close it out was to destroy the economic resources of the region. Then the army should retire behind Cedar Creek. On this line Crook's corps alone could throw back any offensive the Rebels would be able to mount, and the Sixth and Nineteenth corps and most of the cavalry could rejoin the Army of the Potomac. Grant acceded to the wishes of his general on the spot, although with some misgivings. The supreme commander thought that if Sheridan occupied in the Valley a force equal to his own he would be doing as much service as if he brought his own force to before Richmond. Grant also doubted that Sheridan was retaining enough troops to hold his position, and he finally instructed Little Phil to keep the Nineteenth Corps, sending only the Sixth east.[8]

The Army of the Shenandoah started on its return march October 6. As it moved down the pike, its way was lit day and night by the flames from burning barns, grain stacks, fields, and mills. Sheridan was carrying out with exacting detail Grant's instructions to leave the Valley a "barren waste." This was the "Brown October." "This valley will feed and forage no more Rebel armies," Hayes wrote. "It is completely and awfully devastated. . . ." Most of the work was done by the cavalry, which fanned out in a wide arc behind the infantry, but some infantry regiments were allocated to support the horsemen. The Twenty-third drew one of these

---

[8] *Official Records*, XLIII, pt. 2, 187, 196, 209–10, 249–50, 266, 272–3, 307–8, 327; Pond, *Shenandoah Valley*, 192–9.

assignments and possibly because it had absorbed the ideals of its former commander disliked it intensely. Colonel Comly described some of the scenes that ensued as pitiful and said that they fairly broke his heart. "We executed the orders as carefully and tenderly as possible," Comly recorded, burning only stores of military value, "but I hate none the less to have such duty to perform. . . . We ought to enlist a force of damned scoundrels for such work." As for Hayes himself, he said little about the devastation except to note instances of it briefly in his diary. But in one entry, referring to an order of Sheridan's to destroy all the houses along a five-mile stretch of road from whence somebody had fired at the soldiers, Hayes wrote: "not according to my views or feeling." Perhaps he had reached a point where he could no longer bear to contemplate the horrors of war.[9]

When Early at Mount Sidney learned that Sheridan was retiring, he put his own army in motion down the Valley pike. The recently reinforced gray cavalry caught up to Sheridan's cavalry at Tom's Brook on the ninth, and a spirited little battle followed. Sheridan's riders, stimulated by orders from Sheridan to show some aggressiveness and supported by two regiments from Hayes's division, drove back the Rebels with heavy losses. The affair strengthened Sheridan's conviction that he would not be bothered by anything more than enemy cavalry. On the next day the army crossed Cedar Creek and occupied the high ground on the north bank, the Eighth Corps forming on the east of the pike and the Nineteenth on the west. Sheridan directed the Sixth to march to Front Royal, where it would take the rails over the mountains. "I believe that a rebel advance down this valley will not take place," Sheridan assured Grant.[1]

---

[9] Hayes to Mrs. Hayes, October 10, 1864, Hayes MS. Letters; Comly, MS. Diary, October 8; Hayes, MS. Diary, October 4, 8.

[1] Hayes, MS. Diary, October 9, 10, 1864; Hayes to Mrs. Hayes. October 10, Hayes MS. Letters; *Official Records*, XLIII, pt. 2, 395–6.

Hayes agreed with his commander that the Confederates were not much of a threat any more. In camp at Cedar Creek the colonel gave his main attention to supervising the taking of the soldier vote for the Ohio elections. He was delighted with the results. The state regiments in his division rolled up 1,015 votes for the Union-Republican ticket, while giving only 53 to the Democrats.[2] In the elections at home his own candidacy for Congress was at stake. He had not known, and would have been embarrassed if he had, that earlier his friends had asked President Lincoln to promote him to brigadier general to enhance his chances. At it turned out, Hayes did not need the help of this artificial arrangement. He won handily, amassing a majority of 1,700. His reaction to the news of the victory was characteristic. He was pleased, he told Lucy, but primarily for "general reasons." He took more "particular gratification" for winning good opinions in "the more stirring scenes" occurring around him. "My share of *notoriety* here is nothing at all, and my *real* share of merit is also small enough, I know," he conceded, "but the consciousness that I am doing my part in these brilliant actions is far more gratifying than anything the election brings me." He had no intention of claiming his seat until the military crisis had passed.[3]

While Hayes the volunteer officer was busying himself with the politics of war, Early the professional soldier was marching down the Valley pike. Aggressive by nature and emboldened by his reinforcements, the Confederate leader was eager for a chance to resume the offensive. On October 12 he heard that a part of Sheridan's army had gone to Grant's, and he pushed on with new hope. The next day he occupied

---

[2] Hayes, MS. Diary, October 11, 1864; Hayes to Scott Cook, October 12, Hayes MS. Letters.

[3] Edgar Conkling and thirty-two others to Lincoln, September 28, 1864, manuscript in Hayes Library; Hayes, MS. Diary, October 18; Hayes to Mrs. Hayes, October 21, Hayes MS. Letters.

the heights south of Cedar Creek. From one of the ridges he spied a body of Federal infantry lolling at ease in a field below—it was Thoburn's division resting between marches on a scout—and he could not resist letting one of his batteries lob some shells at the men. The Federals scattered hastily but soon re-formed and advanced, and a brisk skirmish ensued before Early retired to Fisher's Hill. Rashly the Confederate had advertised his presence before he had decided on any definite plan of action.[4]

The news that Early was in his front in strength and obviously champing for battle caused Sheridan to reconsider his analysis of the strategic situation. Other influences were working at the same time to alter his thinking. Grant, as tenacious in pursuing an idea as in pushing a foe, had renewed his suggestion that Sheridan should try to strike for Charlottesville. On the day that Early made his dramatic appearance, Sheridan had written Halleck that if he were going to have to go to Charlottesville he would have to retain the Sixth Corps. Early's presence decided Sheridan. With Grant's concurrence, he directed the Sixth to return from Front Royal. When it arrived, Sheridan placed it to the rear of the Eighth and the Nineteenth to act as a reserve. To add to the general's trouble, Halleck and Secretary Stanton besought him to come to Washington to hear their ideas about the strategy that should be employed in the Valley. Suddenly the campaign that was supposed to have ended seemed to be flaring to life again, and Colonel Hayes would see some more of the stirring scenes he had written about before he would see the halls of Congress.[5]

---

[4] Hayes, MS. Diary, October 13, 1864; Comly, MS. Diary, October 13; Hayes to Mrs. Hayes, October 15, Hayes MS. Letters.

[5] *Official Records*, XLIII, pt. 2, 339, 355, 363.

Chapter 15

Surprise at Cedar Creek

THE EIGHTEENTH of October was, even for the Shenandoah Valley in the autumn, a day of exceptional beauty. A golden and mellow sun shone on the Union camps at Cedar Creek, warming the air, which was yet pleasantly crisp, and softening the atmosphere with a delicate haze that hardly obscured the outlines of the mountains stretching to every horizon. The Federal soldiers lolled in their lines, confident that they were secure from any attack and happy over the issuance of fresh uniforms and the promise of being paid in the near future. An unusually large mail arrived in the afternoon and was distributed to the appreciative men. Shortly after five the sun went down in a crimson glow and sudden darkness followed, but at eight a full moon came out to light up the scene. The evening was still and mild, and Sheridan's troops remained outside to enjoy it. Officers sat around fires smoking their pipes and chatting. The enlisted men gathered in groups around a fiddler or flutist comrade and sang the songs of home. Some lay on the grass studying the stars or the heights to the south, the Massanuttens and Fisher's Hill, where Early's army was supposed to be resting. Around ten o'clock soldiers from a New York regiment thought they saw lights flashing from the Confederate signal station on Three Top Mountain and speculated that the Rebels must be up to something, but they figured that their officers must have noted the odd sight and did not report it—and anyway it was after taps and too late to worry about an enemy who had been twice whipped. The army retired, and while it slept, toward morning, a dense fog arose from Cedar Creek and the Shenandoah River and enveloped the fields on either side of both streams.[1]

Sheridan was sleeping elsewhere, and not as easily as his army. On the sixteenth he had proceeded with a part of his cavalry to Front Royal, from whence, after sending the riders south to strike the Virginia Central Railroad, he intended to go to Washington to attend the conference that Stanton and Halleck so ardently desired. Before he could depart, he received a dispatch from General Wright, whom he had left in command at Cedar Creek, stating that Union signalmen had deciphered a message from Three Top indicating that Early had been heavily reinforced. Although Sheridan suspected that the news was a deliberate deception, he was still worried that it might be true. He reluctantly decided to continue to Washington, but he sent the cavalry back to Cedar Creek and warned Wright to be on the alert. At the capital Sheridan concluded his business quickly—he convinced Stanton and Halleck it was impractical for him to operate toward Charlottesville—and entrained for Martinsburg, reaching there by dark on the seventeenth. The next morning he started for Winchester and on arriving late in the afternoon sent a staff officer to Cedar Creek to report on the situation. The officer returned with an assurance that all was quiet. Although he thought that he should be with his troops and was vaguely disturbed, Sheridan retired for the night con-

---

[1] A. B. Nettleton, "The Famous Fight at Cedar Creek," in *Annals of the War*, 658; H. M. Pollard, "Recollections of Cedar Creek," in *War Papers and Personal Reminiscences, 1861–1865. Missouri Commandery of the Military Order of the Loyal Legion of the United States* (St. Louis, 1892), I, 279; James Franklin Fitts, "In the Ranks at Cedar Creek," in *Galaxy* (1866), I, 536; George Haven Putnam, *Memories of My Youth, 1844–1865* (New York, 1914), 365–6; Irwin, *Nineteenth Army Corps*, 417, note.

fident that Wright could handle any trouble which might develop. He was about fifteen miles from Cedar Creek.

Sheridan was basing his confidence on a conviction that the Confederates had been too weakened by the recent battles to mount a dangerous attack. He could not have believed that the Rebels would restrain themselves because of the natural strength of his position. Although Cedar Creek was an obvious line for a force attempting to hold the lower Valley, it was not, as Sheridan well knew, a particularly defensible site. Here the creek made a big bend to the right as it flowed south to join the north fork of the Shenandoah. The blue army was encamped within the bend, on the north (or east) bank, the left, Crook's corps, resting at the confluence of the creek and the river; the center, the Nineteenth Corps, stretching to the right of the Valley pike; and the right, the Sixth Corps, touching the creek again. The pike constituted a gap between Emory and Crook, and Meadow Brook, running parallel to the pike, caused a similar separation between Emory and Wright. The three corps were thus positioned in echelon, the Nineteenth to the right and rear of the Eighth, and the Sixth to the right and rear of the Nineteenth, with all of them facing in a general southerly direction. The creek in front of them, although its banks were high, was fordable along practically its whole course. On the other side wooded ravines concealed the enemy from sight and offered hidden approaches to the Federal line, and because Early's position on Fisher's Hill was only five miles from the creek the Federals could not throw forward pickets to ascertain the intentions of the Rebels.

To General Wright, nervously aware that there were Confederates out in those murky woods, it seemed that an attack, if one came, would strike his right, and on this flank he accordingly placed almost the whole of his cavalry force. His front, held by the Nineteenth Corps and protected by entrenchments, was so strong that Early would never risk an assault against it, Wright judged. He was equally unconcerned about his left, even though it was occupied only by the numerically weak Eighth Corps. The left was safe because of its protecting terrain, the engineers assured Wright, who readily accepted their decision. It seemed so correct. In this sector the Shenandoah River, flowing northeasterly, swept closely past the precipitous northern shoulder of the Massanuttens; and around that rugged slope no flanking enemy force could possibly work its way. If Wright was guilty of the common military sin of believing what he wanted to believe, he was no more culpable than Sheridan. It was the commanding general, after all, who had thus aligned the army, and he too must have felt that the left was safe.

Everybody in the Union high command was, in fact, indulging himself in some wishful thinking, and none more ardently than George Crook. First of all, he had posted his corps, in what was for him a curiously careless fashion. The First Division, Thoburn's, occupied a hill overlooking Cedar Creek, a mile in advance of Crook's camp. Although the division was strong in front, where crude entrenchments had been erected, its flank toward the river was weak, and it was in a dangerously exposed position. Farther back, in the vicinity of the camp, and separated from Thoburn by a ravine was Hayes's Second Division. Back of Hayes was a small provisional brigade under Colonel J. H. Kitching temporarily attached to Crook. Neither Hayes nor Kitching enjoyed the protection of fieldworks. Crook himself was at Belle Grove plantation, the site of Sheridan's headquarters and a mile from his camp. Thus the two divisions of the corps were divided, with considerable distance and a ravine between them; Thoburn's division was isolated and beyond support if attacked; Hayes's division was unfortified and vulnerable to a flank assault; and the corps commander, the only man who might have brought some order to this disordered situation, was not on the immediate scene.[2]

But corps commander Crook took a strangely detached view of the whole security problem, then and later. Security was the business of the cavalry, he seemed to think, and as he did not have enough riders to patrol his line he felt no responsibility. It was true that his cavalry force was small. A part of it was operating by Sheridan's orders in the Luray Valley, and only one brigade was with the corps, posted two miles below the mouth of Cedar Creek, poorly located either to report information or to screen Crook's front. It was also true that Wright, obsessed with the notion that his right might be attacked, erred in placing his cavalry, two divisions, on the right flank instead of distributing some of them on the left. But none of this relieved Crook of the obligation to take some precautions on his own, the kind that even an ordinarily alert infantry general would have seen to in the known presence of an enemy. Crook took almost no precautionary measures. He seems to have disposed his pickets poorly, placing them only a short distance in front of his camp and throwing none below Cedar Creek. The pickets themselves felt no more urgency than their general, and many of them apparently fell asleep toward morning.

Crook was more than an ordinarily alert officer, but on this occasion he was far below par. Like everybody else in the Union command, he was deceiving himself with the assumption that the Confederates would do what they were supposed

[2] De Forest, *A Volunteer's Adventures*, 204–6; Irwin, *Nineteenth Army Corps*, 413–15; Putnam, *Memories*, 361–3; Du Pont, *Campaign of 1864*, 142–3; Morton, *Story of Winchester*, 171; Walker, *Vermont Brigade*, 131–2; Fitts, "In the Ranks at Cedar Creek," *Galaxy*, I, 535; Kennon, "Valley Campaign," *Papers of Military Historical Society of Massachusetts*, VI, 51; Benjamin W. Crowninshield, "Cedar Creek," ibid., 161–5; Hazard Stevens, "The Battle of Cedar Creek," in *Civil War Papers, Military Order of the Loyal Legion, Massachusetts Commandery* (Boston, 1900), I, 185–6; E. D. Hadley, *Cedar Creek* (Des Moines, 1898), 4–5.

to do—which was to retreat. That day Crook had sent out a brigade reconnaissance under Colonel Thomas M. Harris of the First Division. Harris went as far as Hupp's Hill, where Early had first encamped when he moved up before he retired to Fisher's Hill. Finding a deserted camp, Harris reported that Early had probably withdrawn up the valley. Crook, assuming that Harris had gone all the way to Fisher's Hill, transmitted the assuring news to Wright at nine that night. Not quite convinced, Wright decided to send more patrols out in the morning. Probably much more receptive to the good news was the Eighth Corps. Harris's men, returning to camp, must have talked about their scout, and in the small corps the word would have spread fast. Officers and men turned in to their bunks with a comfortable feeling of safety.[3]

That Crook was affected by the prevailing mood was demonstrated by his reaction to an odd incident that occurred during the night. His Officer of the Day, while making the rounds, heard some noise beyond the picket line and went out to investigate. He was captured by lurking Rebels before he could give the alarm. In recounting the episode later, Crook gave no indication that he knew about the officer's misadventure or, if he did know, that he was worried about it. This was a pretty casual dismissal of something very vital. The Officer of the Day was the security representative of the corps commander, charged with the job of inspecting the safety of the command and reporting to his superior any development that portended danger. When such an officer disappeared or went for any length of time without handing

---

[3] Du Pont, *Campaign of 1864,* 144–6; Schmitt (ed.), *George Crook,* 132; Stevens, "Cedar Creek," *Civil War Papers, Massachusetts Commandery,* I, 193–4, 242–3; Moses M. Granger, "The Battle of Cedar Creek," in *Sketches of War History, Ohio Commandery,* III, 110–11.

in reports, Crook should have stormed out of Belle Grove to find out what was wrong.[4]

Plenty was wrong. While the Union army slumbered, thousands of Confederate soldiers had been moving through the dark woods toward Cedar Creek and the Shenandoah, and by early morning the whole gray army was poised across the two streams and waiting only for the word to attack. "Old Jube" Early, as badly defeated as he had been, had yet another battle in him. Stung by his recent reverses and emboldened by his reinforcements, the Confederate general had been champing to get at the Federals ever since he came down the Valley. Reconnaissances had convinced him that he could not hope to surprise the Union right because of its cavalry screen or smash the front because of its strength. There remained the possibility of working around the left, but at first examination this seemed downright impossible. The flanking force would have to move east from Fisher's Hill, cross the bending Shenandoah twice, and finally, and most difficult of all, worm its way between the river and the frowning slope of the northern shoulder of the Massanuttens. It looked impossible—until John B. Gordon, Early's ablest subordinate, and Captain Jed Hotchkiss, expert staff topographer, climbed Three Top Mountain on the seventeenth for a closer look. What they saw caused their fighting hearts to jump with anticipation.

Spread out below them in sharp detail were the camps of the Army of the Valley, its three corps echeloned back five

---

[4] Schmitt (ed.), *George Crook*, 132–3. Unfortunately Crook did not say where or when the OD was captured. Presumably the incident took place near the lines of Hayes or Thoburn. In a modern army the OD would operate in the area around general headquarters, with assistants reporting to him from all over the lines. In the Civil War such an officer was likely to go anywhere. The question of time is important. If the officer disappeared after midnight, when Crook would have retired, it was not so strange that nobody noticed his absence.

The Battle of
CEDAR CREEK
October 19, 1864

air miles from Crook on the left to the cavalry division on
the right. They observed, closest to them and of greatest
interest, the disposition of Crook's command, Thoburn's
detached division on one hill and Hayes's division on another and slightly higher eminence behind it. Quickly Gor-

don's practiced eye took in some salient facts—Crook's front was lightly picketed, and two fords of the river immediately below the mouth of Cedar Creek were practically unguarded. A force crossing one of those fords could pass at once beyond Thoburn to the higher ground on Hayes's left and would be in position to take the Eighth Corps in the rear. It would be able, in fact, because of the echeloned position of Sheridan's corps, to strike the rear of the whole Union army. The problem was to move a flanking force along the base of the mountain to the nearest ford. Gordon and Hotchkiss both believed it could be done, and the staff officer, who made a sketch of the terrain, so reported to Early.

Early wanted to believe the report, but he was not going to act until he could be assured that there was a usable route to the fords. On the morning of the eighteenth he sent Gordon and Hotchkiss out to make a personal examination of the ground at the base of the mountain. They found a winding path to the river, so narrow that an infantry column would have to traverse it in single file. This was enough to satisfy Early. Immediately he decided to launch an attack on the Union left, and because he wanted to get at it right away and because surprise was essential, he ordered the movement to begin that night. He and Gordon, who was to lead the flanking column, calculated that it would take all the hours of darkness to pass a force of corps strength around the shoulder of the mountain.[5]

---

[5] Granger, "Cedar Creek," *Sketches of War History, Ohio Commandery*, III, 101–4; Johnson and Buel (eds.), *Battles and Leaders*, IV, 526, 530; Morton, *Story of Winchester*, 171–2. It is assumed here that Early took into battle a force of 14,000–15,000, of whom 11,000 were infantry, and that the flanking column of three divisions numbered 8,000. From the records it is impossible to establish with any degree of accuracy the size of the Confederate army. The highest Union estimates credit Early with 21,000–22,000 men of all arms, but the Rebel general claimed he commanded no more than 8,800. The extreme figures seem too high and too low. Irwin, *Nineteenth Army Corps*, 436–7; Stevens, "Cedar Creek," *Civil War Papers, Massachusetts Commandery*, I, 187.

Early committed three divisions, around 8,000 troops, to Gordon's command. Gordon was to make his march and be prepared to attack Hayes's division at five in the morning. At the same time two other divisions, under G. C. Wharton and J. B. Kershaw, would move down the Valley pike through Strasburg and at the sound of Gordon's guns would engage the Union front. Later Early sensibly altered this arrangement, directing Kershaw to veer off to the right and, crossing Cedar Creek, to strike the front of the Federal left, which was Thoburn's division. Two brigades of cavalry were to charge over Cedar Creek and attack the blue cavalry on the far right, and another cavalry brigade was to ride through the Luray Valley, cross the Shenandoah, and come up the pike to hit the Federals in the rear. As Early envisioned it, he would take the Federal army in detail, first the Eighth Corps and then the Nineteenth and the Sixth. "Old Jube" had made himself an audacious plan. It was perhaps too audacious for his resources. With a smaller army than his foe, he was proposing to envelop that foe, and to do it with four separate movements that would have to be synchronized exactly. There was an element of desperation in the plan but at this stage of the war Confederate commanders had to take desperate chances. Early was aiming at a big result, to destroy Sheridan's army, which was what Sheridan had been trying to do to his. Whether or not the Confederate commander could bring it off would depend on several things, and first of all on Gordon's being able to conduct his march secretly and deliver his attack as a surprise.

Gordon moved out shortly after dark. He had but a short distance to travel to reach McInturf's Ford, his jumping-off place, no more than six miles, but he had to ford the Shenandoah below Fisher's Hill and then move along a tortuous road to Three Top Mountain, from where the column would have to proceed single-file. At the base of the mountain Gordon halted the men to give them a few hours of sleep. He roused them at one o'clock and resumed the march. They went forward now under orders to preserve the greatest quiet— Gordon had directed that swords, canteens and any other items that might create a noise be dispensed with—and around four they came to the Shenandoah, its current flowing dark under the chill autumn sky. On the opposite banks unsuspecting Union pickets sat in bored immobility. Suddenly, as if to mask the presence of the attackers, the fog arose and shrouded the whole scene. Kershaw's division, accompanied by Early reached its destination about a half hour earlier and also undetected. In the damp woods four gray divisions waited expectantly for five o'clock and the first signs of dawn—and the order to attack.[6]

In the Union camps nobody was stirring, except on the far right and the center, where a cavalry brigade and a brigade from the Nineteenth Corps were leisurely preparing, in pursuance of Wright's order of the night before, to reconnoiter toward Fisher's Hill to determine how far the Rebels had retired. Between four-thirty and five troops in the Nineteenth and Sixth heard the rattle of musketry on both of the Union flanks. They sat up in bed to listen. Some concluded it was only the cavalry or the pickets having a brush with the enemy and went back to sleep. Almost immediately the fire increased in volume and now the boom of artillery could be detected and the sounds were clearly coming from the left flank. Officers and men came tumbling out of their tents, and everybody had the same question: What was happening? A captain in the Nineteenth thought that the Rebels might have been foolish enough to probe at Crook's line and were now being punished for their temerity. He waited to hear the vic-

---

[6] Johnson and Buel (eds.), *Battles and Leaders*, IV, 526; Hadley, *Cedar Creek*, 6–7; Walker, *Vermont Brigade*, 134–5; Stevens, "Cedar Creek," *Civil War Papers, Massachusetts Commandery*, I, 196–7.

tory yells of Crook's men. At Belle Grove plantation, the headquarters staff, which had noted the first shots, and, ascribing them to Emory's reconnaissance brigade, had retired again, came out to examine the situation. Crook was there, and soon General Wright and his staff appeared. An officer came galloping up to Crook, and the Eighth Corps commander rode off toward the noise of the firing. The clinging fog obscured the view in all directions, but sounds were clearly audible. The firing on the left rose to a new pitch, and then the onlookers heard, not the conquering shouts of Crook's troops, but the quavering scream the Rebels always emitted in triumph. That cry seemed to envelop the whole Federal left, the Nineteenth Corps captain wrote, and it was like the howl of wolves around a wagon train on the Western prairies.[7]

The shots which first aroused the Union camps had come from Early's cavalry as it hit the Union right and from Kershaw's troops as they dashed over Cedar Creek and encountered Thoburn's pickets. The swelling roar of battle which followed almost immediately was Gordon's column striking Hayes's division. Shortly after four-thirty Gordon's cavalry brushed aside the weak Federal picket line at the ford and led the infantry across. At the sound of the firing Kershaw's division surged over Cedar Creek and advanced on Thoburn's works. The blow fell so quickly that the Union pickets, who were not very alert anyway, had no chance to give the alarm. Of 349 pickets posted on this section of the line, Kershaw gobbled up all but 40 in an instant. In another

---

[7] Stevens, *Three Years in the Sixth Corps,* 419–20; Putnam, *Memories,* 368–9; Fitts, "In the Ranks at Cedar Creek," *Galaxy,* I, 536–7; Crowninshield, "Cedar Creek," *Papers of Military Historical Society of Massachusetts,* VI, 165–6; S. E. Howard, "The Morning Surprise at Cedar Creek," in *Civil War Papers, Massachusetts Commandery,* II, 417; De Forest, *A Volunteer's Adventures,* 209–10; Pollard, "Recollections of Cedar Creek," *War Papers, Missouri Commandery,* I, 279–80.

instant the yelling gray troops were swarming over Thoburn's parapets, many of them shouting derisively: "Another Union victory." The Federals, falling out of bed and attempting to dress, hardly had time to fire a shot. Thoburn was killed while trying to rally his men. In a broken mass the First Division streamed to the rear. The exultant Confederates seized Thoburn's six guns and turned them on the half-clad fugitives. As soon as he could, Kershaw got his men in hand and put them on the march toward Hayes's position.[8]

A mile to the north, Hayes's division stirred to life at the sound of Kershaw's attack. Counting 2,381 men present for duty, this morning it did not number, because some of its units were on detached service, more than 1,445. The two acting brigade colonels, Devol and Coates, sensibly ordered reveille to be sounded and placed their men under arms. Just then a staff officer from Thoburn came galloping up to inform Hayes that the Rebels were driving the First Division from its position. As experienced a commander as Hayes did not need to be told that something had gone awfully wrong. Through the fog Thoburn's survivors were pouring toward Hayes's camp and behind them could be heard the shouts and the measured steps of Kershaw's pursuing troops. Hayes ordered his division to fall in and prepared to form a battle line. Suddenly General Crook appeared from Belle Grove, followed shortly by Wright and then by Emory, who came over from the Nineteenth Corps to see if he could help. Under the direction of Wright and Crook, a line was hastily thrown up to protect the Valley pike. Emory rushed two brigades over to the road, and to the left of it Hayes placed his division, with his

8 Hadley, *Cedar Creek*, 7; Irwin, *Nineteenth Army Corps*, 418; Gould, *First Maine*, 526; Stevens, "Cedar Creek," *Civil War Papers, Massachusetts Commandery*, I, 198–9; Patterson, MS. Diary, October 19, 1864; Keyes, *123rd Regiment*, 96–7; *Official Records*, XLIII, pt. 1, 373, 384, 392. The Confederate advance went forward sometime after four-thirty, but the main attack fell, as Early scheduled it, around five.

left flank bending northward to connect with Kitching's brigade.[9]

The generals and Hayes breathed more easily as they saw the units file into position. This was a line, they thought, that should be able to stop any attack the Rebels could throw. Ordinarily they would have been right—the Second Division and Kitching's brigade, with Emory's help, was strong enough to halt Kershaw and the remainder of the Nineteenth Corps was adequate to deal with Wharton, who was now probing at its front on Cedar Creek. Hayes felt so certain of the result that he decided to ride to his left to encourage Kitching, whom he barely knew. Approaching the brigade officer, Hayes asked him if he could hold on. "Oh, yes," Kitching replied, "I shall have no trouble. This is a good position, and I can hold on here if you can hold on down there." Hayes was a little nettled by the remark, and he answered, as he admitted later, with the condescension of a veteran to a recruit: "You need not feel afraid of my line. I will guarantee that my line will stand there." Turning his head toward the line as he spoke, Hayes was shocked to see it breaking. He spurred his horse back to rally his men. As he did so, a horde of screaming Confederates burst out of the fog to the left of the position and flung themselves on Kitching's brigade and on the Second Division.

It was Gordon's column, which had crossed the river undetected and was now entering the battle. But the odd feature in the situation was that the Federal left started to break before Gordon really delivered his attack. Suddenly a feeling that was close to panic swept through the ranks of the Second Division, and the men, heedless of the exhortations of their officers, fled in a disordered mass. The eruption into their

---

[9] *Official Records*, XLIII, pt. 1, 403, 406, 410–11; Hayes, MS. Diary, October 19, 1864.

midst of Thoburn's fugitives, crying out a tale of disaster as they passed to the rear, had something to do with it, but essentially Hayes's men were the victims of the same psychology that had caused Early's to depart at Fisher's Hill. They had been surprised and were in danger, and if their officers did not have enough sense to know what to do, they did—which was to get out fast before they were attacked.[1]

The troops of the Second Division mingled with those of the First in the flight, and so the whole Eighth Corps, or what was left of it, moved to the rear and, as an organized unit, out of the battle. Yet it moved in a curiously steady flow and with a strange air of purpose. An officer of the Nineteenth Corps who was taking his outfit up to the front noted with interest that the men of the Eighth were not excited or frantic, but "only stolidly, doggedly determined to go to the rear. . . . They passed around us, through our ranks, and almost over us, insistent, determined. They heeded none of our cries to 'Turn back!' 'Make a stand!' but streamed to the rear." Other officers who tried to appeal to the fugitives remarked on the same phenomenon—the men were not running and they would listen but they were not going to be stopped. Many of them did not pause until they were all the way back to Newtown. Perhaps the most tragic figure in this hegira was Crook, temporarily a general without anybody to command. He did not flee in fright, but for a time he apparently wandered over the field in a state of shock. A colonel in the Nineteenth who had collected some of Crook's troops to guard a wagon train

---

[1] Hayes in his report, *Official Records,* XLIII, pt. 1, 404, implied that Kitching's brigade was the first to break, but in a later and more honest account he admitted that his own division gave way first; Hayes, "Incidents of the Battle of Cedar Creek," *Sketches of War History, Ohio Commandery,* IV, 238–9. Other records of this episode are in Hadley, *Cedar Creek,* 7–8; Stevens, "Cedar Creek," *Civil War Papers, Massachusetts Commandery,* I, 200–2; Granger, "Cedar Creek," *Sketches of War History, Ohio Commandery,* III, 112–14; Carpenter, *Eighth Vermont,* 209.

saw the general riding by unattended even by an orderly. The colonel went over and reported on his action. Crook merely muttered, "All right," and continued on his way.[2]

Not all the men or units in the Eighth Corps gave way to panic. Some squads and companies preserved their identity and retreated fighting. Gradually these outfits joined others like themselves, and as the movement continued the two divisions began to assume again some semblance of cohesion. This was especially true of the Second, which had been hit much less hard by the initial Rebel onslaught. Whether or not the Second would halt and re-form would depend in large measure on the ability of its commanding officer to impose his personality, his quality of leadership on the inchoate mass, on his power to lift up these stunned men who believed they had been beaten, make them think they could still win, and turn them into fighting men again.

For a time after his line broke, Hayes had no opportunity to exercise any leadership. Apparently he realized that he could not rally the fleeing troops and turned to follow them. As he galloped away, a bullet struck his horse, killing it instantly. The animal fell heavily, in Hayes's words, "tumbling heels over head." Hayes was thrown to the ground so violently that he fainted. How long he lay there he did not know, but when he revived he was conscious of a sharp pain in one ankle and thought he was disabled. He put out first one leg and then the other and found to his relief that he could walk. Just then some Rebels charged toward him yelling that he should stop. Hayes took off in a run and escaped into a concealing grove. It was a mark of the demoralization of the men that they saw their colonel fall—some of them carried to the rear a report that he had been killed—and did not even pause to see if

---

[2] Howard, "Surprise at Cedar Creek," *Civil War Papers, Massachusetts Commandery*, II, 417–18; Crowninshield, "Cedar Creek," *Papers of Military Historical Society of Massachusetts*, VI, 170; Stevens, *Three Years in the Sixth Corps*, 421–2; Carpenter, *Eighth Vermont*, 219.

they could help him. Sometime after this Hayes was hit in the head by a spent ball which had no more effect than to shock him slightly. Eventually he caught up to his staff, borrowed a horse from an officer, and after a retreat of two and a half miles conducted his gradually gathering division to a ridge north of Middletown.[3]

It is difficult to recount with any degree of exactness the movements of Hayes in the battle or, for that matter, the movements of any officer and any unit. In the terrible confusion after the surprise attack and in the blinding fog, men did not know where they were going, and when they tried to write it down later they were not sure where they had gone or what they had done. Cedar Creek, in the three hours after its beginning, was one of the most fluid battles of the war. The collapse of the Eighth Corps uncovered the flank of the Nineteenth, which then received the full attention of the combined forces of Gordon and Kershaw. Unnerved by the flight of the Eighth, the Nineteenth was not disposed to make much of a stand. It broke too as the Confederates drove forward, although some of its units fought bravely, and retreated west of the Valley pike. The withdrawal was more orderly than that of the Eighth and the corps preserved its organization, but it was also, for the moment, out of the battle. General Wright, sick at heart as he saw his army apparently going to pieces, hurriedly shifted the Sixth Corps and his unused cavalry divisions to the left (east) to stem the rout.[4]

The battle now developed into a series of attempts by the Federals to establish a line on which they could stand. In the first stages the defenders were not trying to set up a permanent line, but were fighting delaying actions for time, time for the

[3] Hayes, "Incidents of Cedar Creek," *Sketches of War History, Ohio Commandery*, IV, 238–9; Hayes to Mrs. Hayes, October 21, 1864, Hayes MS. Letters; Hayes, MS. Diary, October 19; *Official Records*, XLIII, pt. 1, 404.
[4] Fitts, "In the Ranks at Cedar Creek," *Galaxy*, I, 538–9; Carpenter, *Eighth Vermont*, 218; Walker, *Vermont Brigade*, 139–40.

undamaged Sixth Corps to get into position and time for the damaged Nineteenth to re-form. The bluecoats resisted first north of Belle Grove, then on a ridge west of Middletown, then farther back on the Old Forge Road, and finally, sometime between nine and ten o'clock, they came to a ridge a little over a mile north of Middletown. Here they brought their retreat to a halt and here they prepared to stay. The sun broke through the fog shortly before nine, burning the mists away rapidly, and the Federals could at last see the terrain around them and their enemies as they approached.[5]

The Sixth Corps was the first to reach the ridge, and it apparently arrived at approximately the same time that Hayes guided the remnant of his division there. How many men Hayes brought with him is not clear from the records. One careful observer, who was sympathetic to what had happened to Hayes in the battle, stated that the colonel reported to General George Getty of the Sixth, who was in command of this sector of the line, with only sixty men. Hayes, who understandably wanted to minimize the demoralization of his men, contended later that he had 1,000 to 1,200 troops of the division at his disposal. The truth probably is that Hayes came to the ridge with a relatively small number of his men, that others followed him, and that still others drifted in when they passed the position or heard that a line had been established. There was very evidently a mustering of units from all over the field as the news spread that a part of the army had halted at the ridge. Hayes's division formed between and slightly behind two divisions of the Sixth Corps, which occupied the left of the line, west of the Valley pike. The Nineteenth, as it came up, fell in to the right of the Sixth. Some troops of Thoburn's division ceased their retreat and formed

[5] Hadley, *Cedar Creek*, 9–10; Stevens, "Cedar Creek," *Civil War Papers, Massachusetts Commandery*, I, 207–8, 216–19; Granger, "Cedar Creek," *Sketches of War History, Ohio Commandery*, III, 121–3; George A. Forsyth, *Thrilling Days in Army Life* (New York, 1902), 138–9.

in rear of Hayes, and others rallied on the left side of the pike. General Crook arrived and went around to see where his soldiers had placed themselves. Everywhere along the line there was a rising feeling of confidence as the various segments settled in. The position was strong, the front protected by stone fences, and the troops felt that they could hold it unless outflanked. With dogged determination they waited for the next attack.[6]

Strangely, no attack came. A lull descended over the battle that would last for hours. The Confederates would eventually move up opposite the Union line and they would make one weak assault at it, but there would be no more charges bursting out of nowhere, no more screaming Rebels rushing forward with irresistible momentum. Early's army was by late morning almost fought out. After a night of practically no sleep and hours of fighting, the gray troops were beginning to feel a deadly weariness. Many of them stopped to plunder the Union camps, and often after collecting the loot they returned to the rear instead of rejoining their units. The Federal troops, as roughly handled as they had been, were still in better physical shape than their opponents. The Sixth Corps, because of its echeloned position, was able to move into the battle over a short distance and with relative ease, simply by sliding east, and the Nineteenth, after it re-formed, executed the same maneuver; whereas the Confederates had to traverse longer distances and change front after they swung west of the Valley pike. Early had committed his whole infantry and was without a reserve, while the two powerful Union cavalry divisions, unimpeded by Early's inept horse-

---

[6] Stevens, "Cedar Creek," *Civil War Papers, Massachusetts Commandery*, I, 220; Granger, "Cedar Creek," *Sketches of War History, Ohio Commandery*, III, 123; Hayes, "Incidents of Cedar Creek," *ibid.*, IV, 242–3; Augustus C. Hamlin, "Who Captured the Guns at Cedar Creek, October 19, 1864?" in *Papers of Military Historical Society of Massachusetts*, VI, 187–8; *Official Records*, XLIII, pt. 1, 227, 385, 404; Walker, *Vermont Brigade*, 146–7.

men, had ridden east and were now posted on either flank of the Union line.

Later Early would conclude that his own troops had prevented him from destroying the blue army. He would claim that they had plundered and straggled and left him with no striking power. The charge was untrue as well as ungracious. The Rebel army stood immobile for precious hours because the commanding general could not make up his mind what to do. Early, after an audacious beginning, lost his resolution when the battle took a turn he had not expected. When the Federals made their stand on the Middletown ridge instead of continuing to retire, Early seemed to go to pieces. He could not decide whether to attack in front or by the flank and if the latter, by what flank. While he deliberated, the Union force on the ridge increased in numbers as more and more units attached themselves to it. It is unlikely that Early could have carried the position after eleven o'clock by anything he did, and if left to himself he would probably have retired, leaving the field to the Federals. But by that time the one element that could change the situation from a Union tactical defensive success to a smashing victory had arrived on the scene.[7]

As the Federal troops waited for the expected attack to come, they heard far in the rear the sound of tremendous cheering. They knew that stragglers and fugitives were strung all the way back to Winchester, and they wondered what those men were shouting about. Some of them sprang to their feet to take a better look. They beheld a great black charger galloping up the Valley pike, and on him a small man who waved his hat and cried out something that was lost in the din, and behind him a handful of riders in single file who were having

---

[7] This aspect of the battle receives attention in the two best secondary accounts: Stackpole, *Sheridan in the Shenandoah*, 298–341; Pond, *Shenandoah Valley*, 220–39. Early's report is in *Official Records*, XLIII, pt. 1, 561–4. For the Union reports, see ibid., 32–4, 52–4, 158–61, 284–6, 365–6.

a hard time keeping up. He spurred down the line, and officers and men exploded in a delirium of joy and chanted the
same name that they heard in louder and louder tones from
the mass of men following on the pike: "Sheridan! Sheridan!"
He said many things as he showed himself to the men, and
afterwards they were not sure exactly what he had said and
when they came to write about it they were somewhat embarrassed to put down the words. One observer had him say:
"Men, by God, we'll whip them yet!—We'll sleep in our old
camps to-night!" Hayes probably recorded the most nearly
correct version in his diary. As Sheridan came to the rear of
Getty's Sixth Corps division, he encountered Hayes, and the
colonel heard him say: "We'll whip em yet like Hell!" Hayes's
division welcomed the general by raising its regimental flags,
which Sheridan remembered as seeming to rise "out of the
ground." Sheridan also remembered, for some reason, that
Hayes and a few other officers and some color bearers were the
only representatives of the Eighth Corps on the field.[8]

Sheridan had risen that morning expecting to return to
Cedar Creek in leisurely fashion. At breakfast he and his staff
heard the sound of cannonading to the south, but they attributed it to a reconnaissance in force that Wright was
probably making. Nevertheless, Sheridan was anxious to be
on the way, and with an escort of cavalry he rode out of
Winchester. Hardly had he cleared the town when an appal-
ling sight burst into view—a stream of wounded men and
fugitives coming toward him and as far as the eye could see a
mass of wagons, ambulances, and artillery sections tearing
to the rear. An officer in the crowd came up and said that all
was lost, that the whole army was broken. In an instant Sheri-

---

[8] Walker, *Vermont Brigade*, 147–8; Stevens, "Cedar Creek," *Civil War Papers,
Massachusetts Commandery*, I, 221–2; Granger, "Cedar Creek," *Sketches of
War History, Ohio Commandery*, III, 125–6; Hayes, MS. Diary, October 19,
1864; Sheridan, *Memoirs*, II, 83. The time of Sheridan's arrival is variously
cited as between ten-thirty and eleven-thirty.

dan made his resolution. Directing the cavalry to remain where it was and to try to halt the rout, he dashed forward with twenty staffers. As he rode on, he took off his hat and waved it and shouted at every knot of men he met. Always he said the same thing: Turn around, we must go back. Miraculously, they stopped and listened, and more miraculously, they turned and followed him. He came up to the front with a great irregular crowd of yelling men behind him, men who just a few minutes before had been intent on getting to a place of safety and who were now going back to fight. He did not ride twenty miles, as the poet celebrated him—it was eleven and a half—and he did not gallop all the way—that would have been a poor use of horseflesh—but he did something awfully important. He made an army that had lost its self-respect recover it. It was the most dramatic example in the war of personal leadership, of what one man could do to change the whole face of a battle.[9]

When Sheridan told his men that they would sleep in their camps that night, he was not indulging in empty rhetoric. From the moment he arrived at the front, he had determined to regain the field. His quick eye took in the situation and told him that all the fire had gone out of the Rebel offensive and that his line could hold. He reasoned that if the Federals now went over to the attack, the abrupt turn of events would throw the Confederates off balance and demoralize them. In his usual fashion, having made his decision, he proceeded to plan the execution of it with the greatest care and deliberation, making certain that every unit was exactly where he wanted it and that every subordinate who had a part to play would understand his role. The plan called for a general advance of the whole line, with the Sixth Corps acting as a pivot and the Nineteenth swinging on it to strike the Rebel

[9] Tyler, *Recollections*, 298–9; Forsyth, *Thrilling Days*, 145–6.

left obliquely. Not until nearly four o'clock did Sheridan give
the order to advance. By that time Early had decided that he
had lost the day and was starting to withdraw his wounded and
wagons to Fisher's Hill.

Sheridan, under the impression that the Eighth Corps,
except for a few officers, was not on the field, did not include
it in his plan. Shortly before the attack was to begin, a division
commander in the Sixth rode to his left to make certain that
his flank connected with the adjoining division. He found
some troops that did not belong to the Sixth between him
and the next division, and on inquiring learned that they
were of Hayes's division. He saw Hayes, with his staff around
him, lying on the ground in an attitude of dejected fatigue.
Although the visitor did not know it, Hayes was still suffering from the effects of the fall from his horse. The Sixth Corps
general explained the orders to Hayes and asked that he withdraw his troops so that the two divisions of the Sixth could
unite. Hayes put his hand to his head as though in pain or
shock and then rose and mounted his horse. "I have no
orders," he said, "but, if you are ordered to go forward, I'll
go too, without orders. If your orders are to go forward, I will
fill the gap with my men." His response was a courageous
one, but it was more instinctive than reasoned. Injured and
uninformed of Sheridan's orders, Hayes could take no intelligent part in Sheridan's movement and should not even have
been at the front. Five minutes later he received instructions
from Crook to move his division over to the left of the pike
and to form with the section of the First Division there.
Sheridan had discovered that Hayes's division was on the
main line, and he was not going to entrust any part of his
operation to any troops of the Eighth Corps. Hayes shifted
his men across the road, and while the other two corps went
forward the remnant of the Eighth, perhaps 2,000 strong,

acted as a reserve, following the attack and halting at dusk at its previous camp near Cedar Creek.[1]

Hayes thus had only a secondary role in the Union offensive, which went exactly as Sheridan planned it. The Federal line swept forward, and although it encountered at first some stubborn resistance, this did not last very long. The Confederates were weary after hours of fighting and discouraged at the disappearance of a victory they thought they had won, and, as Sheridan had foreseen, they were utterly overcome at the sight of the supposedly defeated Federal army advancing relentlessly on them. They panicked and stampeded over Cedar Creek in a rout worse than their flights in the battles of September. The Federals followed to Cedar Creek, but dusk, coming around five, prevented any effective pursuit. Early rested his army briefly at Fisher's Hill that night and then before dawn retreated to New Market.

The men of Sheridan's army, as they had at the Opequon and at Fisher's Hill, stood again in the twilight and looked on a field of victory. It was a bitter victory, though, and they looked on a field of death. In the thirteen hours that had elapsed since Early had struck his first blow the Federals had suffered casualties of approximately 5,600, of whom 644 were killed and 3,430 were wounded. Early's losses were at least 3,100, and of his 2,200 killed and wounded many were left where they fell. All the way back to Middletown the dead and wounded of both armies lay side by side, and when the moon came out its pale rays illumined the scene with a special weird effect and a special horror. On the field wounded men were crying for water, for help, or for somebody to put them out of their agony, and mingled with their pleas were the terrible screams of mangled horses, of which there were

---

[1] Kiefer, in *Tributes to Hayes*, 11; Kiefer, *Four Years of War*, II, 145–6; *Official Records*, XLIII, pt. 1, 366, 404; Stevens, "Cedar Creek," *Civil War Papers, Massachusetts Commandery*, I, 232.

a particularly large number. Not many who experienced that night would ever forget it.[2]

Colonel Hayes was pleased that he could report relatively light losses in his division, 221, of whom 25 were killed, 157 wounded, and 39 missing. He was, however, especially concerned about one reported casualty—himself. When he fell from his horse, his men carried to the rear the tale that he had been killed, and this story got in the newspapers. He was worried that Lucy would see it before he could get word to her that it was untrue. He did not know that a considerate officer in the Washington telegraph bureau had already acted to remove any cause for anxiety. This man, who knew the facts, telegraphed Mrs. Hayes: "The report that your husband was killed this morning is untrue. He was wounded, not dangerously, and is safe." The message arrived just as an uncle of Lucy's was trying to keep from her a paper which contained a list of the dead at Cedar Creek and a complimentary obituary notice of Hayes.[3]

The Eighth Corps, which had done a lot of crowing about its role at the Opequon and Fisher's Hill, now came in for some ragging about Cedar Creek. Men from the other two corps asked men in the Eighth how far it was to Harper's Ferry and if Crook's troops had gone back expecting an early mail. Stories in the New York press laid the blame for the surprise on the Eighth Corps. Hayes was enraged at the criticism. He wrote a letter to a friend in Columbus giving what he con-

---

[2] Irwin, *Nineteenth Army Corps*, 435; Pond, *Shenandoah Valley*, 239–40; Stackpole, *Sheridan in the Shenandoah*, 340; Stevens, "Cedar Creek," *Civil War Papers, Massachusetts Commandery*, I, 237; Stevens, *Three Years in the Sixth Corps*, 430–1; Kiefer, *Four Years of War*, II, 145–6; Flinn, *Campaigning with Sheridan*, 230.

[3] *Official Records*, XLIII, pt. 1, 135; Hayes, "Incidents of Cedar Creek," *Sketches of War History, Ohio Commandery*, IV, 240–1. The Eighth Corps as a whole counted 314 killed and wounded and 533 missing. The great majority of the latter were obviously from Thoburn's division and Kitching's brigade.

sidered to be the truth of the case and urged this man to get
the essence of the letter in the Cincinnati press to counteract
the propaganda coming out of New York. As Hayes told it,
General Wright should be blamed for the surprise since he
had not provided sufficient cavalry on the left. And Crook's
corps had not broken any more precipitately than the Nineteenth, which was attacked later and had had more time to
prepare. Hayes's division had, in fact, covered the retreat of
the Federal left and had brought out most of its equipment.[4]

There was some truth in this, and also some partial truths
or evasions. Hayes was agitating himself about issues that
mattered very little, was revealing again that he was becoming
too much influenced by military concepts. After the whole
story was told, the fact remained that the Eighth Corps had
broken. But it broke in a situation which would have caused
any unit to stampede. Hayes had not conducted his retreat in
quite the orderly fashion he imagined. But he had brought his
division out of the carnage in such shape that he could re-form
it. This was a tribute to his leadership. No ordinary divisional
officers could have done what Hayes did. Hayes might better
have reflected on the real lesson of the battle—the importance
of one resolute man in a crisis. Sheridan had demonstrated
the lesson on the army level. On a lower level, but essentially
just as vital a one, Hayes had proved the same truth.

[4] Walker, *Vermont Brigade*, 153; Hayes to B. R. Cowan, October 25, 1864,
in Hayes Papers; Hayes to Mrs. Hayes, October 27, Hayes MS. Letters.

Chapter 16

Not Likely Ever to Forget

LTHOUGH HARDLY ANYBODY knew it, after Cedar Creek the Valley campaign was over. Sheridan had dealt the Confederate army two blows from which it could not recover. He had depleted its manpower so seriously in the autumn battles that it would never again have the capacity to mount a real offensive, and he had devastated the Valley so thoroughly that even if the Confederates had been able to put a larger army in the region they could not have sustained it. But all this was not visible at the moment. Early, lurking in the vicinity of New Market, still seemed to be a menace that required watching. Sheridan meant to watch, but with winter coming on to close out active operations he would do it from a more defensible line and one closer to Winchester. Accordingly, in early November he withdrew from Cedar Creek to a position south of Kernstown. For Crook's troops, it was a return to a spot that was, except for Cedar Creek, the scene of their greatest humiliation.

But Hayes and his men gave little thought to the past as they came to the new camp. They were glad to leave the damp woods of Cedar Creek for the more open country around Winchester, to move, as Hayes put it in a letter to Lucy, "one day's march toward civilization," and they knew that the transfer presaged an early change to the warm comfort of winter quarters. That change appeared especially appealing to the troops when the weather abruptly turned cold and windy on the march. For Hayes, the closing out of active operations meant more than an alteration in the way of camp life. Duval, recovered from his wound and now a brigadier, returned to the army and resumed command of the Second Division. Hayes toyed with the idea of trying to get another division, but he did not want to engage in the pressures and negotiations he would have to employ to secure the post. He consented to take again his old First Brigade. It was a good unit, and he and the men knew and trusted each other, and best of all it included his Twenty-third Ohio. "I prefer the Brigade," he wrote Lucy, and he meant it. He was more at ease with a smaller unit, and if the definition of a small unit could be stretched to include a regiment or a brigade, it could be said that he was a natural small-unit officer.[1]

Although the weather turned ever chillier—Hayes said it was colder than "any huckleberry pudding" he knew of—Sheridan would not let the men build huts for winter quarters until he was certain that Early would remain quiet. When the Confederate general withdrew to Staunton during the first week of December, Sheridan concluded that the possibility of any danger had passed. He sent the Sixth Corps back to the Army of the Potomac and permitted the troops of the Nineteenth and the Eighth to construct the snug shanties that had become universal in the armies—four feet high and eight feet square, half underground and banked up with earth and covered with shelter blankets. Hayes and his staff were comfortable in a structure that was a combination of wooden slab sides and a wall tent. For both officers and men it was a period of restful, pleasant living. Newspapers and magazines of late issue circulated in abundant numbers. Social activities ran the gamut from religious meetings through musicals to

---

[1] Hayes, MS. Diary, November 9, 14, 1864; Hayes to Mrs. Hayes, November 13, 17, Hayes MS. Letters.

horse races. There were a large number of women in camp, officers' wives and relatives and young ladies of Union sympathies from Winchester. Hayes noted that Sheridan was particularly attentive to one of the latter. Food was plentiful and, for the officers, occasionally exotic—oysters, lobster, and fish—and liquor, although expensive, was easily procured. Hayes seems to have consumed his share of the beverages and to have liked it. "A jolly wine-drinking in the evening" was his summation of one affair.[2]

On December 9, a day of raw cold followed by snow in the evening, Crook came to Hayes's headquarters in the afternoon to impart some interesting news—to notify Hayes that he had been named a brigadier general of volunteers. The origin of the promotion went back to Cedar Creek, and the reasons for it are not clear, are obscured by the myth that enveloped Hayes after he became a national figure. According to the most dramatic version, and the most unlikely, Sheridan went up to Hayes on the field at Cedar Creek after the victory and, clasping his hand, said: "Colonel, from this day you will be a Brigadier General." Sheridan had no time to notice Hayes in the heat of the final moment of the battle and no knowledge of Hayes's conduct that would have justified the promise, and if such an episode had occurred Hayes would assuredly have described it in his diary or letters. The true story was much more sober and really more complimentary to Hayes. Sheridan after the battle heard from Crook that Hayes had served well throughout the campaign, and, studying the record himself, the general decided that Hayes deserved promotion. What Sheridan probably said to Hayes, sometime after the battle, was that the commission would date from October 19, for when it came it read: "For gallant and meritorious services in the battles of Opequon, Fisher's Hill, and Cedar Creek."

---

[2] Hayes to Mrs. Hayes, November 20, 23, 1864, and to Mrs. Sophia Hayes, December 4, 6, Hayes MS. Letters; Hayes, MS. Diary, November 26.

Crook did not have the actual commission with him—it was late in arriving—but he gave Hayes a pair of his old shoulder straps to wear. Hayes was proud to accept the insignia from the general he adored, but he was not so sure that the rank was anything to take pride in. It had been "cheapened shamefully" by bestowal on "all sorts of small people," he thought. Still he could feel that his promotion was different—it had come at the close of a hard campaign and with the recommendation of fighting generals. He was overwhelmed with congratulations, and the next day he and Duval and Comly celebrated by drinking some poor whiskey. "A rational way of doing the joyful," he recorded, "but all we have!"[3]

Almost immediately the new general experienced a curious reversion to the psychology of a regimental colonel. Inspecting his brigade, he was pleased to pronounce that the Twenty-third Ohio was the crack outfit in appearance and marching. As he rode down its line, the veterans smiled at him, and he smiled back, and he and they felt that rush of emotion, that sense of mystic communion which often passed between fighting men and a commander they loved. He could not hold back the tears. "I felt as I did when I saw them mustered in at Camp Chase," he wrote Lucy.[4]

On December 19 General Hayes received orders to march his brigade to Stephenson's Depot, north of Winchester and on the railroad to Harper's Ferry. Other units of the army were also pulling back. Sheridan, satisfied that operations were over for the winter and informed that a good part of Early's force had returned to Lee, was redistributing his own strength to the greatest advantage. The First Division of the Eighth Corps he put on the train to join Grant before

---

[3] Otis, "Personal Recollections," Santa Barbara *Daily Press*, November 3, 1876; Williams, *Hayes*, I, 264–5; Hayes to Mrs. Hayes, December 9, 1864, Hayes MS. Letters; Hayes, MS. Diary, December 9, 10.

[4] Hayes to Mrs. Hayes, December 17, 1864, and to Mrs. Sophia Hayes, December 18, Hayes MS. Letters.

Richmond, thus cutting Crook's command down to one division. Hayes believed that the Second Division would soon be ordered to follow the First, and he was not sure that he liked the prospect. "I prefer not to go," he wrote Uncle Sardis, "and yet one feels that it is necessary to be present at the taking of Richmond. I am content however to go." While Hayes speculated on the various camp rumors as to troop movements, new ones started up to stir fresh speculations. He heard that two regiments of the division had been ordered to West Virginia and then that Duval had gone to Cumberland, Maryland, on the Baltimore & Ohio line on the route to West Virginia. Perhaps the mountain men were going back to their old theater. Finally Hayes learned the truth—Duval's command had been ordered to Cumberland to guard the rail line. Sheridan would hold the Valley with only the Nineteenth Corps.[5]

Traveling by rail, Hayes and his command reached Cumberland on the night of the last day of December. He found that he was a part of a reorganized Army of West Virginia. That aggregation now consisted of three divisions: the First under Duval—Hayes's brigade was the First of the First Division; the Second under John D. Stevenson; and the Third under Benjamin Kelley. Duval and Kelley were posted in and around Cumberland, and Stevenson was at Harper's Ferry. Hayes was pleased with everything about the set-up. The camp was comfortable, the duty was light, and the official notification of his promotion finally arrived, making him a legitimate general. The thing Hayes liked most of all was that the present assignment placed him only twenty-four hours by train away from Cincinnati and home. Eager to see Lucy and his family, he applied for a twenty-day leave, which in

---

[5] Hayes, MS. Diary, December 19, 20, 1864; Hayes to Sardis Birchard, December 20, 1864, and to Mrs. Sophia Hayes, December 21, Hayes MS. Letters; *Official Records*, XLIII, pt. 2, 841, 853.

this inactive period was readily granted. He left Cumberland on January 10 and did not return until the ninth of February.[6]

Almost immediately after Hayes returned, Duval departed for Cincinnati. The divisional commander was having trouble with his hearing and took extended leave to secure expert medical attention. In his absence the command of the First Division devolved on Hayes. As always, Hayes took his duties with great seriousness. His regiments were unusually full, having been swelled by an infusion of recently conscripted troops. But the new men were almost completely ignorant of military knowledge, and Hayes therefore felt that it was necessary to put them through a heavy schedule of drill and tactics. He spent most of his time doing the same thing he had done as a fledgling officer in 1861. Because he had to be with the troops so much and because he believed as a matter of principle that an officer should share the life of his men no matter how uncomfortable, he decided to remove his quarters from a hotel in town where he had been staying to his camp. Shortly he would have reason to be thankful that he had observed one of the soldierly virtues. On the night of February 19 a band of Rebel guerrillas, disguised as Federals, made their way into Cumberland and spirited Generals Crook and Kelley away from their hotels. Hayes happened to be in town that night, having gone to Duval's headquarters on some business, but the raiders, knowing that the First Division commander had left, made no search of the premises. "It is a very mortifying thing to all of us," Hayes wrote of the episode, but he attached no blame to his idol Crook for having let himself get captured in much the same circumstances as Scammon had the previous year.[7]

---

[6] Hayes, MS. Diary, January 1–3, 1865; Hayes to Mrs. Sophia Hayes, January 1, 1865, and to Mrs. Hayes, January 5, and to Sardis Birchard, January 8, Hayes MS. Letters.

[7] Hayes to Mrs. Hayes, February 13, 21, 1865, Hayes MS. Letters; Hayes, MS. Diary, February 14; Schmitt (ed.), *George Crook*, 303–5.

Shortly after Crook went to Richmond as a prisoner, Sheridan returned to his cavalry command in Grant's army. The departure of two ranking officers made it necessary for the Union high command to reshuffle assignments all along the Valley–West Virginia line. The command of the department, the Middle Department, went to Winfield Scott Hancock, once a fine corps general in the Army of the Potomac, but who, because he had been weakened by a bad wound, was now placed in charge of this relatively inactive theater. Hancock eventually sent Emory, whose Nineteenth Corps had been scattered to various points, to assume command at Cumberland, and the routine of life for Hayes and his troops went on in the same fashion. But before the situation was resolved, one of the strangest personal controversies in the war broke out. It was a row over an unimportant point of military etiquette, but before it was settled it embroiled some pretty important personages—Secretary of War Stanton, Grant, Hancock, and Crook. Hayes was at first no more than an interested observer, but because Crook was involved he finally mixed in it as a courageous if somewhat imprudent actor. Crook had never stood in very well with Stanton, and when he let himself get captured in such humiliating circumstances he dropped still lower in the Secretary's opinion. Crook did not stay long in prison. Within a month, by late March, he was sent north with a group of parolees, and on his return he said some things publicly about the War Department's failure to get him released which aroused Stanton to the boiling point. Whether or not Crook had a fair complaint, he was unwise to criticize his civilian superior. Although paroled, Crook would not be free to acccept an assignment until a formal and special exchange was made for him, and this only Stanton could conclude. The Secretary naturally showed no indication of urgency. Grant himself had to use his influence before Stanton would effect the transfer.

As tangled and slightly ridiculous as the case had been, it was destined to become even worse. Grant had intervened because he wanted to use Crook in the cavalry of the Army of the Potomac. Crook had no objection to another assignment, but he insisted on first being restored to the command of the Department of West Virginia, if but for one day, to demonstrate to the public that he was not in disfavor. Grant readily consented to the unusual arrangement. Hancock did not like it, however, feeling that the thing was done over his head, and his attitude caused all kinds of wild camp rumors to spring up—Crook was going to resume the command regardless of Hancock's wishes and when he did Hancock was going to arrest him. It was at this point that Hayes was drawn into the situation. He had initially viewed the affair with detachment. He hoped Crook would return, although he thought well enough of Hancock. But when Crook made his reputation an issue and demanded reparation, Hayes could not resist showing his support of the general he admired above all others. On the day that Crook came to Cumberland to assert his command he paid a special visit to Hayes's brigade—Duval was back and directing the division again—and Hayes turned out two bands and the whole unit in a formal welcome. The men yelled at the sight of Crook, giving, as Hayes reported, "forty rousing cheers," and both Crook and Hayes delivered speeches. Although Crook was fairly popular with the troops, he could never have aroused spontaneously such a display of loyalty. The affair was contrived by Hayes to impress on the powers in Washington that Crook's army stood behind its general.[8]

It was a manly thing that Hayes had done but hardly a politic one. If he was ambitious for promotion, he had not

---

[8] *Official Records*, XLVI, pt. 1, 525, pt. 2, 760; Schmitt (ed.), *George Crook*, 305; Hayes to Mrs. Sophia Hayes, March 11, 1865, to Sardis Birchard, March 18, 24, and to Mrs. Hayes, March 21, Hayes MS. Letters.

endeared himself to the powerful Secretary of War. Nothing about his action, in fact, was very analytical or rational. The wonder is not that he made the gesture but why he felt constrained to make it. The controversy he had entered was completely without point, probably the most flagrant case of military ado about nothing in the whole war. In an earlier phase of his career Hayes would have seen it in its true light and would have laughed at its absurdity. That he should take such an episode so seriously now showed how fully he had been caught up in the army way of life and in the army way of thinking. He reacted as a professional soldier would have reacted. R. B. Hayes, civilian, was in danger of losing his perspective.

Hayes did not particularly care if his action had offended higher authority. He had gone up in the military hierarchy about as far as he could go or desired to go. In fact, when in April he was assigned to the command of a force of divisional strength, 5,000 men, and of combined arms—infantry, cavalry, artillery—and with an independent status, he wanted to reject the appointment. His objective, which was to seize Lynchburg, was a link in Grant's grand strategy. As a part of his final campaign to break Confederate resistance, Grant hoped that Hancock would be able to advance several columns up the Valley to seize Rebel communications and cut off Lee's retreat from Richmond. It was one of these columns that Hayes was to lead, and that Hancock would select him was a mark of the high esteem his superiors had for him. Hayes appreciated the honor, but he did not like the mission. Quite rightly, he saw that to take an expedition from Beverly, where he was to rendezvous, over the mountains and through a destitute region was an almost impossible task that could well end in failure. "I hope it will be given up," he wrote Uncle Sardis. There was another element in his reluctance. He did not want to leave his brigade, to break the emotional bond of union with his men, some of whom he had commanded for almost four years. He would take the new command, because it was his duty to do so, but he would rather have kept the old one. In his farewell address to the brigade he referred to the great battles of 1864, but he also went back to West Virginia and Cloyd's Mountain and the burning of New River Bridge and the night march over Salt Pond Mountain. These and other scenes, he reminded the men, formed a part of "our common recollections which we are not likely ever to forget."[9]

To get his expedition organized, Hayes went to New Creek, West Virginia, a short distance southwest of Cumberland and also on the Baltimore & Ohio line. Before he left Cumberland the electrifying news came that Richmond had fallen to Grant and that Lee's army was fleeing west. Hayes knew that this victory portended the speedy end of the war and that now there was no need for the expedition to Lynchburg to go on. He would continue his preparations until he was told to call them off, he informed Lucy, but he expected to be home soon. He wanted to stay in the service until June, so that he could say that he had worn the uniform for a full four years. Most of all, he wanted no more responsibility. "I decide nothing at present," he told Lucy, and said that he was fortunate. His mood was that of thousands of other officers at the war's close. They had been a part of a great experience and they were glad they had been in it and they were proud of their records, but now suddenly it was nearly over and they desired nothing so much as to get out of it without having to make one more decision, without ever again having to control the lives of any men in battle, without having to take any action that might mar their reputations. Hayes's analysis of his own situation was accurate. As

---

[9] *Official Records*, XLVI, pt. 3, 570–1; Hayes to Mrs. Hayes, April 5, 1865, and to Sardis Birchard, April 5, Hayes MS. Letters; printed copy of farewell address in Hayes Library.

Union victory followed on victory in April, the Lynchburg expedition was forgotten, and Hayes remained quietly at New Creek, commanding in what was called, in the last table of organization in which his name would appear, the Second Brigade of the First Division.[1]

Full of mellow reflections about the past, on the morning of April 15 Hayes prepared to run down on the train to Cumberland to transact some routine business. Before he started, the telegraph flashed the news of the assassination of Lincoln. Hayes boarded the cars and rode to Cumberland in a changed mood, crushed by a feeling of despair that was slow to lift. Suddenly he realized that the close of the war did not mean the solution of all the nation's problems or the beginning of a period of placid peace for him or anybody else. In a sober letter to Lucy he reflected on Lincoln's greatness and on his record as a war leader, but significantly Hayes pondered most the effect of the tragedy on the future. "The work of reconstruction requiring so much statesmanship just begun," he wrote, and wondered how it would develop—and how it would finally end.[2]

Increasingly now Hayes was thinking of his own future, and of the part that he would play as a civilian and a political leader in the work of reconstruction. In December he would take his seat in Congress, and he could reasonably look forward to additional political honors. The Ohio troops in the Valley army had passed resolutions booming him for the Republican gubernatorial nomination, and although he tried to stop the proceedings from getting into print he was obviously pleased by the recognition.[3] He was getting more and more anxious to get out of service, but his sense of duty would not let him leave until the government stated in some official way that officers of his grade were no longer needed. While

[1] Hayes to Mrs. Hayes, April 8, 12, 1865, Hayes MS. Letters; *Official Records*, XLVI, pt. 3, 1046.

[2] Hayes to Mrs. Hayes, April 16, 1865, Hayes MS. Letters.

[3] Hayes to H. F. Devol, April 22, 1865, and to Mrs. Hayes, April 23, ibid.

he was waiting for a pronouncement, he wanted to have Lucy with him, and in mid-May she went to Marietta, where he met her and took her by train back to New Creek. "I shall bring Lucy here to await events," he told his mother before he started for Marietta. "I am in a great hurry."[4]

The sight of his wife was all that Hayes needed to reach his own decision, regardless of government policy. He and Lucy arrived in camp on the evening of May 19, and on the next day he wrote an official letter resigning as brigadier general of volunteers. He asked that the resignation take effect as of June 8, just four years after he had entered the service. Then he packed his belongings for shipment home —his chest, his sword, his flags—and gave orders for the transportation of his favorite horse, Old Whitey. It was what he wanted to do, and yet he felt a great sense of sadness, as if he were losing something that he could never recapture. He watched the soldiers as they left for their homes and wrote with words that he meant to apply to himself as well as them: "I have no idea that many of them will ever see as happy times as they have had in the army."[5] With Lucy he journeyed to Washington to attend the grand review of the armies and then went on to Richmond for a brief pleasure trip and was back in Ohio by early June. He was Congressman-elect Hayes now and soon he would be Governor Hayes and one day he would be President Hayes. But no later title he would win would ever mean quite as much to him as the one he wore throughout most of the war. No matter how high he went, he would always be Colonel Hayes of the Twenty-third, and he would always take more pride in the victories he won on the Kanawha or in the Shenandoah than he would in any of his triumphs in Columbus or Washington.

His golden years were over.

---

[4] Hayes to Mrs. Sophia Hayes, May 12, 14, 1865, ibid.
[5] Letter of resignation, May 20, 1865, copy in Hayes Library; Hayes to Mrs. Sophia Hayes, May 20, 1865, Hayes MS. Letters.

Index

A NOTE ABOUT THE AUTHOR

T. HARRY WILLIAMS was Boyd Professor of History at Louisiana State University. Noted for his works on the Civil War, he was the author of *Lincoln and the Radicals* (1941), *P. G. T. Beauregard* (1955), and the popular *Lincoln and His Generals* (1952). Williams also wrote *A History of the United States* (with Richard N. Current and Frank Freidel, 1959), *Americans at War* (1960), *Romance and Realism in Southern Politics* (1961), *McClellan, Sherman, and Grant* (1962), and the classic *Huey Long* (1969). He served as both vice-president and president of the Southern Historical Association.